A comprehensive analysis encapsulating a lifetime of field experience and prodigious research in an arena closely contested by lawyers who guard their words and actions behind a cloak of confidentiality. Sunlight finds it hard to penetrate this thicket; Ciaran O'Faircheallaigh has worked marvels clearing the undergrowth to expose and forensically analyse the detail of negotiations between mining companies and Aboriginal groups.

Bruce Harvey, *University of Queensland*

This is a sensitive and perceptive account written by a scholar who has seen negotiations between indigenous peoples and extractive industries from the inside. These negotiations are where many of the final effects of extractive industry on indigenous communities are worked out, yet until this book we knew very little about the nature, dynamics and outcomes of such negotiations. Ciaran O'Faircheallaigh combines his experience as a direct participant, his longstanding relations with aboriginal groups, a mastery of both the conceptual and empirical literature and an extensive review of documented cases to give us an unparalleled book. Remarkably useful and insightful.

Anthony Bebbington, *Director, Graduate School of Geography, Clark University, and Professorial Research Fellow, School for Environment, Education and Development, University of Manchester*

Negotiations in the Indigenous World

Negotiated agreements play a critical role in setting the conditions under which resource development occurs on Indigenous land. Our understanding of what determines the outcomes of negotiations between Indigenous peoples and commercial interests is very limited.

With over two decades' experience with Indigenous organisations and communities, Ciaran O'Faircheallaigh's book offers the first systematic analysis of agreement outcomes and the factors that shape them, based on evaluative criteria developed especially for this study; on an analysis of 45 negotiations between Aboriginal peoples and mining companies across all of Australia's major resource-producing regions; and on detailed case studies of four negotiations in Australia and Canada.

Ciaran O'Faircheallaigh is Professor of Politics and Public Policy at Griffith University, Australia. He is Director of the Centre for Governance and Public Policy's Program on Environment, Resources and Sustainability. His research focuses on the interactions of large resource corporations with governments and communities, particularly Indigenous communities. For over two decades, he has acted as a negotiator and adviser for Aboriginal communities in Australia and Canada and for customary landowners in the Pacific.

Indigenous Peoples and Politics
Franke Wilmer, General Editor

Inventing Indigenous Knowledge
Archaeology, Rural Development, and the Raised Field Rehabilitation
Project in Bolivia
Lynn Swartley

The Globalization of Contentious Politics
The Amazonian Indigenous Rights Movement
Pamela L. Martin

Cultural Intermarriage in Southern Appalachia
Cherokee Elements in Four Selected Novels by Lee Smith
Kateřina Prajnerová

Storied Voices in Native American Texts
Harry Robinson, Thomas King, James Welch, and Leslie Marmon Silko
Blanca Schorcht

On the Streets and in the State House
American Indian and Hispanic Women and Environmental Policymaking
in New Mexico
Diane-Michele Prindeville

**Chief Joseph, Yellow Wolf, and the Creation of Nez Perce History in the
Pacific Northwest**
Robert R. McCoy

National Identity and the Conflict at Oka
Native Belonging and Myths of Postcolonial Nationhood in Canada
Amelia Kalant

Native American and Chicano/a Literature of the American Southwest
Intersections of Indigenous Literature
Christina M. Hebebrand

Negotiations in the Indigenous World

Aboriginal Peoples and the Extractive Industry in Australia and Canada

Ciaran O'Faircheallaigh

Routledge
Taylor & Francis Group

NEW YORK AND LONDON

First published 2016
by Routledge
711 Third Avenue, New York, NY 10017

and by Routledge
2 Park Square, Milton Park, Abingdon, Oxon OX14 4RN

Routledge is an imprint of the Taylor & Francis Group, an informa business

Library of Congress Cataloging in Publication Data
O'Faircheallaigh, Ciaran.
Negotiations in the indigenous world : aboriginal peoples and the
extractive industry in Australia and Canada / Ciaran O'Faircheallaigh.
    pages cm. – (Indigenous peoples and politics)
    Includes bibliographical references and index.
    1. Aboriginal Australians–Land tenure. 2. Indians of North
America–Canada–Land tenure. 3. Mineral industries–Australia.
    4. Mineral industries–Canada. 5. Concessions–Australia.
    6. Concessions–Canada. I. Title.
    DU124.L35O43 2016
    338.20971–dc23   2015014256

ISBN: 978-1-138-85849-7 (hbk)
ISBN: 978-1-315-71795-1 (ebk)

Typeset in Sabon
by Wearset Ltd, Boldon, Tyne and Wear

Printed and bound in the United States of America by Publishers Graphics,
LLC on sustainably sourced paper.

To my children and grandchildren, Sinead, Kevin, Claire, Liam and Eoin, who have brought me so much joy

Contents

Figures

Tables

Acknowledgements

The book draws heavily on research funded by the Australian Research Council, and its support and that of Griffith University is gratefully acknowledged. So also is the work of Tony Corbett, who provided research assistance for many aspects of the study over more than a decade.

I wish to acknowledge all those Indigenous people who must take hard decisions about whether or not to negotiate with corporations and state agencies that wish to extract minerals from their ancestral lands and, if they do decide to negotiate, face formidable obstacles in seeking to achieve outcomes that benefit their communities.

In Australia and Canada, I acknowledge the Aboriginal community leaders, negotiators and advisers, and company and government officials, who assisted me with my research. I express my special appreciation to those individuals who displayed a high degree of trust in providing me with confidential or sensitive information in relation to negotiations and mining agreements, and in particular to Aboriginal people who spoke frankly about situations in which they were not able to secure the outcomes they sought from negotiations with the extractive industry.

In Australia I also wish to acknowledge the Aboriginal organisations, communities and leaders who over two decades have employed me as an adviser and negotiator, and placed their faith in my ability to support them in negotiations where the stakes for them were extremely high. I am keenly aware that, while I shared in the satisfaction of successful negotiations, they were the ones who had to deal with the consequences of any failures. I especially wish to acknowledge the many Aboriginal people who shared with me information about their families, their societies and their culture, and patiently bore my attempts to familiarise myself with Aboriginal values, priorities and ways of seeing the world. In this latter regard I still have much to learn. I sincerely trust that any limitations in my knowledge evident from what follows are compensated for by the benefit Indigenous people can gain from drawing on the experiences recounted in this book.

Abbreviations

ACI	ACI Industrial Minerals Ltd
ALA	Aboriginal Land Act (Queensland)
ALP	Australian Labor Party
ATSIC	Aboriginal and Torres Strait Islander Commission
BATNA	Best alternative to a negotiated agreement
CARC	Canadian Arctic Resources Committee
CEO	Chief Executive Officer
CIRL	Canadian Institute of Resources Law
CRA	Conzinc Riotinto of Australia Ltd
CHC	Cultural Heritage Corporation
CRL	Consolidated Rutile Ltd
CYLC	Cape York Land Council
DFRL	Diamond Field Resources Ltd
DIAND	Department of Indian Affairs and Northern Development
DME	Department of Mines and Energy (Queensland)
DPC	Department of Premier and Cabinet (Queensland)
DSD	Department of State Development (Queensland)
EAP	Environmental Assessment Panel
EIS	Environmental Impact Statement
FAIRA	Federation of Aboriginal and Islander Research Action
GNWT	Government of the Northwest Territories
IBA	Impact and Benefits Agreement
IEMA	Independent Environmental Monitoring Agency
ILUA	Indigenous land use agreement
LIA	Labrador Inuit Association
LIL	Labrador Inuit Lands
LISA	Labrador Inuit Settlement Area
LRT	Land and Resources Tribunal
ML	Mining lease
MLA	Mining lease application
MRA	Mineral Resources Act (Queensland)
NNTT	National Native Title Tribunal
NSI	North Stradbroke Island
NTA	Native Title Act (Commonwealth)

NTRB	Native Title Representative Body
NTS	Native Title Services
NWT	Northwest Territories
QAL	Queensland Alumina Ltd
QLC	Quandamooka Land Council
QNTG	Quandamooka Native Title Group
RTN	Right to negotiate
VBNC	Voisey's Bay nickel company
WCCCA	Western Cape Communities Co-existence Agreement

1 Introduction

Indigenous peoples, mineral development and negotiation

For most Indigenous peoples who have felt the impact of mineral development, the experience has been negative and often highly destructive. There are numerous historical examples, some discussed in later chapters, which illustrate the substantial costs imposed by mining on Indigenous societies, cultures and economies. Those costs have rarely been balanced by opportunities to share in the wealth created by mineral development. This situation reflects the fact that Indigenous people have had little capacity to set the terms under which mining would occur on their ancestral lands. Companies and governments have made decisions about where and when to mine, and about the distribution of costs and benefits associated with mining, with little or no regard for Indigenous interests.

At least in industrialised countries with substantial Indigenous populations, recent changes in the political and legal environment have created opportunities for Indigenous peoples to shift this pattern of costs and benefits in their favour. Such opportunities have typically resulted from an increasing ability to negotiate agreements with mining companies and, in certain cases, with the government agencies that approve mining projects, agreements which set the terms on which development will occur.

Some Indigenous groups believe that there is a fundamental conflict between mining and the integrity of their ancestral lands and their society and culture and that the only way to avoid the costs associated with mining is to prevent it from occurring in the first place. Many others take the view that the opportunity to negotiate with mining companies does create the possibility of positive outcomes. However, the occurrence of negotiation does not of itself guarantee such a result. Indeed where they involve Indigenous approval for mining under terms unfavourable to Indigenous interests, negotiated agreements may leave Indigenous peoples worse off, because they may prohibit the pursuit of legal and political avenues that could otherwise be used to prevent mining or influence the terms under which it occurs.

What sort of outcomes are emerging from negotiations between Indigenous peoples and mining companies? To what extent are negotiated agreements shifting the costs and benefits that Indigenous people experience from mineral development? What explains the nature of outcomes in particular cases? What negotiation approaches and strategies can be employed to maximise the benefits Indigenous peoples extract from negotiated agreements?

These questions are of great importance to mineral developers and governments as well as to Indigenous peoples. There is a growing realisation within the mining industry that, if its operations are to be sustainable over the longer term, it must establish positive and lasting relationships with Indigenous peoples on whose traditional lands the industry operates or wishes to operate. During recent decades, Indigenous opposition has led to costly delays in project development, to decisions by mining companies to abandon proposed projects and to the premature closure of existing mines. Negotiated agreements offer a way in which the mining industry may be able to address the opposition of Indigenous groups. However, this will only be the case if agreements deal with the issues that underlie Indigenous opposition by achieving a fundamental shift in the balance of costs and benefits faced by Indigenous people affected by mining.

Governments also have a strong interest in the outcomes of negotiations involving Indigenous peoples and resource developers. A sustainable mining industry is important to government revenue streams and to economic growth, while the social and cultural problems generated in Indigenous communities by inappropriate development ultimately result in significant costs to the state.

Little has been written in the academic literature about the outcomes of negotiations between mineral developers and Indigenous peoples, and in particular there have been very few attempts to evaluate or explain outcomes. Yet evaluation and explanation of negotiated outcomes are essential to enable Indigenous people to accurately identify the reasons for success and failure in negotiations, reproduce successful negotiation strategies, allocate their resources appropriately and, in these ways, achieve improved outcomes from future mineral development.

This book sets out to improve understanding of negotiated outcomes, positive and negative, to explain these outcomes and, in the process, add to the knowledge available to Indigenous peoples and their advisers as they seek more beneficial outcomes in the future.

I initially became interested in negotiations between Indigenous peoples and mining companies in the 1980s when undertaking research on the regional economic impact of large mining projects in Australia's Northern Territory. It transpired that a significant part of the positive economic impacts that accrued locally resulted from the success of Aboriginal groups[1] in negotiating revenue sharing arrangements, and Aboriginal employment and business development programs, with mining companies. When I moved to Queensland, I was asked by a number of Aboriginal communities to assist them prepare for and undertake negotiations with mining companies, because of my knowledge of multinational mining companies and of taxation of mineral resources (O'Faircheallaigh 1984, 1986, 1999). I quickly formed the impression that not all Aboriginal groups in

Australia were achieving outcomes from their negotiations with mining companies like those I had observed in the Northern Territory. Indeed outcomes seemed to vary greatly, with some Aboriginal groups gaining substantial economic benefits and enhancing protection of the environment and of their cultural heritage, while others appeared to gain little.

At this point I faced two important questions. First, how could outcomes from negotiations be measured in a consistent and systematic manner, in order to establish whether they were indeed highly variable? Second, assuming this did prove to be the case, why should outcomes be strongly positive in some cases and negative in others? It was essential to address this second question if my research and professional practice were to help Indigenous people use negotiations to achieve more favourable outcomes from mining.

The wider literature on negotiation seemed an obvious place to start in seeking a basis on which to evaluate and explain outcomes in the specific case of negotiations involving Indigenous peoples and mining companies. That literature is discussed in detail in the next chapter. The discussion reveals that existing writing on negotiation has significant weaknesses in terms of evaluating and explaining outcomes from negotiations in the real world. These weaknesses reflect in particular the lack of explicit criteria for gauging 'success' or 'failure' in negotiations; an over-emphasis on negotiation behaviour as opposed to negotiation outcomes; an inability to incorporate wider structural and institutional influences and the power relationships that create the context for individual negotiations; and a reliance on 'experimental' or 'laboratory' methods applied in conditions that depart substantially from those that characterise actual negotiations.

Thus a new approach was required, and such an approach is developed and applied in this book. It involves making negotiation outcomes rather than negotiation behaviour a central focus and developing explicit and robust criteria for evaluating outcomes on a range of negotiation issues that are of critical importance for Indigenous peoples. It involves applying these criteria in analysing the content of 45 agreements negotiated in multiple jurisdictions and industry sectors in Australia, providing a basis for analysing factors that operate at institutional and structural levels, rather than only in the specific context of individual negotiations. It also involves detailed case studies of negotiations between Aboriginal peoples and mining companies in Australia and Canada, and of the agreements they produce, creating an opportunity to see how wider structural factors and power relationships interact with the 'micro level' influences at play in particular negotiations.[2]

The use of a comparative approach further assists in explaining negotiation outcomes. Australia and Canada have large mining industries and substantial and diverse Aboriginal populations, and each has a distinctive history and political and legal context. A comparative analysis provides the opportunity to examine the impact of contrasting approaches to negotiations within different social, political, legal and economic contexts.

It permits an analysis of the various factors that might, in principle, affect outcomes; of the relative importance of these factors; and of the way in which their interaction brings about specific results.

This book focuses on Aboriginal peoples and mineral development and evaluates outcomes from the perspective of Aboriginal interests. However, the analytical and methodological problems it addresses are common to many areas of negotiation. The book can thus help address weaknesses in the general literature on negotiations, especially as it extends the range of contexts within which negotiation analysis has been conducted. Such an extension is, as Dononue notes (2003: 173), essential if shortcomings in negotiation theory are to be addressed.

The next chapter examines the literature on negotiations, particularly in terms of its capacity to evaluate and explain negotiation outcomes. Chapter 3 provides important context for the development of evaluative criteria and the later analysis of specific negotiations by examining the impact of mining on Indigenous societies and, on this basis, identifying critical issues for negotiation from an Indigenous perspective. The chapter also examines the interests of the other key parties to negotiations, mining companies and governments, and provides brief but essential background material on Australia and Canada. Chapter 4 develops evaluative criteria for assessing outcomes on seven issues that are of critical importance to Aboriginal peoples in Australia and Canada and that figure prominently in negotiations between them and mineral developers. Chapter 5 applies those criteria to examine agreements that emerged from 45 negotiations conducted in Australia in recent decades.

The following four chapters present detailed case studies of four negotiations, two in Australia and two in Canada. The cases are chosen because sufficient information is available on the negotiations and agreements involved, and because they include a wide range of outcomes from the perspective of the Aboriginal participants, from the strongly positive to the strongly negative, an important consideration when seeking to explain success and failure in negotiations.

The genesis of the Australian and Canadian case studies and the sources they use are quite different. I was closely involved in the two Australian negotiations, organising preparatory work in the Aboriginal communities concerned and participating in the negotiations which followed. I attended virtually all major negotiation meetings in both cases and had access to all relevant documentation. The Australian case studies are thus written from the point of view of an 'insider'. This raises important ethical issues, in particular my duty of care towards the Aboriginal people and communities involved, expressed in one contract with an Aboriginal organisation as a duty to 'show respect for Aboriginal people and Aboriginal culture and ... observe the trust placed in [me] through the disclosure by Aboriginal people to [me] of knowledge concerning their society, customs and traditions, especially sacred/secret knowledge'. I have sought to ensure that the case studies were written in a way consistent with these obligations and, as part of this approach, had each reviewed by a senior member or members of the Aboriginal peoples involved when they were first completed in 2005–2006. In one case, their advice was that it was too soon after the events described to publish my account. A decade later, I again arranged to have the case study reviewed and was then advised that publication would create no difficulty, subject to a pseudonym being used for one organisation involved. No similar issues arose in relation to the second case study, but here a delay in publication was also required until information on the negotiations had made its way into the public domain through other channels, so allowing me to comply with confidentiality arrangements between the Aboriginal community and the mining company involved.

The two Canadian case studies are research based, drawing on published materials, unpublished documentation, including copies of agreements resulting from negotiations, and extensive interviews with Aboriginal negotiators, advisers and community leaders and company and government officials involved in negotiations. While drawing on different sources of information, each case study follows a standard format to facilitate comparison and generalisation. The mining project and the company operating or developing it are briefly described, and information presented on the Aboriginal groups involved. The course of negotiations is outlined, as is the content of the agreement reached at the conclusion of negotiations. Negotiation outcomes are then assessed, and explanations for these outcomes are developed.

The final chapter draws together the wealth of empirical data generated by the macro-analysis of Australian agreements and the four case studies. It focuses in particular on explaining observed outcomes from negotiations and on what this reveals about the utility of existing negotiation theory and methods. It highlights the critical impact on negotiation outcomes of structural factors affecting the distribution of power between negotiation parties; the capacity of some Indigenous groups to effect shifts in structural power; the key role of political action and community cohesion in allowing them to do so; and the impact of organisational and other resources (or their absence), of alternatives to negotiation, and of time factors on negotiation processes and outcomes. On this basis it revisits the issues raised in the review of negotiation literature in Chapter 2 and seeks to draw lessons that can assist Indigenous peoples to use negotiated agreements as a basis for controlling, and benefitting from, mineral development on their ancestral lands.

Notes

1 Indigenous peoples in Australia (other than Torres Strait Islanders, who are not a focus of this study) and Canada are generally referred to as 'Aboriginal peoples', while specific names are used in referring to particular language or cultural groups, for instance Innu, Labrador Inuit, Tlicho, Wik, or Qandamooka, to cite some examples from the case studies in this book. I follow this nomenclature here, and use the term 'Indigenous' when referring to Indigenous peoples globally.
2 The research studies of agreements were funded by the Australian Research Council (Project A00102914).

References

Donohue, W. A. (2003) 'The Promise of Interaction-Based Approach to Negotiation', *International Journal of Conflict Management*, 14(3/4): 167–76.

O'Faircheallaigh, C. (1984) *Mining and Development: Foreign-financed Mines in Australia, Ireland, Papua New Guinea and Zambia*, London and New York: Croom Helm Ltd and St Martin's Press.

O'Faircheallaigh, C. (1986) 'Mineral Taxation, Mineral Revenues and Mine Investment in Zambia, 1964–83', *American Journal of Economics and Sociology*, 45(1): 53–67.

O'Faircheallaigh, C. (1999) 'Indigenous People and Mineral Taxation Regimes', *Resources Policy*, 24(4): 187–98.

2 Analysing negotiations
Theory and method

Introduction

This book seeks to document, evaluate and explain outcomes of negotiations between Aboriginal peoples and mining companies and so to provide a basis for achieving outcomes that are more positive from an Indigenous perspective. As noted in Chapter 1, little has been written about negotiations involving Indigenous peoples. On the other hand a very large literature exists on negotiation more generally (Lewicki *et al.* 2001; Li *et al.* 2007; Menkel-Meadow 2009). In principle this literature might offer general frameworks for assessing 'success' or 'failure' in negotiations and for explaining the outcomes they produce, frameworks that could be applied to the specific case of Indigenous peoples and mining.

In this Chapter, I analyse the general literature on negotiation in order to establish whether it can offer insights of this sort. To assist in analysing what is a large field of study, Table 2.1 provides an overview of approaches used and issues dealt with in the negotiation literature. I examine these in the order in which they appear in Table 2.1.

For reasons that will become apparent, the utility of the general negotiation literature is limited, because it is weakest in those areas that are of most interest for this study: evaluating and explaining negotiation outcomes. I argue that these weaknesses are fundamental not just from the perspective of research on Indigenous peoples and mining, but in the context of analysing negotiations in general. This study is of wider significance in that it can help address those weaknesses.

Understanding 'negotiation'

A substantial part of the literature seeks to understand and characterise the general nature of 'negotiation' processes. Fundamental questions are 'What *is* negotiation?', 'What is the *purpose* of negotiation?', and 'What *sort of activity* does it involve?'

For example, drawing on the seminal contribution of Walton and McKersie (1965) numerous scholars have sought to characterise negotiation processes as either *distributive* or *integrative* (Elms 2006; Han *et al.*

Table 2.1 Approaches and topics in the negotiation literature (individual studies may address multiple topics)

Studies attempt to:

1 **Understand and characterise the nature of 'negotiation' processes**, to understand **what is happening** when negotiation occurs. Negotiation may be seen as e.g. 'distributive' or value sharing; or 'integrative' or value creating. Studies are either:
   (a) **Descriptive**, stating that negotiations happen in a variety of ways, because of the attitudes, preferences, experiences of the parties; or because of differences in negotiating contexts.
   (b) **Normative**, taking the position that particular ways of negotiating are superior to others (e.g. because they save time, increase chances of getting agreement, maximise benefits to both parties).

2 Deal with the **behaviour** of individuals and parties in negotiations. They may:
   (a) **Describe** behaviour, seeking to answer questions such as 'How do people behave?' 'What tactics do they employ?'
   (b) **Explain** behaviour, in terms either of:
       (i)   Factors 'internal' to the negotiation process, such as the disposition, experience, beliefs, or ambitions of negotiators, or whether the negotiation is part of an ongoing relationship.
       (ii) 'External' or 'Structural' factors relating to the wider institutional/ political/economic/legal context for negotiations.
   (c) **Prescribe** behaviour, offering conclusions or advice on how those involved in negotiations **should** behave based either on:
       (i)   **Ethical standards**
       (ii) What is required to **maximise gains** from negotiation.

3 Deal with outcomes from negotiations by:
   (a) **Defining or assessing outcomes**, e.g. outcomes as negotiator profit, as reaching an agreement, meeting specific objectives.
   (b) **Explaining outcomes** in terms either of:
       (i)   Factors 'internal' to the negotiation (behaviour of parties, tactical competence, resources available to negotiators).
       (ii) 'External' or 'structural' factors relating to the wider institutional/ political/economic/legal context for negotiations to occur.
       (iii) A combination of 'external' and 'internal' factors.

4 Describe, explain or advise on behaviour in **cross cultural negotiations**.

5 Address **methodology** or **how to study** negotiations (as opposed to what is studied or what studies reveal), e.g. through laboratory experiments, surveys of participants, analysis of negotiation transcripts, or in-depth case study analysis. Studies can:
   1 **Describe** methodology employed.
   2 **Critically assess** methodologies in terms of their ability to address Items 1–4 above.

2012; Lewecki *et al.* 2001; Weiss 2010). In distributive negotiation each party tries to maximise their share of fixed-sum pay-offs that are determined through negotiation activity. Any gain for one party is a loss for the other, and consequently behaviour is individualistic, competitive and hostile. Specific examples involve negotiation over the purchase of a motor vehicle or between multinational mining or petroleum companies and governments over the division of revenues from resource projects. A higher price for the car is a win for the seller and a loss for the buyer. A larger government share of mineral revenues is a gain for the government and a loss for the operator of the resource project. The concept of distributive negotiation has given rise to a large literature on bargaining power, which seeks to explain and quantify the relative capacity of negotiating parties to skew the 'pay-off' from negotiations in their direction (Bacharach and Lawler 1980, 1981; Filzmoser and Vetschera 2008; Fisher 1983; Li *et al.* 2007: 225–6).

In *integrative* negotiation, the parties attempt to work together to 'increase the size of the pie' beyond what either can achieve on their own, allowing joint gains to be achieved through the negotiation process. They explore options that will allow *all* parties to be better off, rather than focus on the *division* of pay-offs between them. In this case activity focuses on ways of promoting joint action, on the definition of problems and the search for solutions that maximise joint gains and, critically, on achieving information sharing. For instance, parties must have information on each other's goals and interests if they are to jointly identify options for allowing maximum progress towards achieving goals and pursuing interests. An example of integrative negotiation might involve two firms negotiating a merger. By allowing potential synergies between them to be realised, a merger may allow the production of a larger quantum of wealth than the sum of what the two companies could produce individually, leaving shareholders and employees in *both* companies better off.

In characterising 'negotiation', researchers tend to adopt either a 'descriptive' or a 'normative' approach. Those adopting a descriptive approach accept that in the real world negotiation will take a number of different forms, each of which is equally legitimate. Which form will occur in specific cases will depend on a range of contextual factors, including the nature of the inter-dependence between the parties; the subject matter of the negotiation; the assumptions, attitudes and disposition of individual negotiators; whether negotiations occur between groups rather than individuals; and the composition of negotiation teams, for example in terms of gender or ethnic background (Han *et al.* 2012; Herbst and Schwartz 2011: 149; Lewecki *et al.* 2001: 7, 27; Putnam 1990).

Those adopting a normative approach argue that particular negotiation approaches are inherently more likely than others to generate positive results. For example, they may argue that integrative approaches result in superior outcomes because they are more stable as a result of their tendency to produce win–win solutions; because they are less likely to involve behaviour that is questionable on ethical grounds; or because, over the longer term, they increase the quantum of resources available for distribution rather than simply divide and re-divide existing resources (Elms 2006; Menkel-Meadow 2009: 416; McKersie *et al.* 2004; Ury 1993. For a contrary view on the inherent superiority of integrative approaches, see Gillespie and Bazerman 1997; Weiss 2010).

Negotiation behaviour

Studies that focus on the behaviour of individuals and organisations involved in negotiations account for a very large proportion of the literature. Some of these studies are based on analysis of actual, 'real world' negotiations (Elms 2006; Pruitt 1986: 240–1; Watkins 1998). However, many are what are referred to here as 'experimental' studies, i.e. simulations of negotiations based either on observation of interactions between individual subjects (often students) in a controlled or 'laboratory' environment, or on computer-based models. This heavy reliance on experimental methods, discussed in detail below, reflects the difficulty of observing real-world negotiations that are frequently confidential; the substantial resources and time required to analyse such negotiations; and the belief that experiments can assist in establishing causality by allowing interactions between a limited number of variables to be observed in a 'controlled' environment (Fells 2013: 134–5; Friedman 2004; Moore and Murnighan 1999).

Describing behaviour

Most research on negotiation behaviour begins by describing what happens when people negotiate. Researchers describe, for instance, how people frame and pursue their demands; how they respond to the demands of others; their attitudes to risk and in particular their relative assessment of the possibility of gains and losses; whether and in what circumstances they make concessions and how they respond to concessions; whether, to what extent and in what circumstances they share information; how they respond to information sharing; and how they react to time limitations. As Putnam (1994: 341) notes, the focus is generally on the interests, motivation and behaviour of *individuals*, despite the fact that in the real world negotiation often involves interactions between teams of people representing multiple parties (see also Fisher 1989; Polzer 1996). As with many other facets of the literature, this 'individualistic orientation' reveals the influence of experimental approaches that, reflecting their origins in cognitive psychology and game theory, tend to take the individual as the fundamental unit of analysis.

Explaining behaviour

In principle, the behaviour of negotiators can be explained in terms of two sets of distinct though possibly inter-related factors, referred to here as 'internal' and 'external'. 'Internal' factors are located within the negotiation process itself.[1] They include individual characteristics of negotiators on both sides such as personality, cultural background, attitude to risk, degree and type of negotiation experience, gender and motivation. They also include factors such as whether an ongoing relationship exists between negotiators, whether negotiations are conducted by individuals or by teams, and whether negotiators are operating within time constraints or with or without knowledge of their opponents' positions. In some cases behaviour is explained in terms of the interaction among a range of internal factors. For example, the degree of trust displayed by negotiators or their tendency to embrace or resist compromise may be explained through the interaction of their personal dispositions and characteristics of the negotiation process, such as the absence or presence of time constraints and the availability of information (Ross and LaCroix 1996).

'External' factors involve 'structures and processes of the broader system within which negotiation occurs' (Druckman 1990: 180).[2] They could include time constraints mandated externally (for instance by government), resource availability, organisational politics that may be unrelated to the issue being negotiated but which affect negotiator behaviour, and the wider legal and political context within which negotiations are conducted. For example a negotiator's reluctance to adopt a specific approach that could advance a negotiation may reflect a wider organisational policy that constrains her behaviour, or an acceptance that underlying power relationships between groups and interests in society render it pointless to pursue certain approaches.

Druckman has described 'external' factors as 'uncontrollable' (1983: 76). This may be valid in relation to an individual negotiation occurring in real time, when negotiators have little ability to alter the wider legal or organisational structures or power balances within which they operate. However, over the longer term these structural features may be amenable to change, and indeed in his later work Druckman (2003: 186, 188) acknowledges that negotiation processes and strategies can themselves play a role in bringing about societal change. An important goal of negotiation analysis is to identify how such change is likely to affect negotiation behaviour and outcomes in specific negotiations, and how individual negotiations, in turn, can contribute to system-level change (Sturm 2009). This point is particularly relevant to Indigenous peoples, who occupy a position of *structural* disadvantage in the dominant society (see Chapter 3). Any approach to negotiation analysis that does not address structural, system-level issues is therefore unlikely to assist them (or other marginalised groups) to achieve more positive outcomes.

In fact most of the literature on negotiation behaviour focuses on the influence of 'internal' factors, despite evidence that in the real world 'external' factors may have a greater impact (Druckman 1997, 2003: 181; Li *et al.* 2007; Susskind and Susskind 2008: 203). To the extent that external factors are considered, they tend to involve individual 'events' rather than underlying institutional or structural factors (Crump 2011: 199–200; Druckman 2003: 179–80; Irmer and Druckman 2009: 213; for an exception, see Sturm 2009).

This focus on 'internal' factors reflects the immediacy of their impact, their greater susceptibility to observation and, importantly, the heavy reliance on experimental approaches (see below). Given that a key motivation for experimental work is to isolate the impact of certain variables by controlling for others, such approaches will tend to focus on the variables that are susceptible to control. These are the individual characteristics of 'negotiators' (i.e. study participants) and the 'internal' conditions under which negotiations occur (such as the presence or absence of time constraints). Much less attention is devoted in experiments or simulations to 'external' factors that are harder to control, though in some experiments an attempt is made to replicate their effect, as for instance when time limitations imposed on subjects by the researcher are used to examine the effect of 'externally imposed' time constraints.

Few scholars seek to provide an integrated analysis of how internal and external factors interact to explain behaviour (for some exceptions, see Druckman 2003; Irmer and Druckman 2009; Kumar and Worm 2004).

Behaviour is also 'explained' in the literature by reference to the broad interpretations of 'negotiation' discussed in the previous section. For example, if negotiation is understood as distributive, behaviour which is competitive, aggressive, self-seeking, and information hoarding can be explained as the rational acts of a utility-maximising individual or organisation bent on achieving the maximum gains from a negotiation. Collaborative, information-sharing, problem-solving behaviour can similarly be explained in terms of an integrative understanding of negotiation (Murray 1986: 182–4). In this context the discovery of behaviour consistent with a particular model of negotiation both validates the model and explains the behaviour.

However, there are clearly potential problems associated with this sort of approach. The 'lens' provided by a particular understanding of negotiation may predispose a researcher to 'find' behaviour consistent with that understanding or to explain behaviour in a way consistent with it. This situation can represent a 'closed', circular form of logic, in that a particular conceptual framework is capable of generating only forms of explanation that are consistent with the framework and that are not subject to external validation.

Prescribing behaviour

The literature prescribes negotiation behaviour on two distinct grounds. The first involves ethics, defined by Lewecki *et al.* (2001: 164) as 'broadly applied social standards for what is right and wrong in a particular situation, or a process for setting those standards'. A relatively small but growing body of work identifies the sorts of negotiation approaches and behaviour that raise ethical issues; discusses alternative grounds on which ethical standards can be developed; and examines the practical issues and choices faced by negotiators (see for example Lewecki *et al.* 1997: Chapter 7; Li *et al.* 2007: 240–2; Schroth 2008; Van Es 1996).

Another and much more common approach is to prescribe behaviour regarded as likely to maximise gains from negotiation, on the basis that evidence from experiments or real world negotiations indicates that they are systematically associated with positive outcomes for the parties that adopt them. This may be the case regardless of the specific type of negotiation involved or the negotiation approach of the party concerned, i.e. the behaviour prescribed may be equally relevant to distributive or to integrative negotiation. Examples are Pendergast's work on the use of agendas to shape the negotiation process (Pendergast 1990); Watkins' advice on building momentum in negotiations (Watkins 1998); and Pruitt's discussion of optimum communication strategies for inter-organisational negotiations (Pruitt 1994).

In other cases, prescription may be based more on a general understanding of negotiation processes or contexts. For instance, if a particular negotiation is regarded as distributive, or if distributive negotiation is regarded as inherently superior, then the behaviour advocated will be designed to maximise a negotiator's bargaining power in a win–lose, competitive environment. Conversely, different behaviour will be advocated if a specific negotiation is regarded as integrative or if integrative approaches are regarded as always likely to produce better results (Halpert *et al.* 2010; Fells 2013; Brett *et al.*1998).

Outcomes from negotiation

Defining and assessing 'outcomes'

This book focuses on negotiations between Aboriginal communities, mining companies and the state, and between representatives of those organisations. In this context I define 'outcomes' as the end result of negotiations in terms of the presence or absence of agreement, the content of any agreement reached, and the consequences for negotiation parties of that content. In Underdal's terminology, the first two represent the 'output' of negotiations, and the third their 'impact'. Output combined with impact equals outcomes (Underdal 1991: 100–1).

Little of the negotiation literature focuses on outcomes in this sense. There is a strong tendency to focus on the behaviour and performance of negotiators, rather than on outcomes per se, even in cases where authors explicitly claim to include a focus on outcomes in their research (see for example Kumar and Worm 2004: 305, 308, 321–6). As Weiss notes (1997: 247–8):

> Much existing literature examines negotiation outcomes only insofar as they are affected by or associated with certain behaviors. The emphasis is on the negotiator's effectiveness. Alternatively … a researcher might focus on negotiation outcomes directly and in their own right, treating them as part of the phenomenon of negotiations. He or she could then study different types of outcomes and their determinants. Few researchers have done so, particularly with respect to complex, 'real-world' negotiations.
>
> (1997: 247–8)

This failure to focus directly on outcomes represents a fundamental weakness in the context of this study. In particular, as explained in Chapter 1, a clear focus on negotiation outcomes and on the reasons for them is essential in order to develop a basis on which Indigenous people can enhance the benefits they derive from negotiations.

A specific aspect of the lack of a direct focus on outcomes is that the literature rarely addresses the question of 'Success from whose point of view?' In the experimental context, this question is easy to resolve. The only relevant parties are those participating in the experiment, and so success is measured from their perspective. In the real world those who actually participate in a negotiation may achieve an outcome that is positive from their point of view, but is not highly regarded by their constituents, a possibility we discuss below. Some stakeholders directly affected by a negotiation may have little or no opportunity to influence its outcome or may not even participate in it (Gillespie and Bazerman 1997: 278–9; Pfetsch and Landau 2000: 38), and their assessment may be quite different to those of powerful participants.

The following sub-sections outline approaches commonly found in the literature to the definition of outcomes and to their assessment as positive or negative or favourable or unfavourable.

Outcomes as negotiator behaviour or 'performance'

In laboratory experiments outcomes are often so directly linked to the behaviour of subjects that outcomes are often equated with the behaviour or performance of negotiators. For example, if the focus of the research is propensity to reach an agreement the outcome is either reaching agreement, or failing to do so, which can easily be established. The behaviour of subjects is the only factor involved in determining outcomes. In this case, if that behaviour is conducive to reaching an agreement, this outcome will occur. If behaviour is not conducive to reaching agreement, it will not occur (Ross and LaCroix 1996: 334; Stuhlmacher *et al.* 1998: 99). This helps explain the fact that many studies lack any explicit discussion of negotiation outcomes.

It follows that 'outcomes' are assessed indirectly by assessing the 'behaviour' or 'performance' of negotiators in terms of their capacity to bring about the goal which is specified for the negotiation exercise.

The emphasis on 'negotiation performance' carries over into the analysis of 'real world' contexts. For example, Allred (2000) identifies three key aspects of 'negotiation performance', each of which corresponds to a basic negotiating situation – the ability to 'claim value' (distributive), to create value (integrative) and to enhance relationships with the other party. He identifies two frameworks for managing negotiation performance (best practice and strategic practice). Best practice involves behaviours (for example, effective listening) 'that work well in terms of one or more dimension of negotiating performance without diminishing one's performance on the other dimensions' (Allred 2000: 388). Strategic practices (such as sharing information) work well in terms of one or more dimensions of performance but tend to diminish performance on other dimensions. Allred concludes that success in negotiations will be associated with consistent use of 'best practice' in all situations, and contingent use of strategic practice in appropriate situations, for example, information sharing in situations where the other party is behaving in a cooperative manner (Allred 2000; see also Fisher 1986, 1989; Pruitt 1994; Watkins 1998.)

Two issues arise in relation to approaches that equate outcomes with negotiator behaviour or performance. First, outcomes in the real world cannot be equated with behaviour because they are determined in part by factors *other than* negotiator performance, including other dimensions of negotiation processes and organisational, economic, legal and political aspects of the wider environment within which negotiations occur.

Second, in the real world the issue of whether or not particular behaviours or ways of managing negotiations do generate positive results requires empirical verification. For example, it would be necessary to establish whether Allred's 'best practice' behaviours do in fact enhance performance on one or more dimensions while not diminishing performance on others. However, in many cases claims of this sort are based on a priori argument regarding the superiority of certain approaches to negotiation (see above, and Bartos 1995: 58), or on limited information generated by experiments or surveys, rather than by analysis of real-world negotiations. For example Allred's empirical analysis of whether the practices he discusses do in fact generate the expected performance is based on simulated negotiations among students enrolled in negotiation courses (Allred 2000: 394–5).

Outcomes as private profit

In laboratory studies, 'outcome' is often defined as the 'profit' gained by each individual, or jointly by all individuals, involved in a negotiation, measured numerically. The researcher provides negotiators with a task, for example, negotiation of a contract for the sale of a house or the publication of a book, and allocates points for specific components of the contract (for instance the price for the item being sold, or royalty payable on book sales). At the end of the exercise, the points achieved by each individual, or jointly by the negotiators, are added up, and their sum constitutes the 'outcome'. The researcher can calculate the maximum number of points achievable in the exercise, and negotiator performance can be ranked by either comparing the scores of two negotiators with each other or comparing the scores they achieved with the maximum (Kass 2008: 326; Kirk *et al.* 2013; Miles and LaSalle 2008; Weiss 2010).

The obvious issue with this approach is the impossibility and/or inappropriateness of applying it to 'real world' negotiations. In these there is no equivalent of the researcher who can set a task and allocate scores; many of the issues involved are complex and not subject to computation in the manner that can be applied to the price of a car or a royalty on book sales; and organisational and group interests, not just individual profit or performance, are at stake.

I should stress here that I am not criticising the application of a 'profit calculation' methodology in experiments. The problem is that, as discussed in detail below, experimental approaches dominate the literature and the approach they use in identifying and assessing outcomes is of limited use as a basis for undertaking research on 'real world' negotiations.

Outcomes as 'subjective value'

An approach similar to that focusing on 'negotiator performance' involves the broader concept of 'subjective value', which refers to negotiators' experience of the negotiation process, their assessment of their own performance, their relationship with negotiators 'across the table', and their subjective assessment of the terms of agreements they negotiate. Researchers using a 'subjective value' approach argue that the subjective experience of negotiators is both intrinsically interesting and has important implications for 'objective' outcomes from negotiations, because subjective experience shapes the future behaviour of negotiators, for instance their propensity to engage in integrative behaviour, which in turn will influence 'objective' outcomes (Curhan *et al.* 2006; Kass 2008). For example in one experiment, Curhan *et al.* (2006) found that the subjective evaluations of participants of negotiation processes had a larger impact on their future behaviour than did the 'objective' outcomes of the negotiations. They also argue that subjective feelings of success are usually the only way of gauging negotiators' performance given that the opposing side in negotiations will never reveal whether it would have been prepared to enter a more 'generous' agreement (Curhan *et al.* 2006: 494).

A focus on the subjective experiences of negotiators may indeed be valuable, but it does not in itself allow conclusions regarding the actual outcome of negotiations. Negotiators may not accurately assess outcomes and in particular may be prone to overstate their successes and understate their failures. It is noteworthy in this regard that, in one of the most extensive studies of 'subjective value' undertaken to date, participants themselves nominated an 'objective' measure, 'terms of negotiated agreement', much more frequently than subjective measures in indicating how they would assess their performance as negotiators (Curhan *et al.* 2006: 496–7). The study authors state: 'How to know whether you succeeded in negotiations is critical. The current empirical findings suggest that such knowledge is imperfect ... [a negotiator's] experience can be a lousy teacher if one's conclusions about that experience are flawed' (Curhan *et al.* 2006: 508). More broadly, in the real world negotiators usually represent organisations (Fisher 1989), and outcomes that are optimal for an individual negotiator are not necessarily optimal for the organisation. Thus there is a clear need to go beyond the subjective experience of negotiators in assessing outcomes.

Outcomes as reaching agreement

Since a central purpose of negotiation is to reach agreement, 'outcome' in many studies, both experimental and 'real world', is defined as success or failure in reaching agreement (Bartos 1995: 50; Druckman 2001: 527; Filzmoser and Vetschera 2008: 427; Schiff 2014; Watkins 1998). Reaching agreement constitutes a positive outcome, failure to do so a negative one. In some circumstances, equating 'agreement' or non-agreement with 'outcome' may be appropriate, for example in hostage negotiations where reaching agreement saves lives and failure to reach agreement leads to loss of life. However, the approach does have important limitations.

First, inability to achieve an agreement may not indicate failure in a negotiation. If it transpires that the underlying interests of parties to a negotiation are not compatible, then both sides may be better off without an agreement (Cohen *et al.* 2014). In addition, substantial benefits may emerge from a negotiation in the absence of an agreement, for example in terms of maintaining or fostering positive relations between the parties or in facilitating mutually beneficial information exchange (Druckman 1983: 55–7; Underdal 1991: 103).

Second, in most cases an agreement must be maintained over a period of time if the parties are to realise gains from it, and if this does not occur its conclusion does not represent a robust or accurate measure of 'outcome'. Short-lived cease-fire agreements in regions such as the Middle East and (prior to recent years) Northern Ireland are a case in point. Thus the durability or sustainability of an agreement is as important as the fact of its conclusion (Bottom 2003; Duursma 2014).

Third, success or failure involves the character or content of agreements as well as the fact of their achievement (Duursma 2014: 93). For instance a party that negotiates a series of agreements that contain terms detrimental to its interests would hardly be regarded as achieving positive outcomes. Yet such a result is entirely possible (Cohen *et al.* 2014; Susskind and Susskind 2008: 207; Zarankin 2008). It may occur, for example, if the organisation undertaking negotiations suffers from endemic corruption and negotiators sell out their constituents; or if it faces a chronic shortage of resources, lacks institutional memory because of high staff turnover or operates within a legal system that allows third parties to take unilateral action unless an agreement is reached. An example of the last point is where governments can make unilateral decisions in relation to disposition of mineral resources if Indigenous peoples fail to reach agreements with mining companies. The fact of agreement in this case does indicate that agreement is (at least marginally) preferable to no agreement, but for the Indigenous groups concerned agreement does not signal achievement of a favourable outcome.

Application of available bargaining power

Another possible criterion for assessing outcomes is the extent to which they reflect the full use by each negotiating party of whatever negotiating power is available to it (Drahos 2003; Underdal 1991: 111). For example, Indigenous groups would regard an outcome as positive as long they fully exercised the negotiating power they possessed, even if structural or external factors related to the legal or political framework limited that power and resulted in outcomes that were less than optimal. A focus on bargaining power does not assume a competitive, distributive approach to negotiation. Bargaining power can just as easily be applied in pursuit of integrative outcomes.

In principle this approach could be of considerable utility, providing a basis on which to assess and so improve the various aspects an organisation's performance required to maximise use of its available bargaining power in negotiations. At the same time, as long as 'external' factors affecting negotiations are not ignored, it does not preclude an appraisal of, and possibly attempts to change, the wider context of negotiations so as to shift bargaining power beyond its existing limits. The case studies in Chapters 6–9 and the analysis in the concluding chapter pay careful attention to the factors shaping the bargaining power of parties to negotiations and the extent to which they effectively use the power available to them.

Achievement of goals or interests

Another approach to assessing outcomes would be to establish the objectives or positions of parties to a negotiation and evaluate outcomes on the basis of whether those goals were achieved (Butler 1994: 311). For instance Elms (2006) identifies greater United States access to the domestic car markets of its trading partners as the key goal of US negotiations regarding trade disputes with Japan and Korea, and assesses outcomes on the basis of the extent the which this goal was achieved.

However participants in negotiations may have an incentive to hide their 'real' objectives. To do so might weaken their negotiating position by revealing to their opponents their 'bottom lines' or 'resistance points' below which they will walk away rather than accept an agreement. For example, Matz (2004: 367) argues that negotiators have strong incentives to misrepresent their goals and refers to the 'near impossibility of reliably knowing' what these are (see also Faure 1999: 212). In addition, professional negotiators may express their goals honestly, but their goals may not correspond to those of their constituents (Gillespie and Bazerman 1997: 277), and an analysis that focused on the former and not the latter would be at best partial. There is also the issue of whether the objectives established by negotiators are appropriate and realistic. If they are over-ambitious, failure to achieve them might not indicate an unsuccessful negotiating effort. Conversely, if goals are excessively modest (for example because negotiators are corrupt and have been 'bought off' or because they have not prepared properly and so have underestimated the benefits they could obtain), goal achievement may be a poor indicator of success.

Alternatively, achievement of underlying interests could be used as a measure of success. The obvious problem here is to establish what those interests are. The previous discussion indicates that they cannot be equated with goals. The goals of a corrupt negotiator might be to achieve an outcome that allows him to obtain a pay-off from the other party, while avoiding retribution from the constituency he is representing. Such an outcome would not correspond to the 'underlying interest' of the party he represents.

These problems are not insurmountable. A careful and detailed analysis of the wider social and economic characteristics of particular participants in negotiations and of the aspirations and priorities they pursue over time in a range of negotiations and in wider policy, legal and institutional forums could provide a basis on which to establish their underlying interests (see Chapters 3 and 4). Criteria could then be established against which to gauge achievement of negotiation goals and also the appropriateness of these goals in terms of the underlying interests of parties to a negotiation (see next section).

Standard measures

A final approach is to develop standard measures against which to assess negotiation outcomes. A range of negotiations dealing with the same issues can be examined over time and on this basis a scale of outcomes established. Specific outcomes could then be assessed on this scale and conclusions drawn about the 'success' or 'failure' of negotiations. For example, royalty rates negotiated for extraction of minerals from Indigenous lands in a range of jurisdictions could be documented, with negotiations that achieved rates close to the top of the range regarded as 'successful' and those falling towards the bottom of the range as 'unsuccessful'. Any such judgment would have to consider the possibility of trade-offs against other issues under negotiation. In other words a similar assessment would have to be made across each major issue under negotiation before an overall conclusion was reached. However, if this is done, an approach based on standard measures can offer a viable means of assessing negotiation outcomes and a way of addressing what Zartman refers to as the 'need to address consequences [of negotiations] as well as causes' (2002: 12).

I have identified few existing studies that have tried to adopt such an approach to outcomes. Even where authors recognise the need not only to achieve an 'agreement' but also to achieve a 'good', 'comprehensive' or 'win–win' agreement, they rarely identify standard measures, or indeed any explicit criteria, by which an agreement may be regarded as 'comprehensive' or as 'good' (or 'bad') (see for example Druckman 1990: 197–213, 1997: 402–3; Kumar and Worm 2004).

In summary, much of the negotiation literature is deficient in identifying and assessing negotiation outcomes. Criteria commonly employed are negotiator behaviour, performance or 'subjective value', or reaching agreement, each of which has inherent limitations. An approach based on assessing progress towards achieving underlying interests, gauged through the application of standard measures in relation to specific negotiation issues, offers an alternative approach that may be feasible though certainly not without its challenges. Few studies have attempted to utilise such an approach. I do so in this book (see Chapters 4 and 5).

Explaining outcomes

Not surprisingly given its focus on behaviour, much of the negotiation literature concentrates, to the extent that it seeks to explain outcomes, on the impact of factors 'internal' to the negotiation process. These include the characteristics and disposition of negotiators, the degree to which they maintain unity during the process, internally imposed time constraints, availability of information and the interaction between these factors. These interactions are frequently observed in experimental settings and generate hypotheses that, in principle, are amenable to testing in the real world. However, a review of the literature suggests that such testing is rare (see below).

Negotiation outcomes are also affected by factors external to the negotiation process (Druckman 1990; Li *et al.* 2007: 223–6; Weiss 1997; Putnam and Fuller 2014). A focus on such factors and on the way in which they interact with 'internal' factors is essential in order to explain existing outcomes and to identify ways of bringing about different ones. Events outside the negotiation process, for instance, may have a major bearing on the ability of a negotiating team to maintain its cohesion which, in turn, is widely recognised as important in explaining negotiation outcomes (Downie 1991: 180; Putnam and Fuller 2014; Strum 2009). At a more general level, it is entirely conceivable that substantial change in negotiator behaviour will have only a marginal effect on outcomes unless changes are also made to the legal, organisational or policy framework in which negotiations occur. As Strum points out:

> The outcome of any negotiation is determined by more than the negotiating skills and power each individual brings to the table. These individual level negotiations take place in an institutional and social context, which profoundly shapes what happens in the individual negotiation.
>
> (2009: 93)

This point is well illustrated by the later discussion of the impact of legal and institutional frameworks on the outcomes of negotiations involving Aboriginal peoples in Australia and Canada (Chapters 5–9).

A failure to address causal factors external to negotiation processes can thus lead to a major problem with 'under-explanation' or with erroneous explanation. In the former case there is an inability to fully explain observed outcomes, while in the latter causality may wrongly be attributed to factors internal to negotiation processes. These problems make it difficult for scholars to address what Zartman (1994: 222) describes as 'the basic analytical question for any negotiation analysis.... How to explain outcomes?' They also render it impossible to offer soundly based advice on how to achieve different outcomes, given that the causes of existing outcomes cannot be fully or correctly explained.

While they are rare, a number of studies do focus directly on outcomes and on explaining them in terms of both 'internal' and 'external' factors. One area of research with considerable potential in that regard involves the concept of negotiating or bargaining power and its application, given that the power balance between negotiators will reflect both factors internal to a negotiation, for example the skill levels and experience of negotiators, their effectiveness as advocates for their position, their ability to identify innovative strategies; and external factors such as resource availability, organisational politics and the applicable legal framework. For example, Bacharach and Lawler (1980, 1981, 1986) attempt to use the analysis of bargaining power to 'develop a framework for understanding how parties translate structural or environmental conditions into tactical action and how this tactical action affects the power relationship in the long run' (1986: 167–8). They argue that the implications of particular bargaining strategies have to be understood in terms of their effects on long-term relationships between the parties, and that the concept of 'bargaining dependence' is helpful in this regard. The more one party is dependent on the other, the more bargaining power the second party has. Dependence is created and maintained by generating benefits for the other party in a relationship. Also relevant is the availability of alternative sources of outcomes and the degree of value attributed to the outcomes at stake. A party that obtains substantial outcomes that are highly valued from a negotiation relationship and has no other alternative source of these benefits will be in a highly dependent position. In this situation the other party possesses a high degree of bargaining power.

This situation might be expected to result in exploitation of the dependent party by the powerful one (Rojot 1991: 62–3). Bacharach and Lawler argue that, paradoxically, this does not necessarily occur (see also Zartman and Rubin 2000). If one party applies power in the short term to gain more benefit from a relationship, they reduce their power over the longer term because the other party is receiving fewer benefits and so becomes less dependent. They claim, for example, that if workers apply their industrial muscle to gain short-term concessions from management, managers will respond by reducing their reliance on labour, for instance through technological innovation accompanied by retrenchments or relocation. As a result the benefits generated by labour for management will decline, as will management's dependence on labour and so labour's nego-tiating power (1986: 169–70).

Bacharach and Lawler's work was undertaken in the context of labour–management negotiations, which normally involve the long-term relation-ships and repeated and regular sets of negotiations that are critical to their analysis of dependence and bargaining power. Relationships between mining companies and Indigenous peoples may be quite different, for example because negotiations focus heavily on a single decision to grant or not to grant mining leases whose terms typically exceed 20 years. However, this does not mean that their approach is irrelevant. It would provide a cogent explanation, for example, if it transpired that Indigenous groups obtained more substantial benefits from negotiations with mining com-panies with an interest in establishing long-term relationships with Indi-genous landowners.

Drahos (2003) also focuses on differences in bargaining power in seeking to explain outcomes from trade negotiations involving developed and less developed countries. Such differences are in turn attributed to dif-ferences between countries or groups of countries in market share – diffi-cult to change – and in technical, organisational, analytical and communication capacity. The latter are susceptible to change, and Drahos discusses cases in which less developed countries, in some cases with the assistance of Non-Governmental Organisations (NGOs), have been able to enhance their capacities in these areas, with demonstrable impacts on negotiation outcomes. Drahos also relates the ability to maintain and enhance technical and communication capacities to underlying characteris-tics of different groups of countries (for instance shared political values and histories) and to the structural arrangements they put in place or fail to put in place.

Another and related area of research which may offer useful insights analyses asymmetry of power in negotiations. Bacharach and Lawler argue that the party whose bargaining power is apparently weaker (i.e. is more dependent) may, paradoxically, be able to achieve beneficial outcomes from negotiations. This reflects the fact that potential benefits from negoti-ation are more highly valued by the weaker than by the stronger party, which may lead the former 'to expend more tactical effort to manipulate the other and, thereby, acquire the highly valued outcomes' (1986: 173). Similarly, Pfetsch and Landau (2000: 33–8) argue that the outcomes of international trade negotiations do not mirror the obvious asymmetry between industrialised and Third World countries in terms of conventional measures of power such as material wealth and economic capacity. In asymmetrical negotiations the weaker parties engage in what they describe as a 'search for justice', and in doing so utilise other sources of power, including the ability to infuse moral principles into the negotiations, coali-tion building, their ability to create a sense of crisis, 'creative ingenuity' and strategic use of information (see also Cameron and Tomlin 2000; Zartman and Rubin 2000).

Weiss's work (1997), which seeks to explain outcomes of two negotiations between Toyota and major US car manufacturers, is also of interest. Weiss was concerned to explain why Toyota's negotiations with General Motors in relation to joint vehicle manufacture in the US were successful while 12 months earlier similar negotiations with Ford had failed. He set out to identify causal factors which would explain these contrasting outcomes, starting with the premise that no one factor was likely to offer an adequate explanation for the outcome of complex 'real world' negotiations. He used a review of literature and of information regarding the specific negotiations, followed by interviews with participants, to identify critical factors that militated against and in favour of agreement in each case, and showed how the balance between them explained the (contrasting) outcomes. Factors that Weiss identified as critical were (1997: 298):

- The type and extent of previous experience in similar negotiations;
- Environmental forces acting on each party;
- The degree of fit between parties' negotiation goals;
- Leadership;
- The behaviour of individual negotiators;
- The internal activities (away from the negotiating table) of the parties;
- The benefits and costs of the last proposal on the table.

The comparative element of Weiss's approach was critical in allowing him to interpret his data and to validate what could otherwise be regarded as subjective assessments by participants and observers regarding the significance of possible causal factors. For example, participants ascribed little importance to cultural factors in explaining outcomes, a finding at odds with the significance attached to this factor in the negotiation literature (see the section below on cross-cultural negotiations). Had Weiss studied only one negotiation this finding might have been regarded with scepticism. However the fact that both negotiations occurred in (the same) cross-cultural context and that one 'succeeded' where the other 'failed' indicates that participants were correct not to identify cultural factors as *causal*. This does not mean, of course, that cultural factors might not affect the degree of time, expense or effort required to achieve a particular outcome (see for example Elgstrom 1990: 155–6; Faure 1999).

There are two problems with Weiss's approach. First his understanding of 'outcomes' is limited to the question of whether or not agreement is reached between the parties. However, as noted earlier there is also the very important issue of the *nature* of any agreement that is reached, which must also be analysed and explained. We address this issue by focusing on the nature of outcomes produced by negotiated agreements as well as on the fact of agreement or non-agreement (see Chapters 4–9).

A second difficulty arises from the very general nature of some causal factors identified by Weiss, and in particular the concept of 'environmental forces acting on each party', which is the only one his of his seven causal factors that relates unambiguously to 'external' factors. This concept is extremely broad, and raises the obvious question of which of the numerous components of the 'environment' that act on parties to negotiations are likely to be of critical importance in explaining outcomes. This issue can be addressed by adopting a comparative approach that is more systematic and broadly based than that used by Weiss. The current study involves the analysis of negotiations across a range of different Aboriginal settings, two national jurisdictions and four state/provincial jurisdictions. This allows considerable scope to isolate the relevance or otherwise of specific environmental factors by comparing cases in which they occur (or are absent) and establish whether their presence (or absence) is associated with the occurrence (or non-occurrence) of particular outcomes (Irmer and Druckman 2009; O'Faircheallaigh 2002: 17–18).

Negotiation in cross-cultural contexts

One area of literature that could be of particular relevance to this study involves the analysis of negotiations in cross-cultural contexts. However, I have not been able to identify any studies of cross-cultural negotiations involving Indigenous peoples. More generally, much of the literature that deals with culture and negotiation examines, usually in an experimental setting, differences in the behaviour of people from different cultural backgrounds faced with similar negotiation issues or contexts (Adair *et al.* 2009; Bisselling and Sobral 2011; Fleck *et al.* 2013; Li *et al.* 2007; Salacuse 1999). Few studies focus on whether conducting negotiations in a *cross-cultural* context alters the behaviour of negotiators or the outcomes of negotiations, compared to a situation where negotiations occur between members of a single culture (for an exception, see Drake 1995). As Bulow and Kumar (2011: 350) note, 'the vast majority of these studies are cross cultural comparisons, rather than studies of intercultural interaction'.

A typical approach is for two or more groups of students from different cultural backgrounds to separately undertake a given negotiation task under similar conditions in relation, for example, to time constraints or their absence and to the reward structure of pay-offs. Differences in behaviour are then attributed to the cultural backgrounds of students (Volkema and Fleck 2012; and for a summary of relevant literature, Li *et al.* 2007: 235–7). The (often implicit) assumption of such studies is that 'attitudes' or 'characteristics' of particular cultures can be identified in this way, and awareness of such characteristics can be utilised in 'real-world' cross-cultural negotiations to enhance prospects for positive outcomes (Brett *et al.* 1998).

There are a number of problems with this approach. In fact it cannot be taken for granted that attitudes revealed in negotiations between members of a particular culture will be displayed in cross-cultural negotiations (Drake 1995: 76; Faure 1999: 193). Most obviously, negotiators may seek to behave in a way that, on the basis of their knowledge of the other culture, is likely to achieve the desired results. Aboriginal people have certainly engaged in this sort of adaptive behaviour in other contexts, as for example when they adapt their political behaviour so as to maximise their ability to influence decisions within non-Aboriginal political systems (Sawchuk 1998).

In addition, it can be argued that the impact of culture is contextual rather than causal, depending on a range of context-specific psychological and social factors. In Rubin's words, 'much of what we explain in terms of culture can probably be traced more accurately to an amalgam of culture, situation, personality and interaction' (Rubin 1991: 98; see also Drake 1995: 83; Faure 1999: 194; Ross and LaCroix 1996: 318; and the earlier discussion of Weiss's work on American–Japanese negotiations, which provides empirical support for this view). If this is the case it is not possible to predict behaviour in a general way based on the cultural origins of negotiators.

A further problem is that practical considerations may confound attempts to isolate the effects of culture, for example the fact that a particular negotiating team may be composed of individuals from different cultures. This is often the case in negotiations involving Indigenous peoples. Finally, in common with the negotiation literature generally, existing studies tend to focus on the impact of culture on negotiation behaviour, rather than including a focus on outcomes

Methodology

A final focus of the literature is on methodology or on *how to study* negotiations (as opposed to what is studied or what studies reveal). Methods used include experimental studies (see numerous studies cited elsewhere in the chapter), surveys of participants in negotiations (Hiltrop and Rubin 1981), analysis of negotiation transcripts (Glenn and Susskind 2010; Twitchell *et al.* 2013) and in-depth case study analysis of individual negotiations using multiple sources of information (Downie 1991; Sebenius 2011; Weiss 1997). It is also possible to use large-scale analysis of outcomes from multiple negotiations in particular jurisdictions or in relation to a specific issue (see Chapters 4 and 5), but such an approach is rare in the literature (for one example see Zartman and Rubin 2000).

While some researchers offer a critical analysis of the strengths, weaknesses and limitations of the methodology they adopt (for instance Curhan *et al.* 2006: 507; Drake 1995: 83; Kass 2008: 333; Weiss 2010: 284–5), many do not (for example Cohen *et al.* 2014; Lun 1996; Polzer 1996; Sokolova and Szpakowicz 2007; Weingart *et al.*1990). This is an obvious problem given that a particular methodology may be appropriate for one purpose but not for another. It is a major issue in relation to experimental studies, both because of the quite specific limitations associated with them and because they are used so extensively in the literature. For example, one survey of 1,108 negotiation studies found that 66 per cent used laboratory experiments or computer simulations, whereas only some 5 per cent involved field or case studies of actual negotiations (Buelens *et al.* 2007: 328; see also DeDreu and Carnevale 2005: 196–7; Kumar and Worm 2004: 326).

As indicated earlier, experimental studies abstract from reality by removing the influence of a variety of factors that would normally affect the conduct and outcomes of negotiations in order to observe more clearly the impact and interaction between a small number of variables that are of interest to the researcher. Typically, 'external' factors related to the wider environment within which actual negotiations occur are removed, but most experiments also involve a considerable degree of abstraction from the internal dynamic of 'real world' negotiation. For example, experiments often involve pairs of individuals, whereas most actual negotiations involve teams; in some experiments the individual negotiators cannot communicate face to face, a very unusual situation in the real world, and/or have never met one another before; and negotiators know there will be no repercussions from their behaviour outside the experiment. Typically only one or two issues are dealt with, and the proxies used to represent variables such as 'experience', 'resource constraints' and the passage of time in negotiations are themselves abstractions. As an example of this last point, in one study that investigated the impact of negotiator experience on the use of information, the students who played the role of experienced negotiators had undertaken a single three-hour training session in negotiation, whereas 'inexperienced' negotiators had not (Murnighan *et al.* 1999: 327). More generally, the characteristics of the students often used as subjects in laboratory studies usually depart dramatically from those of experienced negotiators. (For examples of these approaches see Cohen *et al.* 2014; Kass 2008; Kirk *et al.* 2013; Olekans and Smith 2003: 239–40; Urlacher 2014; Wilkenfeld 2004: 435. For critiques of them see Friedman 2004: 376–7; Mintz *et al.* 2006; Poitras 2012; Susskind 2013).

As a result of their abstraction from reality, experimental studies can result in exclusion of precisely those factors that are of most interest to the analysis of real-world negotiations and so lead to conclusions that are an artefact of laboratory methodology rather than a reflection of reality (Bottom 2003: 368; Susskind 2013: 229). For example, many studies ensure that subjects have not met each other before and/or cannot interact face-to-face, lest the influence of personal relationships confound the impact of other variables that are the subject of the experiment. However, as Greenhalgh notes this means that the interpersonal dynamics that are often crucial to negotiations 'are exactly the dynamics that many researchers have so carefully purged from their laboratory simulations as irrelevant distractions' (1987: 235). The exclusion of the effects of relationships is a particular problem, because there is considerable evidence that relationships (existing or potential) do in fact substantially influence the behaviour and goals of negotiators and indeed help define the whole context within which negotiation occurs. In Greenhalgh and Chapman's view, 'the nature of the relationship that has formed [between negotiation parties] is likely to be the strongest predictor of how the negotiation ensues' (1995: 178). The influence of relationships may thus be sufficient to undermine core assumptions of experimental approaches, including the fundamental assumption of many studies that individuals act to maximises their own 'gains' from negotiation (Davidson and Greenhalgh 1999; Kirk *et al.* 2013: 152; Li *et al.* 2007: 231–2; Ross and LaCroix 1996: 32).

In addition, as noted earlier reliance on experimental approaches creates an obvious and unfortunate tendency for scholars to identify negotiation outcomes with negotiation behaviour, because such an approach is reasonable in an experimental context. This has helped contribute to the general tendency in the literature to focus heavily on behaviour and to ignore outcomes (see above), seriously undermining the capacity of negotiation scholars to explain outcomes and so to identify ways of obtaining alternative and preferable outcomes.

Because of the limited nature of the variables they can address, experiments can yield results that could confidently be predicted on the basis of common sense or which are self-evident, in that it is difficult to conceive how any alternative finding could possibly be explained. For example, Hiltrop and Rubin report (1981, 533) that participants in one-off or first negotiations are less sensitive about loss of image than participants in repeated encounters or in ongoing relationships. How could we possibly explain a *contrary* finding, i.e. that negotiators care more about their image in situations where any loss of image would have no consequences for an ongoing relationship? (For other similar examples see Kramer *et al.* 1993; Lun 1996: 183; Murnighan *et al.* 1999: 325; Olekans and Smith 2003: 235, 244; Polzer 1996).

A small number of experimental studies go to considerable lengths to more closely approximate real-world conditions, for example by simulating negotiations involving multiple parties and multiple issues or by using students in graduate courses who have substantial real-world negotiation experience. Such studies are more likely to test hypotheses that are non-trivial and empirically verifiable, and to generate findings that have direct and substantive implications for real-world negotiations. For example, Weiss (2010) included eight negotiation issues of varying types in experiments involving MBA students with an average of 6.5 years work experience, and generated results which led him to question the widespread assumption that integrative approaches result in superior negotiation outcomes (see also Olekans *et al.* 2003). However, even in these cases there are issues about the transferability of findings to actual negotiations, for example because of the limited time (typically an hour or less) available for negotiations (Weiss 2010: 263, 284–5) and because of the impossibility of approximating fundamental features of negotiations in the real world. For instance, the latter are typically carried out by organisations. To note just one consequence of this fact, it allows the possibility of intervention by senior decision makers not directly involved in negotiations, creating a dynamic and bringing about outcomes that simply could not occur in a laboratory context (Fells 2013; see also Susskind and Susskind 2008: 203).

There is a defensible and valid role for the use of experimental studies, including those using students as subjects, in negotiation research (Herbst and Schwarz 2011; Huffmeier *et al.* 2011: 150; Wilkenfeld 2004). They create the conditions that allow researchers to generate and to test hypotheses about the causal links between specific attributes of negotiators and of the conditions (such as time constraints) under which they operate. Such conditions can be difficult and in some cases impossible to replicate in the real world (Carnevale and DeDreu 2005; Moore and Murnigham 1999: 349).

However, given the very clear evidence that findings from experimental studies cannot simply be transferred into the real world (see for example Mintz *et al.* 2006, Poitras 2012), it is essential to test hypotheses generated in experiments through empirical research of actual negotiations. This point is widely acknowledged, including by many scholars who undertake experiments (Bartos 1995: 60; Carnevale and DeDreu 2005; Fells 2013; Huffmeier *et al.* 2011; Moore and Murninghan 1999: 349–50; Zartman 2002: 5–6). However, in practice it rarely occurs, a fact that is a significant problem in seeking to use experimental studies to generate practically useful knowledge (Huffmeir *et al.* 2011: 150).

Indeed many experimental studies fail to consider, in any systematic way, how their findings might or might not be relevant in a 'real world' context. An exception is the study by Rubin and Zartman (1995), who assess the relevance of findings regarding asymmetrical negotiations from a very large number of experimental studies with nine real-world negotiations characterised by asymmetry. They found significant differences between the two, which they attributed in part to the fact that 'the world is a messy place, fraught with intervening, confounding variables, making it exceedingly difficult to find real situations with the hypothetical neatness found in the laboratory' (Rubin and Zartman 1995: 39).

The constraints and limitations attached to experimental methodologies have long been recognised (see for example Kee and Knox 1970, Miller and Komorita 1986), but, despite this, negotiation research still relies very heavily on them. There is an urgent need to redress this bias towards experimental studies by undertaking in-depth detailed studies of real-world negotiations that can test hypotheses and assumptions and help identify the full range of relevant causal factors, internal and external. In this regard it is important to recognise that experimental approaches do not represent the only methodology that can be effective in identifying causal connections. A comparative approach is also powerful in this regard, because as discussed above the comparison of cases where specific factors are absent or present, and observation of negotiation outcomes in these cases, allows a causal connection to be drawn between individual factors and specific negotiated outcomes (Irmer and Druckman 2009: 215–16; Zartman 2005).

As mentioned in Chapter 1, this study adopts a comparative approach at a number of levels. Outcomes from some 45 negotiations in Australia are compared, allowing the influence of different legal, historical and political influences to be examined, and the detailed case studies are undertaken in different jurisdictions, providing further opportunities for comparison and identification of key causal variables and their influence on negotiation outcomes.

Conclusion

To facilitate analysis, I have discussed separately the way in which the negotiation literature deals with a range of key issues, including the definition of negotiation; negotiation behaviour; identifying, assessing and explaining negotiation outcomes; cross-cultural negotiations; and how to study negotiations. In practice there are of course links between the position adopted on any one of these issues and on a number of others. For example, the way in which negotiation is defined will affect how one describes, understands and explains behaviour. In turn, findings in relation to behaviour and the reasons for it support (or conceivably lead to reappraisal of) definitions of negotiation. If a normative stance is adopted on the superiority of a particular approach to negotiation, this will affect the nature of any advice offered in relation to appropriate negotiation behaviour. There will be a link between the methodology employed and the way in which a number of other issues are approached. For example, if laboratory experiments are used, they are unlikely to produce information relating to 'external' factors that might influence negotiator behaviour or explain negotiation outcomes.

This review indicates that the literature focuses heavily on characterising negotiation and on describing, explaining and assessing the behaviour of individual negotiators. A major weakness of the literature is the widespread tendency to equate negotiation outcomes with negotiation behaviour, to focus on the latter to the exclusion of the former and to concentrate on factors 'internal' to negotiation processes in explaining behaviour and outcomes. There are few attempts to develop conceptual frameworks that would integrate analysis of 'internal' and 'external' factors in a coherent way so as to explain outcomes from negotiations. However some of the research on bargaining power does offer insights that can be tested and extended through this study.

The focus of research is overwhelmingly on the individual and their personal experiences of and gains or losses from negotiations, rather than on organisations that engage in negotiations, the constituencies represented by organisations and what negotiation outcomes mean for these constituencies. As Menkel-Meadow (2009: 425) concluded in a review of 25 years of research published in one of the leading academic journals in the field, *Negotiation Journal*: 'We need more rigorous methods of evaluating the work of negotiators and finding out who their constituencies are, what we [negotiators] have (or have not) achieved for them and for those affected by the agreements we mediate or negotiate'.

The weaknesses in the literature are associated with the heavy use of experimental methodologies combined with the lack of a direct focus on outcomes and the limited attention devoted to real-world negotiations. The lack of a direct focus on outcomes and the reasons for them, combined with the lack of attention to 'real-world' negotiations, hides from view the relevance of 'external' influences on negotiations and the reality that outcomes cannot be explained simply by negotiator behaviour. Thus the use of experimental methodologies, the lack of a focus on outcomes, and the limited attention to actual negotiations have a compounding and reinforcing effect, leading often to an inability to fully or correctly describe negotiations, let alone explain their outcomes (Menkel-Meadow 2009: 423).

From the perspective of my research, such findings are disappointing because they suggest that there are few existing conceptual frameworks that could provide a basis for adequately assessing and explaining the outcomes of negotiations between Indigenous peoples and mining companies. On the other hand, they suggest that there is an urgent need for empirical studies of actual negotiations that focus on outcomes, developing criteria for their assessment and seeking to explain them in a systematic way that encompasses both 'internal' and 'external' influences on negotiations. In undertaking such a study, I seek to build on and extend the existing work of Weiss, and of researchers who have sought to explain outcomes by analysing the concept of power as it applies to negotiations. I adopt a comparative approach to assist in identifying key causal factors and demonstrating how they explain negotiation outcomes.

Notes

1 The concept of factors located within the negotiation process itself is sometimes used in another sense in the literature, to refer to variables in a formal model that both influence and are influenced by other variables of the model.

2 I acknowledge that the boundaries between 'internal' and 'external' factors are not always clear, for example because they may be defined differently depending on the specific type of negotiation involved. However, as we shall see, the negotiation literature focuses heavily on factors that are clearly susceptible to influence or manipulation by actors involved in the negotiation process, i.e. factors that are obviously 'internal' in my terms. For reasons explained in detail later in the text, this tendency is highly problematic. Thus the distinction between 'internal' and 'external' factors is both valid and important.

References

Adair, W., Taylor, M. and Tinsley, C. (2009) 'Starting Out on the Right Foot: Negotiation Schemas When Cultures Collide', *Negotiation and Conflict Management Research*, 2(2): 138–63.

Allred, K. (2000) 'Distinguishing Best and Strategic Practices: A Framework for Managing the Dilemma between Creating and Claiming Value', *Negotiation Journal*, 16(4): 387–97.

Bacharach, S. and Lawler, E. (1980) *Power and Politics in Organisations*, San Francisco: Jossey-Bass Publishers.

Bacharach, S. and Lawler, E. (1981) *Bargaining: Power, Tactics and Outcomes*, San Francisco: Jossey-Bass Publishers.

Bacharach, S. and Lawler, E. (1986) Power Dependence and Power Paradoxes in Bargaining, *Negotiation Journal*, 2(2): 167–77.

Bartos, O. J. (1995) 'Modeling Distributive and Integrative Negotiations', *Annals of the American Academy*, 542(1): 48–60.

Bisseling, D. and Sobral, F. (2011) 'A Cross-cultural Comparison of Intragroup Conflict in The Netherlands and Brazil', *International Journal of Conflict Management*, 22(2): 151–69.

Bottom, W. P. (2003) 'Keynes Attack on the Versailles Treaty: An Early Investigation of the Consequences of Bounded Rationality, Framing, and Cognitive Illusions', *International Negotiation*, 8(2): 367–402.

Brett, J. M., Adair, W., Lempereur, A., Okumura, T., Shikhirev, P., Tinsley, C. and Lytle, A. (1998) 'Culture and Joint Gains in Negotiation', *Negotiation Journal*, 14(1): 63–86.

Buelens, M., Van De Woestyne, M. and Mestdagh, S. (2008) 'Methodological Issues in Negotiation Research: A State-of-the-Art Review', *Group Decision and Negotiation*, 17(4): 321–45.

Bulow, A. M. and Kumar, R. (2011) 'Culture and Negotiation', *International Negotiation*, 16(3): 349–59.

Butler, J. (1994) 'Conflict Styles and Outcomes in a Negotiation with Fully Integrative Potential', *International Journal of Conflict Management*, 5(4): 309–25.

Cameron, M. A. and Tomlin, B. W. (2000) 'Negotiating North American Free Trade', *International Negotiation*, 5(1): 43–68.

Carnevale, P. J. and De Dreu, C. K. W. (2005) 'Laboratory Experiments in Negotiation and Social Conflict', *International Negotiation*, 10(1): 51–66.

Cohen, T. R., Leonardelli, G. J. and Thompson, L. (2014) 'Avoiding the Agreement Trap: Teams Facilitate Impasse in Negotiations with Negative Bargaining Zones', *Negotiation and Conflict Management Research*, 7(4): 232–42.

Crump, L. (2011) 'Negotiation Process and Negotiation Context', *International Negotiation*, 16(2): 197–227.

Curhan, J. R., Elfenbein, H. A. and Xu, H. (2006) 'What Do People Value When They Negotiate? Mapping the Domain of Subjective Value in Negotiation', *Journal of Personality and Social Psychology*, 91(3): 493–512.

Davidson, M. N. and Greenhalgh, L. (1999) 'The Role of Emotion in Negotiation: The Impact of Anger and Race', *Research on Negotiations in Organisations*, 7: 3–26.

De Dreu, C. K. W. and Carnevale, P. J. (2005) 'Disparate Methods and Common Findings in the Study of Negotiation', *International Negotiation*, 10(1): 193–205.

Downie, B. M. (1991) 'When Negotiations Fail: Causes of Breakdown and Tactics for Breaking the Stalemate', *Negotiation Journal*, 7(2): 175–86.

Drahos, P. (2003) 'When the Weak Bargain with the Strong: Negotiations in the World Trade Organisation', *International Negotiation*, 8(1): 79–109.

Drake, L. (1995) 'Negotiation Styles in Inter-cultural Communication', *International Journal of Conflict Management*, (6)1: 72–90.

Druckman, D. (1983) 'Social Psychology and International Negotiations: Processes and Influences', in R. F. Kidd and M. J. Saks (eds), *Advances in Applied Social Psychology*, London: Lawrence Erlbaum Associates, 51–81.

Druckman, D. (1990) 'Three Cases of Base-Rights Negotiations: Lessons Learned', in J. W. McDonald and D. B. Bendahmane (eds), *US Bases Overseas: Negotiations with Spain, Greece, and the Philippines*, Boulder, CO: Westview Press, 177–215.

Druckman, D. (1997) 'Dimensions of International Negotiations: Structures, Processes and Outcomes', *Group Decision and Negotiation*, 6: 395–420.

Druckman, D. (2001) 'Turning points in International Negotiation: A Comparative Analysis', *Journal of Conflict Resolution*, 45(4): 519–44.

Druckman, D. (2003) 'Linking Micro and Macro-Level Processes: Interaction Analysis in Context', *International Journal of Conflict Management*, 14(3/4): 177–90.

Duursma, A. (2014) 'A Current Literature Review of International Mediation', *International Journal of Conflict Management*, 25(1): 81–98.

Elgstrom, O. (1990) 'Norms, Culture and Cognitive Patterns in Foreign Aid Negotiations', *Negotiation Journal*, 6(2): 147–59.

Elms, D. (2006) 'How Bargaining Alters Outcomes: Bilateral Trade Negotiations and Bargaining Strategies', *International Negotiation*, 11(3): 399–430.

Faure, G. O. (1999) 'The Cultural Dimension of Negotiation: The Chinese Case', *Group Decision and Negotiation*, 8(3): 187–215.

Fells, R. (2013) 'Negotiation Success – An Application of the Halpert *et al.* Path Model', *Negotiation and Conflict Management Research*, 6(2): 133–50.

Filzmoser, M. and Vetschera, R. (2008) 'A Classification of Bargaining Steps and their Impact on Negotiation Outcomes', *Group Decision and Negotiation*, 17(5): 421–43.

Fisher, R. (1983) 'Negotiating Power – Getting and Using Influence', *American Behavioural Scientist*, 27(2): 149–66.

Fisher, R. (1986) 'The Structure of Negotiation: an Alternative Model', *Negotiation Journal*, 2(3): 233–5.

Fisher, R. (1989) 'Negotiating Inside Out: What are the Best Ways to Relate Internal Negotiations with External Ones?', *Negotiation Journal*, 5(1): 33–41.

Fleck, D., Volkema, R., Levy, B., Pereira, S. and Vaccari, L. (2013) 'Truth or Consequences: The Effects of Competitive-unethical Tactics on Negotiation Process and Outcomes', *International Journal of Conflict Management*, 24(4): 328–51.

Friedman, R. (2004) 'Studying Negotiations in Context: An Ethnographic Approach', *International Negotiation*, 9(3): 375–84.

Gillespie, J. and Bazerman, M. (1997) 'Parasitic Integration Win–Win Agreements Containing Losers', *Negotiation Journal*, 13(3): 271–82.

Glenn, P. and Susskind, L. (2010) 'How Talk Works: Studying Negotiation Interaction', *Negotiation Journal*, 26(2): 117–23.

Greenhalgh, L. (1987) 'Relationships in Negotiations', *Negotiation Journal*, 3(3): 235–43.

Greenhalgh, L. and Chapman, D. I. (1995) 'Joint Decision Making: The Inseparability of Relationships and Negotiations', in R. M. Kramer and D. M. Messick (eds), *Negotiation as a Social Process*, Thousand Oaks, CA: Sage, 166–85.

Halpert, J., Stuhlmacher, A., Crenshaw, J., Litcher, C. and Bortel, R. (2010) 'Paths to Negotiation Success', *Negotiation and Conflict Management Research*, 3(2): 91–116.

Han, I., Kwon, S., Bae, J. and Park, K. (2012) 'When are Integrative Tactics more Effective? The Moderating Effects of Moral Identity and the Use of Distributive Tactics', *International Journal of Conflict Management*, 23(2): 133–50.

Herbst, U. and Schwarz, S. (2011) 'How Valid is Negotiation Research Based on Student Sample Groups? New Insights into a Long-Standing Controversy', *Negotiation Journal*, 27(2): 147–70.

Hiltrop, H. and Rubin, J. (1981) 'Position Loss and Image Loss in Bargaining', *Journal of Conflict Resolution*, 25(3): 521–34.

Huffmeier, J., Krumm, S. and Hertel, G. (2011) 'The Practitioner–Researcher Divide in Psychological Negotiation Research: Current State and Future Perspective', *Negotiation and Conflict Management Research*, 4(2): 145–68.

Irmer, C. and Druckman, D. (2009) 'Explaining Negotiation Outcomes: Process or Context?', *Negotiation and Conflict Management Research*, 2(3): 209–35.

Kass, E. (2008) 'International Justice, Negotiator Outcomes Satisfaction, and Desire for Future Negotiations: R-E-S-P-E-C-T at the Negotiating Table', *International Journal of Conflict Management*, 19(4): 319–38.

Kee, H. W. and Knox, R. E. (1970) 'Conceptual and Methodological Considerations in the Study of Trust and Suspicion', *Journal of Conflict Resolution*, 14(3): 357–66.

Kirk, D., Oettingen, G. and Gollwitzer, P. (2013) 'Promoting Integrative Bargaining: Mental Contrasting with Implementation Intentions', *International Journal of Conflict Management*, 24(2): 148–65.

Kramer, R., Pommerenke, P. and Newton, E. (1993) 'The Social Context of Negotiation: Effects of Social Identity and Interpersonal Accountability on Negotiator Decision Making', *Journal of Conflict Resolution*, 9(4): 633–52.

Kumar, R. and Worm, V. (2004) 'Institutional Dynamics and the Negotiation Process: Comparing India and China', *International Journal of Conflict Management*, 15(3): 304–34.

Lewicki, R., Saunders, D. and Minton, J. (1997) *Essentials of Negotiation*, Boston: Irwin McGraw-Hill.

Lewicki, R., Saunders, D. and Minton, J. (2001) *Essentials of Negotiation, Second Edition*, Boston: Irwin McGraw-Hill.

Li, M., Plunkett Tost, L. and Wade-Benzoni, K. (2007) 'The Dynamic Interaction of Context and Negotiator Effects: A Review and Commentary on Current and Emerging Areas in Negotiation', *International Journal of Conflict Management*, 18(3): 222–59.

Lun, C. D. (1996) 'Power's Effects on the Negotiation Process (A summary of K. W. De Dreu 1995 Coercive Power and Concession Making in Bilateral Negotiations)', *Negotiation Journal*, 12(2): 181–3.

Matz, D. (2004) 'How Much Do We Know About Real Negotiations? Problems in Constructing Case Studies', *International Negotiation*, 9(3): 359–74.

McKersie, R. B., Eaton, S. C. and Kochan, T. A. (2004) 'Kaiser Permanente: Using Interest-Based Negotiations to Craft a New Collective Bargaining Agreement', *Negotiation Journal*, 20(1): 13–35.

Menkel-Meadow, C. (2009) 'Chronicling the Complexification of Negotiation Theory and Practice', *Negotiation Journal*, 25(4): 415–29.

Miles, E. and LaSalle, M. (2008) 'Asymmetrical Contextual Ambiguity, Negotiation Self-efficacy, and Negotiation Performance', *International Journal of Conflict Management*, 19(1): 36–56.

Miller, C. E. and Komorita, S. S. (1986) 'Coalition Formation in Organisations: What Laboratory Studies Do and Do Not Tell Us', *Research on Negotiation in Organisations*, 1: 117–37.

Mintz. A., Redd, S. and Vedlitz, A. (2006) 'Can We Generalize from Student Experiments to the Real World in Political Science, Military Affairs and International Relations?', *Journal of Conflict Resolution*, 50(5): 757–76.

Moore, D. A. and Murnighan, J. K. (1999) 'Alternative Models of the Future of Negotiation Research', *Negotiation Journal*, 15(4): 347–53.

Murnigham, J. K., Babcock, L., Thompson, L. and Pillutla, M. (1999) 'The Information Dilemma in Negotiations: Effects of Experience, Incentives and Integrative Potential', *International Journal of Conflict Management*, 10(4): 313–39.

Murray, J. (1986) 'Understanding Competing Theories of Negotiation', *Negotiation Journal*, 2(2): 179–86.

O'Faircheallaigh, C. (2002) *A New Model of Policy Evaluation: Mining and Indigenous People*, Aldershot, UK: Ashgate Press.

Olekalns, M. and Smith, P. L. (2003) 'Social Motives in Negotiation: The Relationship Between Dyad Composition, Negotiation Processes and Outcomes', *International Journal of Conflict Management*, 14(3/4): 233–54.

Olekalns, M., Brett, J. M. and Weingart, L. R. (2003) 'Phases, Transitions and Interruptions: Modeling Processes in Multi-Party Negotiations', *International Journal of Conflict Management*, 14(3/4): 191–211.

Pendergast, W. (1990) 'Managing the Negotiation Agenda', *Negotiation Journal*, 6(2): 135–45.

Pfetsch, F. R. and Landau, A. (2000) 'Symmetry and Asymmetry in International Negotiations', *International Negotiation*, 5(1): 21–42.

Poitras, J. (2012) 'Meta-analysis of the Impact of the Research Setting on Conflict Studies', *International Journal of Conflict Management*, 23(2): 116–32.

Polzer, J. T. (1996) 'Intergroup Negotiations: The Effects of Negotiating Teams', *Journal of Conflict Resolution*, 40(4): 678–98.

Pruitt, D. (1986) 'Trends in the Scientific Study of Negotiation and Mediation', *Negotiation Journal*, 2(3): 237–44.

Pruitt, D. (1994) 'Negotiation between Organisations: A Branching Chain Model', *Negotiation Journal*, 10(3): 217–30.

Putnam, L. (1990) 'Reframing Integrative and Distributive Bargaining: A Process Perspective', *Research on Negotiation in Organisations*, 2: 3–30.

Putnam, L. (1994) 'Challenging the Assumptions of Traditional Approaches to Negotiation', *Negotiation Journal*, 10(4): 337–46.

Putnam, L. and Fuller, R. (2014) 'Turning Points and Negotiation: The Case of the 2007–2008 Writers' Strike', *Negotiation and Conflict Management Research*, 7(3): 188–212.

Rojot, J. (1991) *Negotiation: from Theory to Practice*, London: Macmillan.

Ross, W. and LaCroix, J. (1996) 'Multiple Meanings of Trust in Negotiation Theory and Research: a Literature Review and Integrative Model', *International Journal of Conflict Management*, 7(4): 314–60.

Rubin, J. (1991) 'Actors in Negotiations', in Kremenyuk, V. A. (ed.), *International Negotiation: Analysis, Approaches, Issues*, San Francisco: Jossey-Bass, 90–9.

Rubin, J. and Zartman, W. (1995) 'Asymmetrical Negotiations: Some Survey Results that may Surprise', *Negotiation Journal*, 11(4): 349–64.

Salacuse, J. W. (1999) 'Intercultural Negotiation in International Business', *Group Decision and Negotiation*, 8(3): 217–36.

Sawchuk, J. (1998) *The Dynamics of Native Politics: The Alberta Metis Experience*, Saskatoon: Purich Publishing.

Schiff, A. (2014) 'On Success and Failure: Readiness Theory and the Aceh and Sri Lanka Peace Processes', *International Negotiation*, 19(1): 89–126.

Schroth, H. (2008) ' "Helping You Is Helping Me" Improving Students' Ethical Behaviours in a Negotiation by Appealing to Ethical Egoism and the Reputation Effect', *Negotiation and Conflict Management Research*, 1(4): 389–407.

Sebenius, J. (2011) 'What Can We Learn From Great Negotiations?', *Negotiation Journal*, 27(2): 251–6.

Sokolova, M. and Szpakowicz, S. (2007) 'Strategies and language trends in learning success and failure of negotiation', *Group Decision and Negotiation*, 16(5): 469–84.

Stuhlmacher, A. F., Gillespie, T. L. and Champagne, M. V. (1998) 'The Impact of Time Pressure in Negotiation: A Meta Analysis', *International Journal of Conflict Management*, 9(2): 97–116.

Sturm, S. (2009) 'Negotiating Workplace Equality: A Systemic Approach', *Negotiation and Conflict Management Research*, 2(1): 92–106.

Susskind, L. (2013) 'Confessions of a Pracademic: Searching for a Virtuous Cycle of Theory Building, Teaching, and Action Research', *Negotiation Journal*, 29(2): 225–37.

Susskind, N. and Susskind, L. (2008) 'Connecting Theory and Practice', *Negotiation Journal*, 24(2): 201–9.

Twitchell, D., Jensen, M., Derrick, D., Burgoon, J. and Nunamaker, J. (2013) 'Negotiation Outcome Classification Using Language Features', *Group Decision and Negotiation*, 22(1): 135–51.

Underdal, A. (1991) 'The Outcomes of Negotiations', in V. A. Kremenyuk (ed), *International Negotiation: Analysis, Approaches, Issues*, San Francisco: Jossey-Bass Publishers, 100–15.

Urlacher, B. (2014) 'Groups, Decision Rules, and Negotiation Outcomes: Simulating the Negotiator's Dilemma', *Negotiation Journal*, 30(1): 5–22.

Ury, W. (1993) *Getting Past No: Negotiating your Way from Confrontation to Cooperation*, New York: Bantam Books.

Van Es, R. (1996) *Negotiating Ethics: On Ethics in Negotiations and Negotiating in Ethics*, Delft: Eburon.

Volkema, R. and Fleck, D. (2012) 'Understanding Propensity to Initiate Negotiations: An Examination of the Effects of Culture and Personality', *International Journal of Conflict Management*, 23(3): 266–89.

Walton, R. and McKersie, R. (1965), *A Behavioral Theory of Labor Negotiations*, New York: McGraw-Hill.

Watkins, M. (1998) 'Building Momentum in Negotiations: Time-related Costs and Action-Forcing Events', *Negotiation Journal*, 14: 241–56.

Weingart, L. R., Thompson, L. L., Bazerman, M. H. and Carroll, J. S. (1990) 'Tactical Behaviour and Negotiation Outcomes', *International Journal of Conflict Management*, 1(1): 7–31.

Weiss, S. E. (1997) 'Explaining Outcomes of Negotiation: Toward a Grounded Model for Negotiations Between Organizations', *Research on Negotiations in Organizations*, 6: 247–333.

Weiss, S. E. (2010) 'Negotiators' Effectiveness with Mixed Agendas: An Empirical Exploration of Tasks, Decisions and Performance Criteria', *Group Decision and Negotiation*, 21(3): 255–90.

Wilkenfeld, J. (2004) 'Reflections on Simulation and Experimentation in the Study of Negotiation', *International Negotiation*, 9(3): 429–40.

Zarankin, T. (2008) 'A New Look at Conflict Styles: Goal Orientation and Outcome Preference', *International Journal of Conflict Management*, 19(2): 167–84.

Zartman, I. W. (1994) *International Multilateral Negotiation: Approaches to Managing Complexity*, San Francisco: Jossey-Bass Pubishers.

Zartman, I. W. (2002) 'What I Want to Know about Negotiations', *International Negotiation*, 7(1): 5–15.

Zartman, I. W. (2005) 'Comparative Case Studies', *International Negotiation*, 10(1): 3–15.

Zartman, I. and Rubin, J. (eds) (2000) *Power and Negotiation*, Ann Arbor, MI: The University of Michigan Press.

3 Aboriginal peoples and mining negotiations in Australia and Canada

Context and issues

This chapter provides essential contextual information both for the development of criteria for evaluating outcomes from negotiations between Aboriginal peoples and mining companies (Chapter 4) and for the case studies of individual negotiations (Chapters 6–9). It offer a general introduction to the histories and present conditions of Aboriginal peoples in Australia and Canada and discusses mining's environmental, cultural, social and economic impact on Aboriginal peoples and lands. It briefly reviews the approaches and motivations of governments and mining companies in relation to negotiation of agreements with Aboriginal landowners; and it provides a general overview of the case study countries, Australia and Canada.

The histories of Aboriginal peoples are characterised by diversity both within and between Australia and Canada, reflecting differences in the timing and nature of colonisation and in the ways in which various Aboriginal groups have responded to colonisation and sought to shape its impact. However, at the same time Aboriginal histories across regions and countries share fundamental features that provide a critical common context for Aboriginal experiences with mining and Aboriginal involvement in commercial negotiations.

The impact of colonisation

In both countries, colonisation was characterised by racism, by underlying beliefs regarding the inherent inferiority and lack of value of Aboriginal societies and cultures. Such beliefs were used by settlers and colonial governments to justify a range of actions and policies that were destructive of Aboriginal societies, including dispossession, removal of children, suppression of Aboriginal cultures and languages and, in some cases, attempts to physically eradicate particular Aboriginal groups. Racism was also used to justify a refusal by state authorities to recognise Aboriginal forms of governance and decision-making or to accept that Aboriginal peoples had either the capacity or the right to influence decisions which affected them, including decisions regarding development of minerals on their ancestral lands. From a European perspective, given the marked inferiority of

Aboriginal societies it was obvious that decision-making should be in the hands of non-Aboriginal government officials or settlers. Such beliefs were used in both countries to justify decisions that accorded neatly with non-Aboriginal economic and political interests (Cocker 1998: Parts 2 and 3; Norris 2010; Pearson 2009: 2–9; Sawchuk 1998: Chapter 5; Wilson 1998).

This history explains why, in the contemporary context, the issue of control over decisions that affect their lives is of fundamental importance to Aboriginal peoples. In their view, only by determining their own futures can they ensure their survival (Coon Come 2004; Pearson 2000; Slowey 2008: 49–50; United Nations 2007: 2). This perspective underlies the more specific demand articulated by many Aboriginal groups that mining should not occur on their ancestral lands without their 'free, prior and informed consent' (O'Faircheallaigh 2012a; Weitzner 2002). However, while Aboriginal peoples are keenly aware of the importance of governing themselves, the policies of colonial governments over successive generations have in many cases undermined their ability to do so by weakening traditional authority structures and decision-making processes. Contemporary government policies designed to maintain control over Aboriginal people and their resources and knowledge often reinforce colonial impacts (Lawrence and Gibson 2007; Nadasdy 2003).

Aboriginal peoples were not only denied the capacity to govern themselves, they were also denied the opportunity to participate in 'mainstream' political processes, because one specific manifestation of racism was the denial of political and constitutional rights enjoyed by non-Aboriginal citizens. In both countries, Aboriginal people were, for various lengths of time, excluded from the census, prohibited from voting, denied access to part or all of personal wage income, prohibited from establishing formal organisations and had their movements controlled (Abele 1999: 447; Chesterman and Galligan 1997; Kidd 1997; Sawchuk 1998: 7). This denial of fundamental human and political rights persisted in both countries at least until the 1960s. It prevented Aboriginal peoples from using 'normal' political channels to pursue their goals, and limited their opportunities to develop the skills required to operate effectively in a non-Aboriginal political context.

One result of this situation, in combination with colonial policies that often denied the legitimacy and relevance of Aboriginal forms of governance, is that Aboriginal communities or groups may have limited organisational capacity (including internal decision-making capacity) to support effective interactions with non-Aboriginal society. As we shall see, this limitation can have a critical impact on negotiations between Aboriginal peoples and mining companies.

A specific impact of colonisation that is particularly relevant in the current context is Aboriginal dispossession or diminution of Aboriginal rights to land, including ownership of mineral rights and control over their disposition. The degree and nature of the impact of this depended on the uses Europeans found for land in particular regions. In areas suitable for intensive agriculture or that held valuable resources such as minerals, timber or fisheries, Aboriginal peoples were usually dispossessed and either relocated elsewhere (often to government or mission reserves) or left to survive as urban fringe dwellers. Where extensive agriculture (ranching or pastoral production) left landscapes essentially intact and created a demand for their labour, Aboriginal peoples might be able to remain on, and maintain spiritual and cultural ties with, ancestral lands even when their status as owners was denied under European law. Where no obvious commercial use existed for Aboriginal land (desert and monsoonal areas in Australia, the Arctic North in Canada), Aboriginal peoples might be left in effective possession of their lands over many decades. However, that possession was always vulnerable to the realisation of some commercial potential, in particular because national or state governments controlled the disposition of mineral rights. For example, in the Cape York region of Queensland, lands that had been reserved for the exclusive use of their Aboriginal owners for a century were alienated to mining companies in the late 1950s when major bauxite discoveries were made (see Chapter 6).

In summary, the rights in land of Aboriginal peoples in Australia and Canada were severely impacted by colonialism, but the nature of that impact and so of residual Aboriginal rights in land varied greatly from region to region. These points represent a critical part of the context for negotiations between Aboriginal peoples and mining companies and they are explored in detail later in the chapter and in the case studies.

Another shared experience of Aboriginal peoples in both countries involves their low economic and social status and poor access to public services such as health and education, relative to non-Aboriginal populations. On average, Aboriginal incomes are substantially lower and unemployment substantially higher than national averages; levels of formal education are relatively low; and access to physical services such as housing, sewage and clean water is poor. Health status also tends to be poor, as indicated for example by high infant mortality rates and low life expectancy. In both countries Aboriginal people are hugely overrepresented in the criminal justice system (ABS 2012a; Government of Canada 2013; Health Council of Canada 2013; SCRGSP 2011).

The reasons for this situation are complex. They include the fact that government expenditure on service provision for Aboriginal communities has historically been extremely low and is still grossly inadequate in some cases; the undermining or destruction of Aboriginal law, society and culture as a result of dispossession and policies such as the forced removal of children; the effect of limited organisational skills and capacity on the ability of Aboriginal groups to deal with the economic, cultural and social issues they confront; and the continued unwillingness of governments to work with Aboriginal peoples to develop and implement policies that reflect Aboriginal values and priorities (Alfred 2009; Anderson and Lawrence 2006; Dillon and Westbury 2007; Pearson 2009; United Nations

General Assembly 2014). In economic terms, dispossession has often denied Aboriginal peoples access to physical resources required to sustain life and health and, combined with government policy, has denied them the ability to benefit from European economic activity on their ancestral lands. In the specific case of mining, for instance, most Aboriginal peoples have until recently not been able to share in the revenues and the direct and indirect employment generated by the industry.

Reflecting the nature of their experiences with government over many generations, Aboriginal peoples are often highly suspicious of, if not openly hostile towards, state authorities. Governments have alienated their lands, taken away their children, suppressed their culture, denied them access to rights and services available to other citizens, and denied them the opportunity to share in the economic benefits created by exploitation of their ancestral land. Government policies in Australia and Canada have of course changed significantly in the contemporary period (see below), but even in recent decades governments have been prepared to abandon policies favourable to Aboriginal people in response to commercial pressures. In the mid 1980s, Australia's federal Labor Government abandoned a proposal for limited national Aboriginal land rights legislation in the face of concerted pressure from commercial interests and their allies in state governments (Stokes 1987). In the late 1990s, Canada's federal Government, having enshrined recognition of Aboriginal rights in Canada's constitution, rejected Aboriginal requests to have land claims settled and so the nature of Aboriginal rights defined, before approving major mining projects (see Chapters 8 and 9).

Aboriginal suspicion of the State, its motives and its actions is deeply entrenched.

'We are still here': survival and continuity in contemporary Aboriginal societies

Some Aboriginal peoples have not survived the impact of colonialism. In both countries, there are instances of Aboriginal peoples who have disappeared as distinct entities. Nevertheless in virtually every region of each country Aboriginal peoples have survived. The degree of continuity between contemporary and pre-contact languages, laws, culture and social forms varies greatly from people to people and region to region, depending on the timing of contact with Europeans and the nature of the colonial impact. However, even in areas that were among the first to feel the impact of Europeans and where legal dispossession was complete, Aboriginal peoples have survived as distinct and vibrant entities (Alfred 1995; Anderson and Lawrence 2006; South West Aboriginal Land and Sea Council *et al.* 2009; Watson 2012).

In discussing contemporary Aboriginal societies, as in analysing the impacts of colonisation, the extent of diversity must be recognised. There are important differences *within* Aboriginal societies, differences whose significance will become obvious during the later analysis of negotiations. Not all members of any Aboriginal society will share the same attitudes to land, to personal economic gain, to kinship obligations or to Aboriginal cultural and spiritual practice. However, there are also commonalities, key characteristics that tend to distinguish Aboriginal peoples from the wider non-Aboriginal society. It is these commonalities I seek to highlight at this point.

Central to the existence and survival of Aboriginal peoples are the connections between land, kinship and social relations, and culture and spirituality. Connection to ancestral land or 'country' (defined here to include fresh and sea waters and air) is fundamental. Land is traditionally the source of physical survival and since time immemorial has sustained life and health. However, land is more than this. Land creates identify. A person is a *Wik Waya* or a *Tlicho* or an *Innu* because they have, usually through blood ancestors but sometimes through their place of birth or by adoption, a connection to Wik Waya, or Tlicho or Innu *lands*. To see one's ancestral lands destroyed, to be forcefully separated from them or to lose the ability to influence what happens on and to them, is not just to lose the source of physical sustenance. It is to lose one's identity or have it threatened. Thus, even if Aboriginal people have alternative sources of income with which they can purchase the physical necessities of life, damage to or separation from their ancestral lands still represents a profound threat.

Kinship is central to social organisation in Aboriginal societies. Extended families or groups consisting of a number of linked families tend to be the basic unit of social and cultural (and often of political) organisation. The nature of inter-personal behaviour and social interaction will be heavily influenced by the precise nature of kin relationships. Primary loyalties tend to be felt and expressed towards one's kin or 'clan', and in many contexts other loyalties (for instance to a community council) will have to take second place. Kinship is of course intimately connected to land. It is kin relationships to ancestors that provide an Aboriginal person with connections to land, and in turn the existence of that common connection and its expression (for example through economic production or cultural practice) reinforce ties of kinship.

The persistence and importance of kinship and of ties to land as a basis for social relationships and for political action is difficult to overstate. This is not to suggest that there are rigid land-owning and kinship structures and social rules that survive from pre-contact Aboriginal society and dictate contemporary behaviour in a mechanistic way. This is far from the case. Both connections to land and kinship systems are dynamic; they have adjusted extensively to the impact of colonisation and they continue to evolve, develop and adapt. However, kinship and connection to land are still fundamental in defining Aboriginal responses to issues such as mineral development.

Culture and spirituality are also closely linked to land. Much of Aboriginal cultural practice revolves around caring for and extracting resources from the land, while Aboriginal spiritual beliefs are often related to the existence of a creator-being or beings who are believed to have shaped the landscape and created people and other living creatures. Sites of cultural and spiritual significance are often associated with landscape features linked to those creation processes and to the spiritual entities involved in them. For some Aboriginal peoples those entities continue to reside in the land (Carmichael *et al.* 1994; O'Faircheallaigh 2008; Rose 1996, 2001; Watson 2012: 41).

Fundamental to Aboriginal welfare is the ability to care for the land and the cultural or spiritual sites that form a part of it (Angelbeck 2008). Such activity ensures that the land maintains its capacity to support people and at the same time protect the spiritual well-being of the individuals concerned because it allows them to fulfil their spiritual obligations. It follows that physical damage to the landscape, or an inability to carry out essential land management practices, can have serious cultural, spiritual and physical ramifications. The fact that damage is caused by external agencies over the opposition of Aboriginal custodians or that custodians are physically prevented from caring for country does not reduce the gravity of the situation. Custodians will still have to answer to other Aboriginal people with interests in that country and to the relevant creator or spirit beings (Dixon and Dillon 1990). Such considerations are central in identifying Aboriginal interests in negotiations relating to large mining projects.

A final and critical point to stress is that in talking separately about the past and the present and separately about land, about people (kinship and social relations) and about culture and spirituality, this discussion treats separately matters that Aboriginal people see as inseparable and in a holistic manner. They not only place a different emphasis on these matters or understand them differently from non-Aboriginal people, they do not believe they can be separated in the way that often occurs in non-Aboriginal society (Brody 2000; Randall 2003; Rose 1996).

The impact of mining on Aboriginal peoples

Large-scale modern mining involves clearing of land; the removal of huge quantities of mineral-bearing material ('ore') and waste rock and other materials ('overburden'); the disposal of tailings (the material remaining after the extraction of minerals, which typically account for only a small proportion of the total volume of ore extracted); and in some cases the disposal of other wastes such as treatment water and process chemicals. It also involves the development of extensive infrastructure, such as railways, roads and ports, and in most cases an influx of large numbers of outsiders into mining regions. The scale of mining's impact varies, of course, with the size of the project and the type of mining involved. However, nearly all modern mining operations have substantial impacts on Aboriginal landowners. The nature of those impacts, not all of which are negative, are discussed extensively in the literature (Altman and Martin 2009; Blaser *et al.*

2004; Langton 2013; Rumsey and Weiner 2004; O'Faircheallaigh and Ali 2008; Sawyer and Gomez 2012). The following is intended only as an overview to indicate the sorts of issues that mineral development is likely to generate for Aboriginal peoples. Again, impacts are discussed separately to facilitate the analysis, but such an approach does not sit comfortably with Aboriginal understandings.

Environmental impacts

Large-scale mining can have enormous environmental impacts. It can completely transform landscapes, for example where it involves the removal (literally) of entire mountains, strip-mining and lowering of land levels over wide areas, draining of lakes, diversion of rivers, or inundation of rivers or lakes with tailings. Impacts on this scale are not always involved, though many specific mines discussed later in the book certainly do have such effects and in general the trend in the world mining industry is to larger and larger projects. However, even smaller underground mines that have little obvious effect on the landscape can have major environmental impacts, for example because of the impact of their demand for water or their disposal of waste.

Mining and infrastructure development can also have location-specific impacts on areas of particular importance to Aboriginal peoples, for example sites of high spiritual significance or locations that are vital in the breeding cycle of important food species. Exploration, mining, infrastructure development and in-migration can have substantial effects on wildlife, for example where roads cross animal migration routes, where changes to water quality affect fish populations or where mine workers engage in hunting. Population growth associated with large mines can place more general strains on environmental resources, for instance because of their demand for water.

Given what has been said about the significance of their ancestral lands to Aboriginal peoples, the environmental impacts of mining are obviously of central concern to them.

Social and cultural impacts

The social effects of mining on Aboriginal peoples are complex and can be extensive and severe. Loss of land has serious social consequences as it threatens identity and the foundation for social relations. Similar effects can result where mining affects the ability to undertake subsistence food production, either because of its physical effects or because Aboriginal landowners are denied access to mining lease areas. For instance Freeman notes that, for the Inuit, inability to hunt '[denies] in one essential way the living connection with one's ancestral roots.... Hunting provides a focus for the ordering of social integration, political leadership, ceremonial activity, traditional education, personal values and Inuit identity' (1985: 254, 257).

Other social and cultural problems can arise because of in-migration of outsiders associated with major mineral developments. Aboriginal people can be culturally and socially 'swamped' by members of another culture who regard themselves as superior and who come to occupy positions of authority and influence in local governance institutions such as community councils and school boards. Outsiders can also cause problems by sexually exploiting Aboriginal women and by introducing or facilitating access to alcohol, and the higher incomes and superior level of services they usually enjoy can cause envy and resentment among Aboriginal people whose land is generating the wealth that supports their lifestyles.

As discussed below, mining can generate positive economic impacts by creating new sources of income for Aboriginal people. However in social terms these new sources of income can give rise to major problems because they are often distributed unevenly and can create or sharpen internal social divisions. This can occur directly and in the short term, for example because job opportunities are focused on a minority of the population that has substantial formal education, or because royalty income accrues mainly to individuals who occupy positions of authority in the organisations that receive royalties. More fundamental social conflict can arise over the longer term between those who receive incomes from mining and therefore wish to ensure its continuation or expansion and other community members who oppose mining because of concerns regarding environmental or cultural impacts.

Mining can also generate social tension through its impact on existing structures of authority. The additional incomes it provides can reduce the importance of access to land, underlining the authority of elders. The breakdown of traditional hunting, food sharing and other practices that were used to transmit knowledge to younger people can have similar effects, as can the absence of parents who are employed in mining operations that are distant from their home communities.

An important social impact, but one that is often difficult to document, involves an individual and collective loss of self-esteem by Aboriginal people. The influx of outsiders with scant respect for Aboriginal peoples or their cultures, the erosion of traditional authority structures, the inability to prevent damage to sites and country and more generally the lack of control over events that are shaping their lives can lead to loss of self-respect and to pervasive social problems. Jackson talks about messages Aboriginal people 'constantly receive about their inferiority and their inability to control their own lives' and the damage these do 'to Aboriginal people's sense of self-worth and capacity for self-determination' (1984: 24–5).

Mining can also generate positive social impacts in Aboriginal communities, for example where education and health services are improved as a result of project development and these services are accessible to Aboriginal residents. Upgrading of transport infrastructure can facilitate social interaction within and between Aboriginal groups that are widely dispersed, while income derived from royalties or wages can support community development initiatives or cultural or ceremonial activities. In some cases, cash incomes are also used to support traditional subsistence activities, for example through purchase of hunting equipment or development of 'outstations' or 'homeland centres' on hunting grounds distant from major settlements. More generally, where Aboriginal peoples succeed in exercising control over mineral development on their lands, it can enhance their self-esteem and help build Aboriginal capacity for self-governance.

Economic impacts

Mining creates both negative and positive economic impacts for Aboriginal communities. On the negative side, it can create a loss of economic resources though its impact on environment and wildlife, and so on Aboriginal capacity to produce food and other necessities of life. Such impacts can arise from loss of land used for mining and infrastructure development; restrictions on access to land covered by mining leases; or from the harmful effect of waste disposal on food species.

Positive effects arise from the creation of additional incomes, usually from four main sources. The first involves wage employment with mining companies. With some exceptions such employment has historically been limited, as mining companies have tended to import non-Aboriginal labour, especially for skilled positions. In recent decades, Aboriginal employment has increased, though to varying degrees across different mining companies, regions and communities. Where substantial Aboriginal employment does occur, the economic effect can be substantial given that wages in the mining industry are well above the average. The second source of income arises from Aboriginal involvement in provision of goods and services to mining companies on a contractual basis, in areas such as transport, contract mining, catering and food production, cleaning and security. In this area also, Aboriginal involvement has been limited but has grown substantially though unevenly in recent decades. A third potential source of income involves the use of infrastructure developed for mining projects in other forms of economic activity. For example, roads and air strips may be used by Aboriginal groups to undertake tourism ventures or to export artefacts to urban markets, while accommodation and other mine facilities may support other economic ventures once mining has ceased.

Finally, Aboriginal people may be able to generate additional income by imposing rentals, royalties or other similar charges on mining companies operating on their ancestral lands. Their ability to do so varies considerably depending on the legal context and a range of other factors that are discussed in detail in the case studies. Many Aboriginal groups still obtain no payments from mining on their lands, while others obtain substantial income in this way. The economic effects of this income depend on the quantum involved and on the way in which it is employed. Where income is distributed to individuals and spent on imported consumer goods, the effect will be slight. Where it is invested in service provision and community infrastructure it may help raise living standards as long as the income lasts and assuming there is no corresponding decrease in general government expenditure on services and infrastructure. If income is successfully invested in income-generating assets in the community or elsewhere, it can have a long-term positive effect on living standards that can survive the closure of the mine involved (O'Faircheallaigh 2012b).

Government

Governments tend to have four general and sometimes contradictory imperatives in dealing with mineral development on Aboriginal lands (Martin and Hoffman 2008; O'Faircheallaigh 2006: 10–16). The first is to ensure that mineral resources are exploited as quickly and as cost-effectively as possible, maximising their contribution to government revenues and to economic growth. The second is to either actively defend or promote Aboriginal interests or alternatively to avoid criticism that Aboriginal interests are being ignored. The political imperative in this case generally results not from the electoral influence of Aboriginal people themselves, who account for only a small proportion of voters, but from the desire of governments to retain or attract the support of non-Aboriginal voters sympathetic to Aboriginal interests. The third imperative is to pursue a 'strategic' political advantage, in other words an advantage in another area not directly related to the issue of Aboriginal people and mining. For example, a conservative government under threat from a radical right-wing party may reject recognition of Aboriginal rights in land in order to emphasise its conservative 'credentials', and not because it is intrinsically opposed to allowing a degree of Aboriginal control over mining. The fourth is to avoid setting precedents regarded as likely to create problems for government. For instance, recognition of Aboriginal rights in remote mining regions may be opposed because of a fear that this will encourage land claims by Aboriginal groups in 'settled' regions, creating a risk of a backlash against government from non-Aboriginal property owners.

The relative strength of these imperatives in particular cases will depend on a range of factors including:

- The budgetary significance of mineral revenues for the government concerned and the overall importance of mining to the relevant national or state/provincial economy;
- The scale of potential economic benefits associated with the particular mining project concerned;
- The stage of the electoral cycle and the general political prospects of the government concerned;
- The general state of the economy;
- The identity of the political party holding office;

- Attitudes towards Aboriginal peoples among the general voting population;
- Existing constitutional or legal protection of Aboriginal rights.

In broad terms, these factors can generate three possible policy positions on the part of governments in relation to negotiation of agreements between Aboriginal groups and mining companies. The first is outright opposition to such agreements, based on a rejection of Aboriginal claims to have a say about development on their ancestral lands. Governments refuse to cooperate with or assist the negotiating parties in any manner, and may invoke sanctions against mining companies and Aboriginal groups that seek to enter agreements. Historically, provincial or state governments in mineral-rich regions have tended to adopt this approach (Dixon and Dillon 1990; Martin and Hoffman 2008).

The second involves a laissez-faire approach in which governments play no active role in negotiations and are not parties to agreements, but do not oppose any agreements reached as long as these do not seek to impinge on government powers or revenues. Government may enable the conclusion of agreements, though in a passive manner, for example by not objecting to administrative procedures that allow agreements to be registered in mining courts, thus facilitating their enforcement.

The third approach involves an active role by government. It might undertake obligations as a party to an agreement, for example by agreeing to channel a portion of its statutory royalties from a project to the Aboriginal parties to an agreement. Alternatively it might facilitate the conclusion of agreements without participating directly, for example through legislation or policy requiring companies to negotiate with Aboriginal landowners, or by providing funding to Aboriginal parties to assist in the conduct of negotiations.

Mining companies

The major concern of companies operating on Aboriginal land is to achieve access and secure title to minerals they wish to exploit and to extract those minerals as efficiently and cheaply as possible.

This general statement must be qualified in a number of ways. A first point, obvious but important, is that mining companies are run by people who share the beliefs, values and prejudices of the wider society within which they live and which, in some cases, are not conducive to efficiency. For example, company officials may fail to train and employ Aboriginal people because they share racist attitudes prevalent among the non-Aboriginal population, even though in economic terms it might be considerably cheaper to use Aboriginal rather than imported labour.

Second, companies will wish to maximise efficiency, access and security of title across all of their operations and over the longer term, considerations of particular importance for larger companies. This may require them to behave in a manner other than that required to maximise efficiency *in a specific project*. For instance, a company may expend money at one operation to achieve a higher level of environmental protection than is required by law, because it fears that otherwise adverse publicity associated with the impact of this operation may restrict its access to resources in other jurisdictions. The growing importance of such considerations is reflected in the adoption by many major companies of 'corporate social responsibility' policies that commit them to levels of environmental protection and of engagement with communities affected by their operations that go beyond, and in some cases well beyond, what is required by law (Louche *et al.* 2010; O'Faircheallaigh and Ali 2008).

Third, mining companies operate within specific legal and administrative contexts that constrain their ability to pursue corporate goals in an untrammelled way. The extent to which they are so constrained can vary greatly over time and between jurisdictions.

Historically, the fact that they were operating on Aboriginal lands had little specific impact on the ability of miners in Australia and Canada to pursue their commercial goals. They were generally not required to have any direct dealings with Aboriginal landowners. Even where Aboriginal land ownership was recognised, companies usually dealt with government agencies whose primary interest tended to be the promotion of economic development on tribal lands. In the large majority of cases, no royalty or other specific payments were required to Aboriginal landowners. General legislation sometimes existed that purported to protect Aboriginal sites of cultural or spiritual significance, but such legislation was frequently ineffective or allowed for the exercise of administrative discretion that was applied to the benefit of mineral developers (Dillon 1990; O'Faircheallaigh 2008).

In recent decades, mining companies have been required to pay greater heed to Aboriginal interests, for a number of reasons (ICMM 2013; O'Faircheallaigh and Ali 2008; Owen and Kemp 2012). Corporate behaviour in general has come under greater public scrutiny, and this scrutiny has extended to mining company operations on Aboriginal lands. As noted above, there have been growing pressures on companies to exercise 'corporate social responsibility', to go beyond legal requirements in individual jurisdictions and behave in a way that reflects respect for the environment and for human rights. Such pressures result, in part, from consumer boycotts of prominent companies involved in contentious activities, and the growth of 'ethical investment funds' that refuse to invest in firms regarded as undertaking activities that threaten the environment or ignore human rights. In addition, Aboriginal peoples have increasingly asserted their right to determine what occurs on their ancestral lands. A number of high-profile cases (for example, the permanent closure of the Bougainville copper mine in Papua New Guinea after an armed rebellion by local landowners, and the abandonment of proposed projects due to Aboriginal opposition) have highlighted the risks to companies of ignoring Aboriginal demands. The risk of being excluded from access to low-cost reserves is of particular concern to companies, given the increasingly competitive nature of global mineral markets (Ethical Corporation 2015). Finally, legal and policy changes have occurred in the case study countries that place additional obligations on companies operating on Aboriginal lands.

While change has certainly occurred in the operating environments of companies and so in their policies and behaviour, its impact is highly uneven (O'Faircheallaigh and Ali 2008; Sawyer and Gomez 2012). For instance, large international firms that operate in multiple jurisdictions, whose ownership is dominated by major institutional investors, and who are household names (Shell, Rio Tinto) tend to readily accept the need to be seen as socially responsible. The same imperative does not exist for privately owned companies operating in one or two jurisdictions and whose existence is unknown to most members of the public. (For a specific illustration of this contrast, see Phillips 2000.) In addition, implementation of policy change within large companies can be uneven. It is one matter to introduce a policy initiative at central office in London, Amsterdam or New York, quite another to ensure that the new policy is complied with by operating divisions in Australia or Canada. The *extent* of change in law and government policy relating to Aboriginal peoples and lands is another source of variability. Law and policy in some jurisdictions has remained basically unchanged for decades, while in others change has been fundamental. In addition, Aboriginal peoples vary in their ability to assert their rights and in their capacity to take advantage of changes in corporate and public policies.

More generally, not all of the influences acting on mining companies encourage change, and in particular cost pressures may militate against change that comes at a significant financial cost. Competition in the mining industry has sharpened during recent decades, increasing the pressure to minimise costs in all areas of company operations. Growing competition reflects the inter-related factors of technological innovation, greater integration of regions and countries into global trading networks, increases in the minimum scale of viable mining projects and the long-term downward trend in real mineral prices. Only those firms that can consistently reduce real unit production costs over time can survive, and many are unable to do so. The mining industry is dominated by fewer and fewer large producers, and many mining companies that operated 20 or 30 years ago no longer exist. For most companies, it is no longer an option to ignore Aboriginal interests, and, to the extent that they must address those interests in order to remain competitive (particularly in terms of maintaining access to low-cost mineral resources), they will do so. It is also the case that highly profitable projects may be able to accommodate the costs of meeting Aboriginal demands with ease. However, competitive pressures mean that in general companies will carefully calculate those costs relative to the benefits they expect to result from positive relationships with their Aboriginal neighbours (Ethical Corporation 2015; O'Faircheallaigh 2006: 8).

The Australian context

Some 2.5 per cent of Australia's population, or 550,000 people, are Indigenous and of this number about 90 per cent identify as Australian Aborigines. About 5 per cent are Torres Strait Islanders, a Melanesian people who occupy the islands between the Australian mainland and Papua New Guinea, and the remaining 5 per cent are of mixed Aboriginal/Torres Strait Islander descent. Two-thirds of indigenous people live outside capital cities, compared to about a third for the population as a whole (ABS 2012b).

Colonisation and settlement

British settlement in Australia commenced in 1788, and over the following century much of the continent that was capable of supporting agricultural activity was appropriated from its original owners. Away from high rainfall coastal areas, agriculture consisted primarily of land-intensive production of sheep and cattle on large farms ('pastoral properties' or 'stations') leased from government. Virtually no land remained under Aboriginal ownership in Victoria, New South Wales and the southern portions of Queensland, South Australia and Western Australia. It is estimated that the Aboriginal population declined from between 1,000,000 and 1,500,000 in 1788 to around 100,000 in 1900 (Butlin 1993: 139, 229), reflecting the impact of introduced diseases, settler violence, competition from settlers for land and water and the profound impact of depopulation and dispossession on the social structures of Aboriginal peoples. In regions of Australia remote from major urban centres and unsuited to agriculture, Aboriginal people were generally left in possession of their traditional lands. However, no legal recognition was accorded to Aboriginal interests in land (see below). While such areas might be classified as Aboriginal reserves and set aside for the use of Aboriginal people, their reserve status could be revoked at any time at the discretion of government and the land made available to miners or pastoralists.

Political structures

Until federation in 1901, Australia consistent of six separate colonies that were responsible for most aspects of government other than foreign relations, where the imperial power in London played the major role. Australia's Constitution established two houses of parliament, the House of Representatives and the Senate, the latter a 'states house' with equal representation from each state, regardless of population. The Constitution creates a division of powers, based on enumerating specific responsibilities that are the preserve of the Commonwealth or federal government, based in Canberra, with the remaining or 'residual' powers vested in state governments. Matters related to mining and land management were generally the responsibility of the states. Aboriginal affairs were also a state responsibility, as a result of the fact that the Constitution (s51 (xxvi)) prohibited the Commonwealth from making 'special laws' in relation to 'the aboriginal race in any State'. The Constitution also stated that 'Aboriginal natives' should not be counted in the census (s127). The Commonwealth did have responsibility for Aborigines living in the Northern Territory, which was under federal jurisdiction until 1978 when it achieved self-government (a limited form of statehood).

In the decades since World War II, Australia's party system has been dominated by the Australian Labor Party (ALP), established by trade unionists at the end of the nineteenth century, and by the more conservative Liberal Party, which usually governs at a federal level in coalition with the rural-based National Party (formerly the Country Party). Until the 1980s, the ALP was generally regarded as a social democratic party that supported an extensive social welfare system and an active and at times interventionist role for government in the economy. However, between 1983 and the 1990s the federal Labor government strongly espoused a policy agenda emphasising trade liberalisation, economic deregulation and a 'winding back' of the welfare state. All three major political parties have supported this policy agenda since the 1980s, with only the Australian Greens and a number of non-aligned or 'independent' members of the federal parliament adopting policy positions outside this consensus.

Australia's state and federal governments, regardless of their political hue, have been strongly and consistently supportive of Australia's resource development industries.

Indigenous affairs policy

As mentioned earlier in the chapter, successive governments in Australia adopted policies that were designed to, and/or had the effect of, removing Aboriginal people from their traditional lands, denying them their political rights, threatening their social and cultural identity, and leaving them economically marginalised. Until World War II, policies were generally based on the assumption that Aborigines were a 'dying race' and that government should either step aside and not seek to slow their demise or, at best, to keep their last days 'as free from misery as we can' (Chesterman and Galligan 1997: 19–20). By the 1950s, it was clear that the Aborigines were in fact not going to disappear, and the focus of policy shifted to their assimilation into the wider non-Aboriginal society, though in reality government did little to provide Aboriginal people with the means to enter that society on anything like equal terms.

By the mid 1960s, Aboriginal people and their supporters were demanding legal, political and economic equality for Aborigines, and in 1967 referendum proposals to remove the constitutional prohibition on the Commonwealth enacting special laws and to include Aborigines in the census were carried by an overwhelming majority. In subsequent years, but particularly after 1972, with the election of Australia's first federal Labor government in 23 years, the Commonwealth became much more extensively involved in provision of education, health and other services to Aboriginal communities. In addition, during the late 1970s and the early 1980s there was bi-partisan support for Aboriginal people to maintain their distinct identity and have greater control over their own affairs. However, there were significant differences between the ALP's commitment to Aboriginal 'self-determination' and the Liberal Party's more restricted vision for 'self-management'. The commitment to self-determination found its clearest expression in the establishment in 1990 of the Aboriginal and Torres Strait Islander Commission (ATSIC). ATSIC consisted of an elected national representative body for indigenous Australians, which played a key role in formulating overall policy and in resource allocation, and a bureaucracy responsible for key areas of service delivery and reporting to the federal Minister for Aboriginal Affairs.

The election of a Liberal/National party coalition government in 1996 signalled a major shift in federal Aboriginal affairs policy. Coalition leaders, and in particular the new Prime Minister John Howard and his deputy and leader of the National Party Tim Fischer had been highly critical of the establishment of ATSIC in 1990 and had also attacked the Labor Government's legislative recognition of inherent Aboriginal rights in land in the *Native Title Act 1993* (see below). The Liberal government abolished ATSIC in 2004, reduced the autonomy exercised by federally funded Aboriginal organisations and wound back the rights enjoyed by Aboriginal landowners under the *Native Title Act* (see next section). These initiatives were not reversed when Labor returned to government in 2007.

Land rights and native title

For nearly 200 years after the arrival of Europeans, no recognition was afforded to the rights of Aboriginal people in their traditional lands. Aboriginal people sought to assert those rights on many occasions, in part through armed resistance, but resistance was in most cases futile. From the mid 1960s, Aboriginal peoples began to use their newly won political rights to push for legal recognition of their status as landowners. In 1976 this pressure had its first tangible result when the federal government introduced the *Aboriginal Land Rights (Northern Territory) Act 1976* (the *Land Rights Act*).

The *Land Rights Act* allows Aboriginal people in the Northern Territory to claim ownership of their traditional lands and, where they are successful, to determine whether or not mineral exploration and development should occur on their land. Where mining is allowed, the landowners concerned receive a portion of the statutory royalties that would normally accrue to government, as well as any private royalty they negotiate with the developer. Since 1976, Aboriginal people have successfully claimed ownership of nearly half of the Northern Territory's land area. In the years after 1976, a number of governments introduced state Aboriginal land rights legislation. However, this generally applied to limited areas of land, and in no case were Aboriginal people granted control over exploration or mining or access to statutory royalties.

Major changes occurred in 1992 as a result of the Australian High Court's decision in the *Mabo* case. The Court found that the inherent rights in land of the inhabitants of Mir, an island in the Torres Strait, were not extinguished by the imposition of colonial rule. Those rights could survive, as long as they had not been extinguished by valid government grants of interests to third parties and as long as the Indigenous people involved had maintained their connection with their traditional lands. The Court's decision did not threaten existing non-Indigenous interests in land, including mining interests. However it did have far-reaching implications, because it set aside the fundamental assumption of land law in Australia, that inherent indigenous interests in land were extinguished as Britain established its colonial rule.

The Australian Government responded to the *Mabo* decision by introducing federal legislation, the *Native Title Act 1993 (NTA)*. This validated existing titles in land but also created a process through which Aboriginal and Torres Strait Islander people could claim land in which native title survived. In addition, it created what is called the 'Right to Negotiate', which provides groups that have registered native title claims with an opportunity to negotiate about the terms of any mineral development with the company involved and with the state government that proposes to issue the relevant mining interests. If negotiations do not lead to an agreement after six months, either party can refer the matter to arbitration by an administrative body established under the Act, the National Native Title Tribunal (NNTT). Decisions of the Tribunal are not final, but may be set aside by the responsible government minister (Bartlett 2004). (See Chapter 5 for more details.)

Unlike the *Land Rights Act*, the *Native Title Act* does not confer on Aboriginal landowners a veto over exploration or mining, and neither does it give them access to statutory royalties. Rather it gives them a limited opportunity to sit down and negotiate with developers, limited in the sense both that it is subject to a time constraint and that a developer can, if negotiations do not produce agreement, seek the grant of the mining interest from a government administrative tribunal whose decisions can, in turn, be reversed by a government minister.

The introduction of the *NTA* was strongly opposed by the Australian mining industry (Lavelle 2001), and by the Liberal and National opposition parties. When the latter came to office in 1996, they immediately indicated their intention of amending the Act to reduce the procedural rights of native title claimants. They did so in 1998, for instance imposing much more stringent requirements for the registration of native title claims, and removing the Right to Negotiate from renewal of mining leases and from mine infrastructure such as railways, ports and transmission lines. The amendments also allowed state governments to extinguish native title over hundreds of categories of tenures, and to introduce state native title legislation that would offer minimal procedural rights to native title interests (Bartlett 2004: 52–64).

The Australian mining industry

The large majority of Australia's 22 million people live along the country's eastern and southern coasts, in most cases far removed from the country's major mining regions. Mining accounts for between about 7 and 10 per cent of GDP, depending in part on commodity prices, and directly employs less than 5 per cent of the workforce. However the industry's economic significance is much greater than these figures would suggest, for a number of reasons.

First, significant employment is created indirectly by mining as a result of its demand for inputs and the processing of minerals into semi-finished and finished metal products, and a number of towns and regions rely heavily on this indirect or 'multiplier' employment. Second, non-fuel minerals continue to be Australia's largest single export, accounting for nearly 60 per cent of all exports of goods and services in recent years (ABS 2012b). Third, mining plays an important role in the economies of some states and territories, in particular Queensland, Western Australia and the Northern Territory. It accounts, for example, for over 20 per cent of Gross Industry Output in Western Australia, and mineral royalties contribute more than 20 per cent of state government revenues (ABS 2012b). Two other factors enhance the perceived importance of mining, both for political decision-makers and the wider public. The first is that some individual mining projects can generate large absolute increases in employment, with thousands of jobs being created during project construction and hundreds of permanent jobs generated during the operational phase. As a result the industry tends to draw the attention, and the support, of politicians anxious to demonstrate their ability to create jobs. Second, historically Australia's economic fortunes have been tied to those of the industry, which has allowed industry leaders to argue that what benefits the mining industry also benefits Australia (Lavelle 2001; Stokes 1987).

The mining industry has represented an active and powerful political force in Australia, mobilising its substantial resources in extensive publicity campaigns on the issue of Aboriginal land rights. It successfully opposed the introduction of Aboriginal land rights legislation in Western Australia and nationally in the mid 1980s and lobbied hard against the introduction of the *NTA* in 1993 and in favour of amendments to reduce its scope during the period 1995–1998 (Lavelle 2001; Libby 1989; Marsh *et al.* 2014; Stokes 1987).

The Canadian context

Some 4.3 per cent of Canada's population, or 1.4 million people, are Aboriginal. Of this number, about 61 per cent are 'First Nation' or Indian, 4 per cent are Inuit and 32 per cent are Metis, the descendents of unions between Aboriginal women and (predominantly French and Scottish) trappers and traders. Nearly seven out of ten Aboriginal people live outside metropolitan areas, the same proportion as in Australia.

Colonisation and settlement

European settlement of Canada commenced in the early seventeenth century, and during the next 200 years focused primarily on the extraction of natural resources, in particular furs, fish and timber. Particularly in the fur industry, much of the required labour was undertaken by Aboriginal people, and the extent and intensity of European settlement was therefore limited. From the early nineteenth century large-scale agricultural development increased, particularly in Ontario, Quebec and the Prairie provinces of central Canada. The European population expanded greatly and as this occurred Canada's Aboriginal people experienced patterns of colonial impact similar to those experienced in Australia – large-scale dispossession in regions suitable for agriculture; precipitous decline in populations; and the weakening and in some cases destruction of Aboriginal social and governing structures (Alfred 2009).

However, two fundamental differences existed between the colonial contexts in Australia and Canada. First, in the latter, Aboriginal peoples played, at least initially, a key role in allowing economic exploitation to occur. Because of the economic importance of fur bearing animals, a resource absent in Australia, the ability of Aboriginal people to travel into and hunt in remote and inhospitable regions secured for them an important place in the colonial economy. No such place was available in Australia's colonial economy, and indeed the animals hunted by Aborigines competed directly with the sheep and cattle of the colonisers, leading the latter to push the Aborigines aside. Only in Australia's far north, where the climate and the marginal nature of the land made it uneconomic to employ white labour, did Aboriginal people gain a significant foothold in the new economy, albeit under conditions that were at times little better than slavery (Norris 2010: 135–7).

The second key difference was that, while Australia had but one colonial power and no adjacent colonies of any significance, Canada had two colonial powers in Britain and France and had America as its neighbour. This situation resulted in a series of military conflicts between the two colonial powers and between the English and the American colonists that made Aboriginal peoples valuable allies, allowing them to gain political leverage by playing the colonial powers against each other (and also against their traditional Aboriginal enemies).

In combination, these factors resulted in recognition of Aboriginal political and economic rights in ways that have no precedent in Australia. Two specific aspects warrant mention. The first was the Royal Proclamation of 1763. This recognised Aboriginal title insofar as it established a lawful process for obtaining Aboriginal lands by negotiation and treaty and stated that, until that process had occurred, Aboriginal peoples were to remain unmolested in their use of land and under the protection of the Crown. Only the Crown, not private individuals, could acquire land from Indians. The second was that the British Crown, and subsequently Canada, signed treaties with numerous Aboriginal nations in eastern and central Canada, though treaty making had come to an end by the time that Canada came to engage in a systematic way with Aboriginal populations in much of British Columbia and the far north (Russell 2006: 42–40).

During the nineteenth and much of the twentieth century, Canadian governments may have ignored the spirit of the 1763 Proclamation and both the spirit and the letter of the treaties (Jull 2001: 14; Usher 1997). Yet, as we shall see, their existence represented certain underlying legal and political realities that would have important implications for Aboriginal peoples in the contemporary period.

Political structures

Canada was created by the confederation of four colonies in 1867, with a further five colonies joining the union during the succeeding decades and Newfoundland and Labrador finally joining in 1949. The federal government had jurisdiction over the Yukon and Northwest Territories, which covered much of Canada's far north. The eastern portion of the Northwest Territories, where Inuit account for a majority of the population, gained self-government as the territory of Nunavut in 1999.

In contrast to Australia, both the provinces and the federal government hold specific powers under Canada's constitution, and residual powers adhere to the federal government. Provincial powers include responsibility for mining and other land management issues (*Constitution Act*, s92). Again in contrast to Australia, responsibility for Aboriginal affairs lies at the federal level, with Ottawa given exclusive authority to legislate with respect to 'Indians and land reserved for the Indians' (*Constitution Act*, s91 (24)). This reflects the influence of the Royal Proclamation of 1763, which had mandated that dealing in Aboriginal lands was a Crown prerogative, and the Crown's role in treaty making.

The shape of party politics in Canada is more complex than in Australia. The Liberal and Progressive Conservative formed Canada's federal governments for much of the period between World War II and the turn of the century. However in recent years both parties have suffered serious electoral defeats. The Progressive Conservatives have been replaced by the Conservative Party of Canada (in government since 2006), and in 2011 the Liberal Party lost its status as the official opposition to the social democratic New Democratic Party (NDP). Major parties have not dominated Canadian politics to the same extent as the ALP and the Liberal/ National parties have dominated in Australia. This reflects the powerful impact of regional factors in Canada. For instance, resentment in Western Canada against what is seen as its political marginalisation has generated support for the NDP and the conservative Reform Party. The NDP has won office in a number of western provinces and has exerted significant influence in federal politics, for instance allowing a number of minority Liberal governments to retain office. For different reasons, the Parti Quebecois, formed in 1968, has also had a major impact on national politics, as well as winning power in Quebec.

The existence of a substantial minority of French-speaking Canadians, accounting for 25 per cent of the population and a majority of voters in Quebec, has had a major influence on Canadian politics. It has resulted, it can be argued, in an acceptance of the need to accommodate ethnic differences, which has also affected Canada's approach to its Aboriginal peoples, and led to a major focus on the role of constitutional arrangements in entrenching such an accommodation. This focus is evident, for example, in the repatriation and extensive amendment of Canada's Constitution in 1982. As part of this process, Aboriginal rights were entrenched in the Constitution, a point discussed below.

Indigenous affairs policy

Canada's indigenous affairs policy, reflecting in particular the context of treaty making, was from the start more highly formalised and based in legislation than was the case in Australia. Treaties were agreements between the Crown and members of 'Indian' tribes or bands, under which the groups involved recognised the authority of the Crown and ceded parts of their territories for use by the Crown. In return they were allocated reserves (usually covering only a small part of their traditional lands) on which to live, and were paid annuities by the Crown. Numerous treaties were signed by the British Crown prior to confederation. During the decades between 1857 and the late 1920s, when treaty-making ceased, the federal government signed a series of additional numbered treaties with the result that treaties covered most of Canada apart from northern British Columbia, the Northwest and Yukon Territories, northern Quebec and Labrador. It is now clear that, while the federal government assumed that treaties involved a surrender of Aboriginal sovereignty and of Aboriginal rights on non-reserve land, Aboriginal signatories saw them quite differently, regarding them as 'treaties of peace and friendship' rather than as measures extinguishing their political autonomy or their rights in land (Russell 2006: 44–5; Usher 1997: 104).

The *Indian Act*, originally passed in 1876 and regularly amended thereafter, distinguished between 'status' and 'non-status' Indians. 'Status'

Indians were people who were registered by the federal government as 'Indians', and included members both of groups which had signed treaties and of groups which had not. They were entitled to benefits under the *Indian Act*, including the right to reside on reserves and, where relevant, to receive treaty payments. The *Indian Act* allowed the federal government to exercise control over almost every aspect of the lives of status Indians, in a manner that was at best paternalistic and at worst designed to destroy the distinct identities, cultures and economies of Aboriginal peoples (Alfred 1995: 56–8; Crane 1994: 408).

Indigenous Canadians who were not treated as 'status Indians' included Indian and Inuit groups whose members had never been recognised as status Indians and individuals who had lost their status, as occurred for example when an Aboriginal woman married a non-Aboriginal man or when Aboriginal people surrendered their status to enjoy rights they could otherwise not avail themselves of (for instance, to consume alcohol or to vote in elections). They also included the Metis, who lacked a land base, resided mostly in the prairies and in the NWT's Mackenzie Valley and, according to Canada, were the responsibility of the provinces.

During the period after World War II, Canadian government policy was based on the assumption that Aboriginal peoples would gradually become assimilated into mainstream Canadian society. This approach was reflected, for instance, in the centralisation of dispersed Aboriginal populations into settlements where they could access mainstream government services, and in the widespread removal of Aboriginal children to residential schools where use of Aboriginal languages and other traditional practices were forbidden. In 1969, the Liberal Government of Pierre Trudeau published a white paper on Aboriginal affairs policy that explicitly articulated an assimilationist agenda. The government proposed to terminate all special relationships, including treaty relationships, with Indians and encourage their rapid integration into the dominant society so that they would become 'Canadians as all other Canadians' (Asch 1984: 63).

The white paper resulted in a widespread backlash among Aboriginal people, further galvanising a growing political movement for greater recognition of Aboriginal political rights. In the early 1970s, a number of national and regional Aboriginal and Inuit political leaders started to push hard for major changes in government policy. Their cause was assisted by a landmark Supreme Court decision recognising Aboriginal rights in land in 1973 (see next section) and by political and constitutional debates surrounding the position of French Canadians. During the remainder of the 1970s and the early 1980s, the federal government significantly modified its Indigenous policies, abandoning the push for assimilation and accepting the legitimacy of Aboriginal claims for self-government.

This shift in policy is reflected in a number of areas. One is the entrenchment of Aboriginal rights in Canada's constitution when it was repatriated in 1982. The *Constitution Act 1982* states:

35(1) The existing aboriginal and treaty rights of the aboriginal peoples of Canada are hereby recognised and affirmed.
(2) In this Act, 'aboriginal peoples of Canada' include the Indian, Inuit and Metis peoples of Canada.

The new policy orientation is also reflected in the increasing devolution of control over delivery of public services on Indian reserves; in the creation of the Inuit-dominated territory of Nunavut; in the Canadian government's negotiation of a series of comprehensive land claim settlements with groups in western and northern Canada; and in its increasing willingness to include in these settlements provisions relating to Aboriginal management of government programs, and co-management of natural resources (AANDC 2014).

Land rights and native title

Aboriginal groups that signed treaties continued to occupy and use (small) portions of their traditional territories. However, reserves were held in trust on behalf of band members by Canada, which exercised substantial control over land use and over time allowed substantial areas of reserve land to be alienated and/or used for commercial purposes. The Canadian government's view has been that native title is extinguished in areas subject to treaties, a view rejected by many affected Aboriginal people. Where mineral development has occurred on reserve lands, Indian bands have had little say in determining the commercial and other conditions under which this occurs, with conditions being determined by the *Indian Mining Regulations*. In a limited number of cases, for example the Hobema in Alberta, substantial revenues accrued to bands from exploitation of mineral resources on reserves.

As in Australia, Canada's legal system did not recognise the existence of any *inherent* Aboriginal rights in land. This changed in 1973 when Canada's Supreme Court, in the *Calder* case, recognised that such rights did exist at the time of European settlement and could continue to exist under certain circumstances. While the 1982 Constitution entrenches 'existing Aboriginal and treaty rights', it does not define those rights, and subsequent attempts to define them in negotiations involving Canada, the provinces and Aboriginal groups failed (Abele 1999: 449–50). In the area of land and native title, it has been left to the Supreme Court to do so. In a series of decisions including *Delgamuuk, Sparrow, Haida Nation*, and *Mikisew Cree First Nation*, it has both helped define the content of Aboriginal rights, which importantly are deemed to confer the right to a share of mineral and other resources extracted from the land, and laid down substantial requirements for government to consult with Aboriginal groups before granting any rights in their traditional lands to third parties (AANDC 2014; Bankes 2005; Christie 2007; Gibson and O'Faircheallaigh 2010: 29–31).

As noted earlier, treaty-making ceased in the late 1920s and left large areas of northern Canada and British Columbia without treaties. After the Calder case, the Canadian government began to negotiate a series of land claim settlements or 'modern treaties', designed in part to address issues of native title and resource development. While land claim settlements have evolved over time and differ significantly in their specific provisions, their basic structure is similar. The Aboriginal groups are granted surface and sub-surface rights to a portion (usually less than 10 per cent) of their traditional lands, typically around communities and in areas of critical importance for key food species, and resource development cannot occur on these areas without their consent. They also hold surface rights to somewhat larger areas, and potential developers of resources in these areas will have to negotiate access before developing them. Finally, native title rights will be extinguished over the remainder of the groups' traditional lands, though the Aboriginal groups typically retain rights to hunt and fish and to be involved with government in management of wildlife (Gibson and O'Faircheallaigh 2010: 31–3; Usher 1997). Negotiation of land claims is time consuming, in part because of the reluctance of many Aboriginal groups to accept extinguishment of native title rights over large parts of their traditional lands.

The Canadian mining industry

Canada is the world's leading producer of uranium and potash, its third largest producer of diamonds, and ranks in the top five producers of primary aluminium, nickel, and platinum group metals. About 20 per cent of world expenditure on exploration occurs in Canada. Mining and mineral processing contributes 3.0 per cent of Canada's GDP and 53,000 people are employed in mining, 61,000 in smelting and refining and 194,000 in the manufacture of mineral and metal products. Exports of mineral products are some C$85 billion, equivalent to about a fifth of total domestic exports. In 2010, weekly average earnings in the industry were C$1,079, compared to $853 for the economy as a whole, and freight of minerals and metal products account for nearly 60 per cent of Canada's rail freight traffic (Natural Resources Canada 2013). As in Australia, the substantial employment and foreign exchange earnings associated with large individual projects serve to highlight the industry's economic importance and attract the attention of the media and policy-makers (see for instance 'Canadian diamonds add sparkle to EU trade', *National Post*, 29 March 2006; 'No Vacancy: Boomtown Alberta', *National Post*, 1 April 2006).

During recent decades, Canada's mining industry has not had as high a political profile as its Australian counterpart. It has not launched major publicity campaigns in relation to Aboriginal land rights and indeed until quite recently the industry's top body, the Minerals Association of Canada, did not have a policy on Aboriginal land rights. The industry has certainly been concerned with the potential impact of land claims, and of a failure to settle them expeditiously, on investment in exploration and mining. However, it has generally taken the view that land claims and native title are matters to be resolved between Aboriginal peoples and government, and its public pronouncements have involved encouraging them to do so quickly and in a manner that promotes a stable and transparent regulatory regime (Crane 1994: 420; Mining Association of Canada 2012: 11–12).

Conclusion

Aboriginal peoples in Australia and Canada have survived a colonial experience that subjected them to systemic racism, denied them the ability to govern themselves, largely dispossessed them of their lands, and sought to undermine their cultures. It has left them, relative to the non-Aboriginal population, economically deprived and with poor access to public services and infrastructure and, in particular, poor access to the education and health services that are so fundamental to human well-being. Yet, even where European impact has been most severe, many Aboriginal peoples have survived as distinct and vibrant societies, displaying beliefs, values and social structures that are distinctive and that place a high value on maintaining, in a holistic way, a world based on inter-locking connections between land, people, culture and spirituality.

For Aboriginal peoples, mining poses a major threat to the maintenance of such a world. It can destroy the land that is at its heart, destroy sites of particular cultural or spiritual significance, perpetuate the denial of self-determination that was at the heart of the colonial experience, create divisions among people and threaten the economic basis of their existence. On the other hand, mining has the potential to raise Aboriginal incomes, improve access to services and infrastructure, support Aboriginal cultural and economic activity and provide an opportunity to assert the right to self-determination and build self-esteem and institutional capacity.

Against this background, Aboriginal peoples tend to approach negotiations about mining projects with three fundamental objectives. The first is to ensure that their status as the original owners of the land is recognised and that on this basis they are able to control or at least influence development on their ancestral lands. This is essential both for the achievement of other objectives and because it relates to the fundamental and wider goal of asserting their right and ability to govern themselves. Second, Aboriginal peoples wish to minimise the negative effects of mining on country and on people. Third, they wish to maximise the economic opportunities mining provides to progress towards standards of living that are taken for granted by the non-Aboriginal population.

Governments may have an incentive to participate in agreements between miners and Aboriginal peoples or to support their conclusion in order to ensure that mineral development proceeds smoothly and that any political costs associated with Aboriginal opposition to mining are avoided. However, government may perceive those costs as negligible given that few voters are Aboriginal, the typically low political profile of Aboriginal issues and the continued salience of anti-Aboriginal feeling in the wider electorate. Mining companies are increasingly required to address Aboriginal concerns, though the degree of pressure they face varies considerably depending on the type of company involved, the prevailing legislative and policy environment and the political capacity of the Aboriginal people and organisation they are dealing with. Growing competitive pressures in the mining industry impose contradictory pressures on companies. On the one hand, they cannot afford to be excluded from access to low-cost reserves by Aboriginal opposition. On the other, they must constantly seek to minimise their production costs, including the cost of entering agreements with Aboriginal landowners.

Against this background, we next consider criteria that might be applied in evaluating the outcomes of negotiations between Aboriginal people and mining companies.

References

AANDC (Aboriginal Affairs and Northern Development Canada) (2014) *The Government of Canada's Approach to Implementation of the Inherent Right and the Negotiation of Aboriginal Self-Government*. Online. Available www.aadnc-aandc.gc.ca/eng/1100100031843/1100100031844#inhrsg.

Abele, F. (1999) 'The Importance of Consent: Indigenous Peoples' Politics in Canada' in J. Bickerton and A.-G. Gagnon (eds), *Canadian Politics* 3rd ed., Peterborough: Broadview Press, 443–61.

ABS (Australian Bureau of Statistics) (2012a) *Census of Population and Housing: Characteristics of Aboriginal and Torres Strait Islander Australians, 2011*. Online. Available www.abs.gov.au/ausstats/abs@.nsf/mf/2076.0.

ABS (Australian Bureau of Statistics) (2012b) *Year Book Australia 2012*. Online. Available www.abs.gov.au/ausstats/abs@.nsf/mf/1301.0.

Alfred, T. (1995) *Heeding the Voices of Our Ancestors: Kahnawake Mohawk Politics and the Rise of Native Nationalism*, Toronto: Oxford University Press.

Alfred, T. (2009) 'Colonialism and State Dependency', *Journal of Aboriginal Health*, 5(2): 42–60.

Altman, J. and Martin, D. (eds) (2009) *Power, Culture and Economy: Indigenous Australians and Mining*, Canberra: ANU E-Press.

Anderson, K. and Lawrence, B. (2006) *Strong Women Stories: Native Vision and Community Survival*, Toronto: Sumach Press.

Angelbeck, B. (2008) 'Archaeological Heritage and Traditional Forests within the Logging Economy of British Columbia', in C. O'Faircheallaigh and S. Ali (eds), *Earth Matters: Indigenous Peoples, the Extractive Industries and Corporate Social Responsibility*, Sheffield: Greenleaf Publishing, 123–42.

Asch, M. (1984) *Home and Native Land: Aboriginal Rights and the Canadian Constitution*, Toronto: Methuen.

Bankes, N. (2005) 'Mikisew Cree and the Lands Taken Up Clause of the Numbered Treaties', *Resources*, 92/93: 1–8.

Bartlett, R. (2004) *Native Title in Australia,* 2nd ed., Chatswood, NSW: LexusNexis Butterworths.

Blaser, M., Feit, H. A. and McRae, G. (2004) *In the Way of Development: Indigenous Peoples, Life Projects and Globalization*, London: Zed Books.

Brody, H. (2000) *The Other Side of Eden: Hunters, Farmers and the Shaping of the World*, Vancouver: Douglas and McIntyre.

Butlin, N. G. (1993) *Economics and the Dreamtime: A Hypothetical History*, Cambridge: Cambridge University Press.

Carmichael, D. L., Hubert, J., Reeves, B. and Schanche, A. (eds) (1994) *Sacred Sites, Sacred Places*, London and New York: Routledge.

Chesterman, J. and Galligan, B. (1997) *Citizens without Rights: Aborigines and Australian Citizenship*, Melbourne: Cambridge University Press.

Christie, G. (2007) *Aboriginal Nationhood and the Inherent Right to Self-Government*, Research Paper for the National Centre for First Nations Governance. Online. Available http://fngovernance.org/ncfng_research/gordon_christie.pdf.

Cocker, M. (1998) *Rivers of Blood, Rivers of Gold: Europe's Conflict with Tribal Peoples*, London: Jonathan Cape.

Coon Come, M. (2004) 'Survival in the Context of Mega-Resource Development: Experiences of the James Bay Crees and the First Nations of Canada', in M. Blaser, H. A. Feit and G. McRae (eds), *In the Way of Development: Indigenous Peoples, Life Projects and Globalization*, London: Zed Books, 153–65.

Crane, B. A. (1994) 'Native Rights and Resource Development in Canada', *Journal of Energy and Natural Resources Law*, 12(4): 406–23.

Dillon, M. (1990) ' "A Terrible Hiding": Western Australia's Aboriginal Heritage Policy', in R. Dixon and M. Dillon (eds), *Aborigines and Diamond Mining: the Politics of Resource Development in the East Kimberley*, Nedlands, WA: University of Western Australia Press, 40–54.

Dillon, M. and Westbury, N. D. (2007) *Beyond Humbug: Transforming Government Engagement with Indigenous Australia*, West Lakes, SA: Seaview Press.

Dixon, R. and Dillon, M. (eds) (1990) *Aborigines and Diamond Mining: the Politics of Resource Development in the East Kimberley*, Nedlands, WA: University of Western Australia Press.

Ethical Corporation (2015) *Commodity Prices Briefing: Building a CSR Strategy During an Era of Low Commodity Prices*. Online. Available http://s3.amazon-aws.com/cms_assets/accounts/690b848f-131d-4af6-a319-824db8c89e5b/site-50109/cms-assets/documents/193715-56143.commodity-price-briefing.pdf.

Freeman, M. M. R. (1985) 'Effects of Petroleum Activities on the Ecology of Arctic Man', in F. R. Engelhardt (ed), *Petroleum Effects in the Arctic Environment*, London and New York: Elsevier, 245–73.

Gibson, G. and O'Faircheallaigh, C. (2010) *IBA Community Toolkit: Negotiation and Implementation of Impact and Benefit Agreements*, Ottawa: Walter & Duncan Gordon Foundation.

Government of Canada, Office of the Correctional Investigator (2013) *Aboriginal Offenders – A Critical Situation*. Online. Available www.oci-bec.gc.ca/cnt/rpt/oth-aut/oth-aut20121022info-eng.aspx.

Health Council of Canada (2013) *Canada's Most Vulnerable: Improving Health Care for First Nations, Inuit and Metis Seniors*. Online. Available www.hhr-rhs.ca/images/stories/Senior_AB_Report_2013_EN_final.pdf.

ICMM (International Council on Mining and Metals) (2013) *Indigenous Peoples and Mining: Position Statement May 2013*, London: ICMM.

Jackson, J. E. (1984) 'The Impact of the State on Small-Scale Societies', *Studies in Comparative International Development*, Summer 1984, 3–32.

Jull, P. (2001) ' "Nations with Whom we are Connected" – Indigenous Peoples and Canada's Political System', *Australian Indigenous Law Review*, 6(3): 1–15.

Kidd, R. (1997) *The Way we Civilise: Aboriginal Affairs – the Untold Story*, St Lucia: University of Queensland Press.

Langton, M. (2013) *Boyer Lectures 2012: The Quiet Revolution: Indigenous People and the Resources Boom*, Sydney: Harper Collins.

Lavelle, A. (2001) 'The Mining Industry's Campaign Against Native Title: Some Explanations', *Australian Journal of Political Science*, 36(1): 101–22.

Lawrence, R and Gibson, C. (2007) 'Obliging Indigenous Citizens? Shared Responsibility Agreements in Australian Aboriginal Communities', *Cultural Studies*, 21 (4–5): 650–71.

Libby, R. (1989) *Hawke's Law: The Politics of Mining and Aboriginal Land Rights in Australia*, Nedlands, WA: University of Western Australia Press.

Louche, C., Idowu, S. O. and Filho, W. L. (eds) (2010) *Innovative CSR: From Risk Management to Value Creation*, Sheffield: Greenleaf Publishing.

Marsh, D., Lewis, C. and Chesters, J. (2014) 'The Australian Mining Tax and the Political Power of Business', *Australian Journal of Political Science*, 49(4): 711–25.

Martin, T. and Hoffman, S. M. (eds) (2008) *Power Struggles: Hydro Development and First Nations in Manitoba and Quebec*, Winnipeg: University of Manitoba Press.

Mining Association of Canada (2012) *Improving the Investment Climate in Canada's North*. Online. Available http://mining.ca/sites/default/files/documents/ImprovingInvestmentClimateintheNorthApril2012.pdf.

Nadasdy, P. (2003) *Hunters and Bureaucrats*, Vancouver: UBC Press.

Natural Resources Canada (2013) *Additional Statistics – Minerals and Metals*. Online. Available www.nrcan.gc.ca/publications/statistics-facts/1245.

Norris, R. (2010) *The More Things Change … The origins and Impact of Australian Indigenous Economic Exclusion*, Brisbane: Post Pressed.

O'Faircheallaigh, C. (2006) 'Aborigines, Mining Companies and the State in Contemporary Australia: A New Political Economy or "Business as Usual"?' *Australian Journal of Political Science*, 41(1): 1–22.

O'Faircheallaigh, C. (2008) 'Negotiating Protection of the Sacred? Aboriginal-Mining Company Agreements in Australia', *Development and Change*, 39(1): 25–51.

O'Faircheallaigh, C. (2012a) 'International Recognition of Indigenous Rights, Indigenous Control of Development and Domestic Political Mobilization', *Australian Journal of Political Science*, 47(4): 531–46.

O'Faircheallaigh, C. (2012b) 'Curse or Opportunity? Mineral Revenues, Rent Seeking and Development in Aboriginal Australia', in M. Langton and J. Longbottom (eds), *Community Futures, Legal Architecture: Foundations for Indigenous People in the Global Mining Boom*, Abingdon and New York: Routledge, 45–58.

O'Faircheallaigh, C. and Ali, S. (eds) (2008) *Earth Matters: Indigenous Peoples, the Extractive Industries and Corporate Social Responsibility*, Sheffield: Greenleaf Publishing.

Owen, J. R. and Kemp, D. (2012) 'Social Licence and Mining: A Critical Perspective', *Resources Policy*. Online. http://dx.doi.org/10.1016/j.resourpol.2012.06.016.

Pearson, N. (2000). *Our Right to Take Responsibility*, Cairns: Noel Pearson and Associates.

Pearson, N. (2009) 'Radical Hope: Education and Equality in Australia', *Quarterly Essay* Issue 35, Melbourne: Black Inc.

Phillips, S. (2000) 'Enforcing Native Title Agreements: Carriage v Duke Australia Operations', *Indigenous Law Bulletin*, 5: 14–16.

Randall, B. (2003) *Songman: the Story of an Aboriginal Elder*, Sydney: ABC Books.

Rose, D. B. (1996) *Nourishing Terrains: Australian Aboriginal Views of Landscape and Wilderness*, Canberra: Australian Heritage Commission.

Rose, D. B. (2001) 'The Silence and Power of Women', in P. Brock (ed.) *Words and Silences: Aboriginal Women, Politics and Land*, Crows Nest, NSW: Allen and Unwin, 92–116.

Rumsey, A. and Weiner, J. (eds) (2004) *Mining and Indigenous Lifeworlds in Australia and Papua New Guinea*, Wantage, UK: Sean Kingston Publishing.

Russell, P. (2006) *Recognising Aboriginal Title: The Mabo Case and Indigenous Resistance to English-Settler Colonialism*, Sydney: UNSW Press.

Sawchuk, J. (1998) *The Dynamics of Native Politics: The Alberta Metis Experience*, Saskatoon, Purich Publishing, 1998.

Sawyer, S. and Gomez, E. T. (eds) (2012) *The Politics of Resources Extraction: Indigenous Peoples, Multinational Corporations and the State*, London: Palgrave Macmillan.

SCRGSP (Steering Committee for the Review of Government Service Provision) (2011) *Overcoming Indigenous Disadvantage: Key Indicators 2011: Overview*. Online. Available www.pc.gov.au/__data/assets/pdf_file/0010/111610/key-indicators-2011-overview-booklet.pdf.

Slowey, G. A. (2008) 'The State, the Marketplace and First Nations: Theorizing First Nations Self-determination in an Age of Globalization', in T. Martin and S. M. Hoffman (eds), *Power Struggles: Hydro Development and First Nations in Manitoba and Quebec*, Winnipeg: University of Manitoba Press, 39–54.

South West Aboriginal Land and Sea Council, Host, J. and Owen, C. (2009) *"It's still in my heart this is my country": the single Noongar claim history*, Perth: UWA Publishing.

Stokes, J. (1987) 'Special Interests or Equality? The Mining Industry's Campaign Against Aboriginal Land Rights in Canada', *Australian–Canadian Studies*, 5(1): 61–78.

United Nations (2007) *United Nations Declaration on the Rights of Indigenous Peoples*, Online. Available www.un.org/esa/socdev/unpfii/documents/DRIPS_en.pdf.

United Nations General Assembly (2014) *The Situation of Indigenous Peoples in Canada: Report of the Special Rapporteur on the Rights of Indigenous Peoples, James Anaya*, A/HRC/27/52/Add.2. Online. Available http://unsr.jamesanaya.org/docs/countries/2014-report-canada-a-hrc-27-52-add-2-en.pdf.

Usher, P. (1997) 'Common Property and Regional Sovereignty: Relations between Aboriginal Peoples and the Crown in Canada', in P. Lamour (ed.), *The Governance of Common Property in the Pacific Region*, Canberra: Australian National University, 103–22.

Watson, J. (2012) *Never Stand Still: Stories of Life, Land and Still in the Kimberley*, Derby, WA: Jarlmadangan Burru Aboriginal Corporation.

Weitzner, V. (2002) *Through Indigenous Eyes: Towards Appropriate Decision-Making Processes Regarding Mining on or Near Ancestral Lands: Final Synthesis Report Phase 1*, Ottawa: The North–South Institute.

Wilson, J. (1998) *The Earth Shall Weep: A History of Native America*, London: Picador.

4 Criteria for evaluating negotiation outcomes

Introduction

Negotiations between Aboriginal people and mining companies result in agreements dealing with a range of issues that are important to both parties. Agreements do not, in themselves, represent the totality of outcomes from negotiations. Agreements have to be put into effect, and their implementation (or lack of it) will have consequences that, it could be argued, constitute another dimension of 'outcomes' from negotiations. However, agreements do represent a central and fundamentally important component of negotiation outcomes, for three reasons.

First, certain provisions immediately and automatically generate impacts and outcomes, for instance those involving Aboriginal consent to mining or recognising Aboriginal title to land. Second, even if agreement provisions do not of themselves determine the final outcome of negotiations, they do *determine the range of possible outcomes*. For example, the financial provisions of an agreement directly determine what financial flows can actually occur. They also have a critical role in shaping the ultimate impact of these flows on recipients and communities, by determining the quantum of payments, the form in which they accrue and also, in many cases, to whom they will accrue in the first instance and how they will be spent. Third, agreement provisions dealing with implementation will be critical in determining whether an agreement is actually put into effect (O'Faircheallaigh 2002a), and so in shaping the ultimate outcome of negotiations.

In this chapter, I develop criteria for evaluating agreements that have emerged from 45 negotiations between Aboriginal peoples and mining companies in Australia, negotiations that have occurred across a range of jurisdictions, under different legal regimes and in a variety of political contexts. This will provide a basis on which to assess the impact on outcomes of structural, system-level influences. In developing these criteria, I consider the interests of the Aboriginal participants in negotiations, but a similar approach could be applied by using the interests of other participants as a starting point. In this and the next chapter, I ask: 'In terms of Aboriginal interests, how should individual agreements be evaluated and how, at a broad level, can the outcomes represented by these agreements be explained?' As noted in Chapter 2, questions of this type have rarely been asked let alone answered in the negotiation literature, and the failure to do so represents a basic weakness in negotiation scholarship.

The first task is to identify issues that are critical for Aboriginal people in Australia in their negotiations with mining companies. My choice of issues is based on the following sources of information. The first is the discussion in Chapter 3 regarding the impacts and potential impacts of mining on Aboriginal peoples. Issues related to major impacts are likely to be of central interest to Aboriginal participants in negotiations. The second source of information is my 25 years of professional experience in working with Aboriginal communities in Australia to prepare for and undertake negotiations with mining companies (see for example O'Faircheallaigh 2000, 2013). This experience provides first-hand evidence regarding the issues that are most important for the Aboriginal groups concerned. The third source is information on the content of some 70 agreements negotiated between Aboriginal people and mining companies in Australia, stretching over the period 1977–2013. This provides a profile of the issues that tend to recur across all agreements or a high proportion of agreements. (I discuss the way in which access to these agreements was obtained and ethical issues associated with their use in Chapter 5.)

These extensive and varied sources of information all indicate that seven issues are central to the interests of Aboriginal people in negotiations with mining companies. The first three are *environmental management, cultural heritage protection* and *rights and interests in land*. These are crucial in minimising negative cultural and social impacts and in allowing Aboriginal people to fulfil their responsibilities for looking after country and to protect and promote their cultural integrity and social vitality. The next three issues, *financial payments, employment and training* and *business development* are, along with rights and interests in land, critical in gaining economic (and associated social and cultural) benefits for Aboriginal people from development on their country. The final issue, *implementation measures*, is vital in determining whether provisions related to the other six are actually put into effect.

The 'success' or 'failure' of a negotiation will be reflected in outcomes in relation to these seven issues, and the following sections explore them one by one and develop criteria for evaluating outcomes in relation to each. It is of course the aggregate outcome across all seven issues that will determine whether a negotiation is regarded as 'successful' or not (see Chapter 5). However the only practical way to proceed is to examine outcomes in relation to each issue separately, and then assess the combined result achieved across all seven.

Different sorts of criteria are developed to address each issue, depending on the nature of the matters involved and the way they are dealt with in agreements. For instance, with financial provisions, the payments provided in individual agreements can be recalculated to a standard measure (total expected payments over the life of an agreement as a percentage of the expected value of project output), allowing comparison across agreements. In other cases (for example environmental management, rights and interests in land) a numerical scale is employed, with each step in the scale (0, 1, 2, 3 etc) reflecting an increase in the likelihood that Aboriginal interests will be served. A third option (applied to employment and training, business development and implementation) is to adopt a cumulative approach. A series of relevant initiatives is identified (indicated by the use of bracketed letters (a), (b), (c) etc) with the prospect that Aboriginal interests will be achieved increasing with the number of these initiatives included in an agreement. The way in which these approaches operate is set out in the following sections. Each point of the scale in relation to the first issue addressed, environmental management, is discussed in detail to illustrate how a scale is developed and applied. My assumptions regarding Aboriginal interests in relation to each issue are also outlined.

Environmental management

For many Aboriginal groups entering negotiations with mining companies in Australia, a central goal is to use agreements to help minimise adverse impacts on 'country', a term that refers to the totality of the biophysical environment and areas and sites of cultural or/and religious significance associated with it. (It is not assumed that this goal is held *equally* by all Aboriginal people: see Chapter 3.)

Three sets of provisions commonly found in mining agreements are relevant here – those dealing with environmental management, with cultural heritage protection and with Aboriginal rights and interests in land. These three issues are dealt with separately in mining agreements, reflecting the fact that separate legal and regulatory regimes apply to each issue under Australian law. The same approach is followed here. However, as noted in Chapter 3, for many Aboriginal people such a separation has little validity, because distinctions are not made between the biophysical environment and areas or sites of cultural significance associated with it and because they regard recognition of their rights as landowners as integral to their capacity to look after country.

In terms of Aboriginal interests, environmental provisions of agreements can be regarded as positive to the extent that they facilitate and encourage Aboriginal participation in environmental management. By 'Aboriginal participation in environmental management' I mean the capacity of Aboriginal people, in relation to mineral development on their traditional lands, to directly shape the way in which environmental issues and impacts are identified and defined and the manner in which such issues and impacts are addressed over the project life cycle, from project design through project operation, to project decommissioning and rehabilitation. Use of the term 'directly' is important in this definition. Responsibility for protecting the viability and sustainability of their traditional waters and lands is not something that Aboriginal peoples can delegate to others, for example government regulators or company environmental staff (Brody 2000; Randall 2003). In addition, as mentioned earlier, Aboriginal people have little faith in the inclination or ability of mining companies or governments to protect their country. Only by having a major say in environmental management themselves can they ensure that adverse effects on country are minimised. Thus the central purpose of including environmental provisions in negotiated agreements is to ensure that *Aboriginal people themselves* are placed in a position where they can ensure the protection of their ancestral estates.

On this basis, Table 4.1 presents a scale against which the environmental provisions of mining agreements can be assessed. The scale encompasses eight possible scores, from a negative score of −1 (i.e. worse than zero) at one end to a positive score of 6 at the other. The scale includes a negative score for the following reason. Aboriginal people have rights under general environmental legislation, for example the right to object to a development, to request a higher level of environmental assessment, to demand modifications to a proposed project or to sue for damages arising from environmental impacts. An agreement may limit the ability of Aboriginal people to exercise those rights. For instance, under the terms of one agreement included in the analysis, the Aboriginal parties undertake not to 'lodge any objections, claims or appeals to any Government authority … under any [state] or Commonwealth legislation, including any Environmental Legislation…'. In relation to their ability to influence environmental outcomes, such provisions may leave Aboriginal people worse off than in the absence of an agreement, thus the need for a negative score.

Agreements may contain no provisions in relation to Aboriginal involvement in or responsibility for environmental management of the projects concerned. Such agreements are regarded as achieving a score of 0. They

Table 4.1 Criteria for assessing environmental management provisions

−1 Provisions that limit existing rights.

 0 No Provisions.

 1 Mining company commits to Aboriginal parties to comply with environmental legislation.

 2 Company undertakes to consult with affected Aboriginal people.

 3 Aboriginal parties have a right to access, and independently evaluate, information on environmental management systems and issues.

 4 Aboriginal parties may suggest ways of enhancing environmental management systems, and project operator must address their suggestions.

 5 Joint decision-making on some or all environmental management issues.

 6 Aboriginal parties have the capacity to act unilaterally to deal with environmental concerns or problems associated with a project.

neither detract from, nor add to, the position that would exist in the absence of an agreement. Positive provisions are ranked from 1 to 6 as indicated below, with each step in the scale reflecting an increase in the likelihood that Aboriginal parties will become substantially and effectively involved in environmental management. It is not assumed that each step involves an *identical* increase in this likelihood.

The first positive step on the scale, 1, involves the mining company making a commitment *to the Aboriginal parties* to comply with environmental legislation, regulations and management plans. Such provisions allow the Aboriginal parties to take legal action if they believe that a breach of environmental legislation or regulations has occurred, because such a breach constitutes breach of the agreement. Their inclusion removes any doubt about the 'standing' of Aboriginal people in legal proceedings, because they are parties to a legally binding contract with the project operator. In addition, such provisions help address the concerns of Aboriginal people about having to rely on government regulators to deal with any breaches of environmental law or regulations. However, provisions of this sort have a key limitation in that they do not allow traditional owners to play a *positive* role in avoiding breaches of laws or regulations and/or negative environmental impacts in the first place, except to the extent that a company may apply higher environmental standards in the expectation that traditional owners may take legal action if breaches of laws or regulations occur.

Point 2 on the scale requires the project operator to consult with affected Aboriginal people regarding major environmental management issues, and structures (such as consultative committees) are put in place to ensure that this happens. Such provisions can offer the operator an understanding of environmental issues and impacts that reflects Aboriginal values, knowledge and priorities; facilitate the application of Aboriginal knowledge in allowing the operators to meet its obligations; and ensure that greater weight is attached to environmental risks or impacts that are of particular concern to Aboriginal landowners. However, such provisions have a serious weakness. There is no guarantee that the project operator will respond to Aboriginal concerns, take advantage of Aboriginal knowledge or heed suggestions for improving management systems. This is likely to be a particular problem where Aboriginal values or insights run counter to assumptions and priorities of project operators and environmental regulators.

At point 3 of the scale, Aboriginal parties have a right to access, and independently evaluate, corporate information on environmental management systems and activities.

Access to information and technical expertise can facilitate Aboriginal participation in a number of ways. First, it can be essential in determining whether breaches of environmental regulations are occurring or likely to occur, and provides a firmer basis for threatening or taking legal action if this proves necessary. Second, the information obtained may support the concerns or positions of Aboriginal landowners, and make it harder for project operators and regulators to ignore these. However, access to corporate information does not of itself ensure that companies or regulators will be responsive to the concerns or priorities of Aboriginal landowners.

Point 4 of the scale involves provisions allowing Aboriginals to suggest ways of enhancing environmental management systems, and the project operator undertakes to implement these or some agreed alternative. This approach explicitly recognises the positive value of Aboriginal participation in environmental management. It also addresses the possibility that project operators might ignore proposals put forward by Aboriginal parties through consultative structures, by introducing a mechanism that requires the mine operator to respond to Aboriginal initiatives. It is an approach adopted in a number of recent Australian agreements, which also include dispute resolution procedures for dealing with situations where suggestions by Aboriginal parties are not acceptable to the operator.

Point 5 involves a requirement for joint decision-making in relation to some or all aspects of environmental management. Under this approach the project operator no longer makes unilateral decisions on environmental management, possibly after consultation with or input from traditional owners. Aboriginal landowners are now incorporated into environmental decision-making in a structural and permanent fashion. This is in contrast to their historical marginalisation from such decision-making and greatly increases opportunities for introducing Aboriginal values, perspectives and knowledge into environmental management. While they represent a major departure from historical patterns, joint decision-making structures do not necessarily place Aboriginal landowners in a position to prevent environmental damage. For example, if serious differences emerge between the parties, time-consuming dispute resolution procedures may be required, and their outcomes will not necessarily favour the Aboriginal participants.

At point 6 on the scale, Aboriginal parties have a capacity under specified conditions to act unilaterally (for example by suspending mining operations) where they believe that environmental damage is occurring or may occur. Provisions of this sort allow Aboriginal people to act themselves to protect their traditional lands if companies or regulators do not respond to their concerns. They can be of particular value where there is a belief that serious environmental damage may occur if immediate action is not taken to halt mining in general or some specific aspect of project operations, for example use of a pipeline traversing highly sensitive areas. Such provisions not only recognise the custodial obligations of Aboriginal landowners but accept that in some circumstances these obligations can outweigh the commercial imperative to maintain production. Provisions of this sort can have substantial effects even if they are rarely (or indeed never) invoked, because they create a compelling incentive for the project operator to work closely with Aboriginal traditional owners to avoid the possibility of environmental damage or risk that might lead to suspension of production.

The different approaches outlined above are not mutually exclusive. For example, it may be that an Aboriginal party will seek a commitment to comply with environmental legislation so that it can take legal action if adverse impacts do occur (Point 1), while at the same time wishing to contribute to enhancing environmental systems (Point 4) in order to minimise the chances that environmental damage will happen. However, on the other hand, the scale does represent a clear hierarchy in terms of the potential for allowing Aboriginal influence in relation to environmental management, and a commitment to provisions further up the scale will often also result in adoption of points lower on the scale even if these are not explicitly required by an agreement. For example, it is most unlikely that a mine operator would not consult with Aboriginal parties in relation to environmental management issues (Point 2) or fail to involve them in decision-making (Point 5) if those parties have a capacity to halt project operations if they believe environmental damage is likely to occur (Point 6).

In terms of Aboriginal interests, points on the scale between −1 and 1 could be classified as a 'poor' outcome, because they would allow no positive Aboriginal participation in environmental management. Points 2 or 3 could be classified a 'moderate' outcome, because they would involve Aboriginal consultation but would not guarantee any response from the mining company and points between 4 and 6 would be classified as a 'strong' outcome as they would require project operators to take Aboriginal interests and perspectives into account.

Cultural heritage protection

Any approach to protection of Aboriginal cultural heritage has two critical components. (For a detailed discussion of this point and the wider context for protection of Aboriginal cultural heritage, see O'Faircheallaigh 2008.) The most important is the level of protection that is sought; also critical are the means available (activities, processes, resources) to ensure that this level of protection can actually be secured in practice. The two are inextricably linked. For example, a mining agreement may specify avoidance of any damage to areas or sites of cultural significance as the required level of protection. However, if the processes used to pursue this goal make it difficult or impossible to involve the Aboriginal people who hold relevant cultural knowledge, important sites or areas may be left unprotected or managed inappropriately and the goal will not be achieved. Experience with Australia's state cultural heritage laws, where an absence of appropriate resources and processes has at times resulted in a complete absence of the protection legislation is supposed to provide, highlights the importance of considering both components (O'Faircheallaigh 2008).

Five general levels of protection can be envisaged and can be seen as points along a spectrum that reflects increasingly positive outcomes for Aboriginal custodians. These are presented in Table 4.2, in ascending order according to the level of protection offered to Aboriginal cultural heritage. They range at one extreme from a complete lack of protection (Level 1) to a situation where agreements contain an unqualified commitment to avoid

Table 4.2 Levels of protection in relation to Aboriginal cultural heritage

1 Sites or areas of significance may be damaged or destroyed by project development without any reference to Aboriginal people.

2 Sites or areas of significance may be damaged or destroyed, and Aboriginal parties only have an opportunity to mitigate the impact of the damage, for example by removing artefacts or conducting ceremonies.

3 The mining company must 'minimise' damage, to the extent that this is consistent with commercial requirements, for example by re-routing infrastructure to avoid areas of significance.

4 The company must avoid damage, except where to do so would make it impossible to proceed with the project (for instance where a major site is co-located with the ore body to be developed).

5 There is an unqualified requirement to avoid damage.

any damage to cultural heritage (Level 5). In considering the first alternative, agreements cannot be in breach of the law prevailing in the relevant jurisdiction, and thus an agreement could not condone damage that is prohibited by legislation. However the protection offered by cultural heritage legislation is often limited, and in addition agreements may require that Aboriginal custodians refrain from triggering relevant legislative provisions. A score of 4 or 5 could be regarded as a strong outcome for Aboriginal interests in this case, as each is likely to ensure a high degree of protection in most (4) or all (5) circumstances.

Turning to the activities, processes and resources applied to securing a desired level of protection in practice, Table 4.3 indicates a range of elements that mining agreements can include and which contribute to the appropriate and effective achievement of cultural heritage protection. For example provisions that allocate to Aboriginal traditional owners control over relevant site identification and management processes and over associated information flows increase the likelihood that protective provisions will be implemented effectively (element (a)). Traditional owner control is also important to ensure that the process of 'protecting' cultural heritage does not itself create damage as a result of inappropriate uses of information. Implementation of protective provisions cannot occur without access to financial and other resources, such as appropriate transport (element (b)). Cultural heritage protection of individual areas or sites does not occur in a vacuum. The efficacy of relevant provisions will be influenced by the availability of resources to support the internal capacity of relevant Aboriginal groups (element (d)), and by measures designed to ensure the cooperation of the project workforce and to control the activities of tourists or other visitors to the project area (element (f)).

The potential contribution to effective protection depends on how many of the elements listed in Table 4.3 are present in an agreement. In other words, this list is *cumulative*. The more of the elements an agreement includes, the greater the likelihood that a desired level of protection will

Table 4.3 Activities, processes and resources applied to securing protection of Aboriginal cultural heritage

---

(a) Provisions that maximise Aboriginal control of site clearance and heritage management processes, for example by making them the judges of cultural 'significance', and by allowing them to choose technical staff who assist in surveys, to organise field trips, and to control the flow of information to the company.

(b) Provision of financial and other resources to support cultural heritage clearances, facilitating the effective participation of the appropriate Aboriginal people (for example transport, accommodation and meals).

(c) Explicit protection of any cultural knowledge provided by Aboriginal people as part of the cultural heritage protection regime.

(d) Measures to enhance an Aboriginal community's internal capacity for cultural heritage protection, for example by supporting a ranger program or funding activities to promote cultural vitality.

(e) Provisions that allow traditional owners to at least temporarily stop project activities where sites or areas of significance are threatened or damaged, so as to allow protective or remediation measures to be put in place.

(f) More general measures designed to reinforce the *system* of cultural heritage protection established by an agreement, which might include cultural awareness training for mining company employees and contractors to make them aware of the need for cultural heritage protection or the rehabilitation of unused roads to reduce the possibility that e.g. tourists might gain access to protected sites.

---

actually be achieved in practice. This is in contrast to Table 4.2, which present *alternative* approaches organised in a hierarchy. So, for example, an agreement containing no provisions in any of the categories in Table 4.3 achieves a score of 0; an agreement containing only provisions of type (a) and (d) achieves a score of 2; an agreement containing provisions in all of the categories in Table 4.3 achieves a score of 6. In this case a score of between 4 and 6 could be regarded as a strong outcome for Aboriginal interests.

Rights and interests in land

In a minority of cases (most importantly Aboriginal freehold land in the Northern Territory) Aboriginal people are recognised under Australian law as owners of land subject to development. In such cases, Aboriginal rights and interests in land do not arise as an issue in negotiations. In presenting data on the 45 agreements in Chapter 5, such cases are indicated by the term 'Does Not Apply' (see Table 5.1). However, for many Aboriginal groups in Australia a key goal in negotiating agreements is to be recognised by mining companies and governments as the owners of their ancestral lands, and to have title to these lands recognised, or conferred on them, under Australian law. This may involve recognition of native title, or grant of freehold or other title under relevant state or territory legislation. Typically, an agreement will relate only to land covered by mining interests dealt with in that agreement. However, some agreements (for instance that for the Century zinc/lead mine in Queensland) provide for the transfer to Aboriginal people of tenure to other areas of land held by the mining company.

Any legal recognition or conferring of title requires the support of the relevant state or territory government, as mining companies have no power to deal in title. This support may be expressed as an obligation accepted by government as a party to an agreement, or it may arise from a policy decision by a government that is not a party. Destruction or diminution of existing Aboriginal rights in land can also only be effected by government.

Agreement provisions are contrary to Aboriginal interests where they destroy, reduce, or require the surrender of existing rights in land; deny the existence of Aboriginal rights in land; require that the exercise of such rights be limited or suspended during a project's life; or lessen the possibility that rights or interests will be recognised in the future, for example by leaving the mining company free to oppose a future application for determination of native title. Provisions create benefits for Aboriginal parties to the extent that they recognise and protect any existing rights and interests; increase the possibility of a future recognition or grant of rights or interests; or have the immediate effect of recognizing or creating rights or interests. Recognition or conferring of rights or interests as an integral part of an agreement is preferable to commitments by non-Aboriginal parties to promote such an outcome in the future, given the uncertainty that inevitably surrounds the realisation of those commitments.

On the basis of this discussion, Table 4.4 sets out criteria in relation to Aboriginal rights and interests in land. These cover a spectrum from comprehensive extinguishment or surrender of existing rights and interests; through partial extinguishment of rights or constraints on their exercise; to company undertakings not to oppose, or to support, Aboriginal attempts to achieve recognition; and to immediate recognition or grant of new rights or interests.

Applying these criteria in practice involves a number of complexities. First, for consistency all provisions that represent any diminution of Aboriginal rights or interests, or reduce the possibility that such rights and interests may be recognised in the future, are given a negative sign. However, this does not mean that inclusion of any provision designated as negative would, in the overall context of provisions dealing with land, represent a poor outcome for Aboriginal parties. For example, in some cases it may be difficult for a mining project to proceed and so generate benefits for Aboriginal people in the absence of *any* suspension or limitation of Aboriginal rights or interests in land. Thus an individual agreement might involve a suspension of limited and specific Aboriginal rights, for instance to hunt on parts of a lease where mining is under way, and so attract a score of –2. However, if the agreement also contained a provision involving transfer of

Table 4.4 Criteria for assessing provisions related to Aboriginal rights or interests in land

---

-5 Provisions that have the *general* effect of extinguishing or requiring the surrender of existing rights or interests in land.

-4 Provisions that extinguish or require surrender of *specific* rights or interests in land (e.g. rights in minerals or in areas on which infrastructure is constructed).

-3 Provisions that define Aboriginal rights or interests in a narrow or restricted manner (for instance by defining native title rights more narrowly than might occur under the common law).

-2 The exercise of Aboriginal rights or interests is suspended or restricted during project life.

-1 There is no immediate effect on Aboriginal rights or interests, but non-Aboriginal parties reserve the right to oppose any future application for legal recognition of Aboriginal title.

0 There are no provisions in relation to Aboriginal rights and interests in land.

1 While no recognition of Aboriginal rights or interests is made or proposed, there is an explicit statement that the agreement is not intended to extinguish any rights or interests that do exist.

2 Companies undertake not to oppose any future recognition of Aboriginal title.

3 There is no recognition of Aboriginal rights or interests under European law, but Aboriginal people are recognized as having rights or interests under Aboriginal law and custom, recognition which may hold symbolic value for Aboriginal people.

4 Companies or/and governments make positive commitments in relation to a future recognition or grant of rights or interests to Aboriginal parties.

5 The agreement has the effect of recognising or conferring Aboriginal rights or interests in land, by effecting a transfer of interests in land from companies or/and government to the Aboriginal parties.

---

title to other parts of a mining lease, or to separate areas of land, to the Aboriginal parties, as a package, the agreement might represent a strongly positive outcome for Aboriginal interests.

Second and more generally, because different parcels or categories of land may be dealt with differently, agreements may contain multiple provisions in relation to land. However, in contrast to environmental protection (Table 4.1), these may not represent points in a hierarchy, and thus it may not be appropriate to simply award the agreement a score corresponding to the most favourable provision. For example an agreement could involve an immediate transfer to the Aboriginal parties of an area of land off the mining lease (a 5), and also recognition of customary Aboriginal rights in the mining lease (a 3).

To address these issues, where appropriate I allocate multiple scores (for example '3, 5' or '-2, -3') to each agreement. This should still allow an overall judgment regarding negotiation outcomes on this issue. For instance an agreement with a high positive score and a low negative one

(5, –1) or a combination of positive scores (2, 3) would represent a positive outcome; an agreement with a low positive score and a high negative one (1, –4) represents a negative outcome (see Table 5.1 in the next chapter).

Financial payments

Financial payments represent the least complex of the seven issues in terms of establishing criteria for assessing outcomes. As long as details of payments under an agreement and of the actual or likely economic scale of the project are available, it is possible to establish a common measure against which to assess individual agreements. Total annual payments (regardless of the basis on which they are imposed) are aggregated and calculated as a proportion of annual revenues from the sale of minerals, and the resulting ratio used to compare different agreements. This approach has the advantage that it takes into account a critical contextual factor, project scale. For example it will rate highly an agreement that provides for small payments in absolute terms if those payments are substantial relative to the earning capacity of the project.

To illustrate this approach, an agreement might provide for a payment of $1 million on signing, a payment of $2 million on the grant of a mining lease, an annual rental of $300,000 a year during each year of production, and a royalty equal to 1 per cent of annual revenues. If revenues are expected to be $30 million per annum and production is expected to continue for ten years, total payments under the agreement will be $36 million, equal to 1.2 per cent of total project revenues. A comparable figure (referred to as a 'royalty equivalent') can be calculated for any number of agreements with quite different payment structures. For the agreements I analysed, the range of royalty equivalents is from 0 per cent to 3.05 per cent (see Chapter 5). Given this range, a royalty equivalent of between 2 and 3 per cent could be regarded as a strongly favourable outcome for Aboriginal negotiators.

Employment and training

Mining generates comparatively few jobs relative to the investment involved. However, in the regions in which many Aboriginal people live, mining represents one of the few sources of wage employment. In addition, wages in the mining industry are considerably higher than the national average. Employment in mining can help people develop skills that can be used in establishing small businesses, in other industrial employment and in community development work. Where substantial numbers of Aboriginal people are employed in mining, expenditure of their wages can generate significant additional employment in local retail and service industries and can support non-market economic activity such as fishing and hunting. For all of these reasons, Aboriginal communities usually wish to use agreements to help achieve a high level of Aboriginal participation in a project's workforce.

However, Aboriginal people face major barriers in achieving this goal. A review of the extensive literature on Aboriginal employment in the mining industry in Australia and Canada, including case studies of successful and failed employment initiatives (O'Faircheallaigh 2006), indicates that these barriers relate in particular to:

- lack of the skills and work experience required to compete on the open job market or to achieve advancement to more senior positions, and an absence or scarcity of affordable opportunities to upgrade existing skills;
- a tendency for managers to prioritise the demands of production and cost containment over Aboriginal employment and training in allocating financial and other resources, including their own time;
- racism towards and stereotyping of Aboriginal people by senior company managers, supervisors and co-workers;
- alienation and loneliness among Aboriginal workers, arising from the unfamiliarity of industrial environments and distance from home communities, leading to a failure to complete training and education programs, irregular work patterns and high turnover;
- the reluctance of Aboriginal people to forgo land-based activities such as hunting and fishing that may conflict with regular wage employment.

The literature indicates that general commitments by project operators to maximise opportunities for Aboriginal employment tend to be ineffective unless they are supported by specific initiatives and resources directed at overcoming the barriers listed above. On this basis, Table 4.5 identifies key provisions whose inclusion in an agreement will enhance the prospects for substantial and sustained Aboriginal employment. The approach here is cumulative and is similar to that applied to cultural heritage protection in Table 4.3, i.e. the more of the elements in Table 4.5 an agreement contains, the greater the likelihood that Aboriginal employment opportunities will be maximised. An agreement that lacked provisions in any of the six categories in Table 4.5 would score 0, an agreement that included provisions (a) and (b) or (a) and (d) would score 2, and so on. A strong outcome for Aboriginal interests would involve a score of 5 or 6.

Business development

Many Aboriginal groups are keen to take advantage of business opportunities associated with a mining project, because of the employment and income they generate. Such opportunities are also valued because they can allow creation of sustainable enterprises that can continue after a specific mining project has ended selling goods and services to other mines or to other industrial or commercial customers. However, most Aboriginal communities and organisations face serious constraints in pursuing available

Table 4.5 Provisions to encourage Aboriginal employment and training

---

(a) A general commitment is made to maximise opportunities for Aboriginal employment and training.

(b) Specified resources are committed to Aboriginal employment and training, for example in dollar terms or in the form of numbers of apprenticeships or provision for dedicated training staff.

(c) Concrete goals are specified for employment and training programs (for instance specific and rising proportions of Aboriginal employees), and incentives (or sanctions) are created for the achievement (or non-achievement) of these goals.

(d) In relation to recruitment to training positions and jobs, an explicit statement of preference is made in favour of Aboriginal people who are suitably qualified or capable of becoming so, and resources are committed to ensuring that such people are made aware of employment opportunities.

(e) An explicit developmental component is included, by setting out a staged progression through levels of skill and responsibility for Aboriginal trainees/employees.

(f) Measures are required to make the workplace conducive to recruitment and retention of Aboriginal workers. These might include cross-cultural awareness training for non-Aboriginal employees and supervisors; adjustment to rosters or rotation schedules to acknowledge cultural obligations; initiatives to maintain contact between trainees and their families and home communities.

---

business opportunities, because of (i) the high transaction costs that can be involved in standard tendering and contracting arrangements; (ii) scarcity of capital for business investment; (iii) lack of relevant skills; (iv) their competitive disadvantage in relation to large, well-established non-Aboriginal businesses (O'Faircheallaigh 2006).

The need to overcome these barriers is used as a basis for assessing business development provisions (Table 4.6). The absence of any provisions related to business development attracts a score of 0. An agreement that merely expresses general support for Aboriginal business development but contains no specific provisions designed to overcome the barriers listed above attracts a score of 1. An additional point is added to the score for each provision or set of provisions that address a barrier in a specific manner, by inclusion of initiatives of the sort listed in Table 4.6. Thus an agreement that contained provisions in relation to two barriers would score a 3; an agreement that addressed all four barriers would score a 5. A score of 4 or 5 could be regarded as a positive outcome in relation to business development.

Implementation measures

A range of factors influences the prospect that an agreement will actually be put into effect. Some of these relate to the wider economic, political and social context within which an agreement operates, rather than to the

Table 4.6 Criteria for assessing business development provisions

---

(a) General commitment by the mining company to promote Aboriginal business opportunities.

(b) Initiatives designed to minimize transaction costs for Aboriginal businesses, for example by provision of information on upcoming contracts in a form and within a time frame that facilitates tendering; 'unbundling' of large contracts into smaller contracts that are more easily managed by Aboriginal businesses; offering of contracts to Aboriginal businesses on a 'cost plus margin' basis, as an alternative to competitive tenders.

(c) Initiatives designed to overcome paucity of relevant expertise, for example by giving Aboriginal enterprises access to the business expertise of staff employed by the company; funding Aboriginal people to undertake business management training, possibly by providing them with preferential access to relevant public programs; provision of expertise via joint ventures between the company and Aboriginal businesses during their start-up phase.

(d) Initiatives designed to overcome paucity of business capital, for example by providing 'bankable' long-term contracts to Aboriginal enterprises to assist them in obtaining finance from commercial lenders; giving Aboriginal businesses preferential access to government 'start-up' loans for new businesses; provision of expertise via joint ventures between the company and Aboriginal businesses during their start-up phase.

(e) Initiatives designed to overcome disadvantage of Aboriginal enterprises relative to large well-established non-Aboriginal businesses, for example preference clause for competitive Aboriginal businesses; specification of a margin in favour of Aboriginal businesses in assessing tenders (e.g. an Aboriginal business tendering at no more than 10 per cent above the lowest bid is awarded the contract).

---

provisions of an agreement itself. They include, for instance, the degree of political support mobilised for an agreement; prevailing conditions in regional, national and corporate economies; and broader policy and legislative frameworks within which agreements operate. For example, the prospects for successfully implementing Aboriginal employment and training initiatives contained in an agreement will be affected by general conditions in regional labour markets.

However, the prospects for success are also greatly influenced by the degree to which agreements contain the means for their own implementation. It is on this latter issue that I focus here. Research on implementation of agreements (O'Faircheallaigh 2002a) and the extensive literature on policy implementation generally (O'Faircheallaigh 2002b: Chapter 2) highlight the critical need to allocate human and financial resources *specifically* to the task of implementation, including in some cases to developing general organisational capacity. Other key prerequisites for successful implementation include creation of structures whose *primary* purpose is implementation; measures to ensure that senior decision makers maintain a focus on implementation; clarity in the obligations of each party combined with explicit incentives for performance and sanctions for non-performance; regular and systematic monitoring of performance; and regular review processes to identify and address any gaps in implementation. Agreement provisions that address prerequisites for successful implementation are listed in Table 4.7. A cumulative approach applies in this case also. The more of these categories of provisions that are included in an agreement, the greater the likelihood of successful implementation. Agreements are allocated scores in the same manner as for employment and training and business development, with a score of 5 or 6 indicating a strongly favourable outcome.

Conclusion

In this chapter, I have developed eight sets of criteria (two dealing with cultural heritage protection) for assessing, from the perspective of Aboriginal interests, provisions dealing with seven key issues addressed in agreements between mining companies and Aboriginal peoples. The criteria are not intended to allow an overall quantitative assessment of the negotiation outcomes represented by agreements. In other words, is not possible to 'add up' the scores achieved by an agreement in relation to each issue, because the matters dealt with vary greatly and as a result the approaches adopted in developing relevant criteria and in 'scoring' agreement provisions are qualitatively different. However, in combination the eight sets of criteria do provide a basis for a rigorous, systematic and comparative assessment of the outcomes represented by negotiated agreements. I undertake such an assessment in the next chapter, by applying the criteria to 45 Australian agreements.

Table 4.7 Criteria for assessing implementation provisions

(a)	Allocation of human and financial resources specifically to the task of implementation.
(b)	Creation of structures (such as monitoring and management committees) whose *primary* purpose is implementation of the agreement.
(c)	Establishment of processes that require senior managers in each signatory organisation to focus on implementation on a systematic and regular basis.
(d)	Clear and explicit statements of each party's obligations, with specific incentives for parties to fulfill these obligations and/or credible and appropriate sanctions and penalties for non-performance.
(e)	Regular and systematic monitoring of relevant activities and initiatives to provide reliable information on the extent of implementation or non-implementation.
(f)	Periodic and adequately resourced review processes to establish whether specific measures are creating the outcomes anticipated by the parties and to address any implementation failures, where necessary by amendment of agreements.

References

Brody, H. (2000) *The Other Side of Eden: Hunters, Farmers and the Shaping of the World*, Vancouver: Douglas and McIntyre.

O'Faircheallaigh, C. (2000) *Negotiating Major Project Agreements: The 'Cape York Model'*, Canberra: Australian Institute for Aboriginal and Torres Strait Islander Studies.

O'Faircheallaigh, C. (2002a) 'Implementation: The Forgotten Dimension of Agreement-Making in Australia and Canada', *Indigenous Law Bulletin*, 5: 14–17.

O'Faircheallaigh, C. (2002b) *A New Model of Policy Evaluation: Mining and Indigenous People*, Aldershot: Ashgate Press.

O'Faircheallaigh, C. (2006) 'Mining Agreements and Aboriginal Economic Development in Australia and Canada', *Journal of Aboriginal Economic Development*, 5(1): 74–91.

O'Faircheallaigh, C. (2008) 'Negotiating Protection of the Sacred? Aboriginal–Mining Company Agreements in Australia', *Development and Change*, 39(1): 25–51.

O'Faircheallaigh, C. (2013) 'Extractive Industries and Indigenous peoples: A Changing Dynamic?', *Journal of Rural Studies*, 30: 20–30.

Randall, B. (2003) *Songman: the Story of an Aboriginal Elder*, Sydney: ABC Books.

5 Outcomes from negotiations in Australia

A macro analysis

Introduction

In this chapter, I analyse agreements that have resulted from 45 negotiations conducted in Australia. The agreements represent a wide range of contexts in terms of time, political jurisdiction, scale of project, legal regime, and characteristics of mining companies and Aboriginal communities and organisations. A comparison of the agreements, using the criteria developed in Chapter 4, thus provides an opportunity to assess the impact of a wide range of factors on negotiation outcomes. It also provides an opportunity to assess, at a broad level, whether general structural factors shape outcomes or whether outcomes reflect 'micro level' negotiation processes leading to individual agreements.

The chapter begins by describing the research approach, including the way in which ethical issues are addressed, and outlining key characteristics of the agreements that are examined. It then brings together an analysis of individual provisions in each agreement to provide a composite picture of negotiation outcomes. It examines a range of potential explanations for the observed outcomes, discarding some that lack explanatory power and identifying others that offer a credible explanation.

Research approach, ethical issues and agreement characteristics

Almost all agreements between Aboriginal peoples and mining companies in Australia contain legally binding confidentiality clauses. Their presence represents a fundamental problem in learning about, presenting and analysing agreement provisions, as they prevent researchers from discussing the content of individual agreements or, in some cases, even from revealing which agreements are included in an analysis.

My strategy in dealing with this issue was to seek access to a sufficiently large number of agreements so that I could discuss aggregate findings about their content without revealing the content or identity of individual agreements. I achieved this over time by gaining access to agreements through a variety of avenues, including professional practice as a negotiator; being given copies of agreements by individual informants; accessing the small number of agreements on the public record; and, in particular, by obtaining copies of agreements under research protocols with a number of leading Aboriginal regional land organisations ('land councils') that have been widely involved in negotiations with mining companies. This last approach was especially important both because of the large number of agreements it yielded (over half the total) and because I focused attention on land councils in regions where I did not already have substantial coverage of agreements. In this way, I gained access to 45 agreements governing the development and operation of hard rock mining projects in Australia.

Ethical issues were addressed as follows. In relation to agreements obtained under research protocols, I undertook in the protocols to protect the confidentiality and intellectual property rights of the parties to agreements. I comply with this undertaking here by not revealing the identity or content of any of the 45 individual agreements included in the analysis (see Table 5.1 and discussion of the agreements below). This approach does not constrain the analysis, because the purpose of this chapter is to map broad relationships between agreement outcomes and the political, legal, and institutional contexts within which agreements are negotiated. This approach also allows me to comply with any confidentiality obligations in relation to agreements included in the study which I helped to negotiate.

Turning to the characteristics of the agreements, they were negotiated under a variety of legislative regimes, in particular the *Aboriginal Land Rights (Northern Territory) Act 1976* ('*Land Rights Act*') (four agreements), Queensland's *Mineral Resources Act 1989* (MRA) (two agreements) and the federal *Native Title Act 1973* (35 agreement). The dominance of *NTA* agreements reflects the national application of the Act and the increase in agreement-making since its introduction (see Chapter 3). In addition, four agreements result from policy initiatives by the mining companies concerned, in contexts where no legal requirement existed to negotiate. The agreements were concluded over the period 1978–2006, with two signed in the 1970s; three in the 1980s; 11 between 1990 and 1998; and 29 since 1998, reflecting the impact of the *NTA*. The agreements cover a wide range of projects in terms of scale, with actual or planned revenues from as little as A\$20 million to as much as A\$700 million per annum. They cover a wide variety of minerals, including bauxite, coal, diamonds, gold, gypsum, iron ore, nickel, heavy minerals (rutile and ilmenite), silica sand, zinc/lead and uranium. They involve 37 different companies ranging from the world's largest multinational mining companies to small, single project operators.

Agreements differ in terms of their size and complexity, but most are extensive documents and some run to hundreds of pages and incorporate numerous schedules and attachments. Each agreement was analysed in full, because provisions relating to the seven issues identified as of central importance in Chapter 4 are not necessarily contained under relevant section headings such as 'Environmental Management'. For example one agreement had no such section heading, but under a heading dealing with relations between the parties creates a joint decision-making body that has responsibility for environmental issues related to the project.

Provisions from each agreement relating to each of the seven issues were consolidated and then rated according to the criteria set out in Chapter 4. Agreements were rated independently by an individual familiar with agreement-making in Australia but who had no involvement in negotiating any of the agreements, as well as by the author. In most cases, ratings coincided; in rare cases where this did not occur, the relevant provisions were re-examined, and an agreed score determined.

Where criteria involve a scale that represents a hierarchy of outcomes (for example environmental management, levels of cultural heritage protection) and agreements contain provisions that match more than one point on the scale, agreements are allocated to the 'highest' point they contain. For example, if an agreement provides both for consultation on environmental matters (a 2 on the relevant scale) and also for joint decision-making on environmental matters (a 5 on the relevant scale), the agreement is awarded a 5.

In applying the criteria for assessing cultural heritage provisions, it proved difficult to assign certain agreements unambiguously to a particular level, because some provisions in individual agreements indicated a commitment to, for instance, Level 2 protection, while others implied a commitment to Level 3 protection (see Table 4.2 above). (No agreement included individual provisions separated by more than one Level, e.g. Level 2 and Level 4). To reflect this situation, some agreements have been allocated a score midway between the two levels concerned, indicated for instance by the use of the numerals 2/3 for an agreement containing both Level 2 and Level 3 provisions.

The criteria developed in Chapter 4 proved robust and effective in allowing the agreements to be evaluated. This is indicated by the facts that no provisions were encountered that were not amenable to classification using the criteria, and that the criteria made it possible to discriminate clearly between the provisions of various agreements dealing with a particular issue.

Outcomes from negotiations

Table 5.1 presents the results of the analysis. Each agreement has been allocated a number, indicated in the first column. The second column indicates the year in which the agreement was concluded, and the third the legal or policy regime under which the agreement was negotiated. Use of the term 'Policy' in column 3 indicates that there was no legal requirement for an agreement to be negotiated. The following columns indicate the scores achieved by each agreement in relation to the seven issues, with the cultural heritage provisions being broken down into their two components, cultural heritage levels of protection (CHLP) and cultural heritage

Table 5.1 Agreement ratings for 45 Australian agreements, grouped by environmental rating

Agreement	Year	Legislation	Environment	Land	Employ & Training	$ (%)	CHLP	CHAPR	Business Develop	Implementation
1	2001	NTA	−1	−2, 2, 3	3	1	2	3/4	1	1
2	1999	NTA	−1	1, 2	2	0.016	2/3	2	2	0
3	1994	NTA	0	−5, 5	0	0	0	0	0	1
4	1994	NTA	0	−5	1	0	2/3	3/4	0	0
5	2003	NTA	0	−5, −1, 2, 5	2	0.01	3/4	3/4	2	4
6	2003	NTA	0	1, 2	1	0.75	2/3	5	0	0
7	2001	NTA	0	2, 3	4	0.75	3	4	4	2
8	2003	NTA	0	3	4	0.45	3	4	2	2
9	2003	NTA	0	−5, 1	2	0	2	2/3	4	3
10	1980	Policy	0	0	1	0.13	1	0	0	0
11	2003	NTA	1,−1	1, 5	1	0.1	3	4	3	4
12	1997	NTA	1,−1	−4, −3, −1	2	0.82	2	2	0	0
13	1978	ALRA	1	DNA	2	2.8	4	2	2	2
14	1993	NTA	1	−5, 3, 5	3	0	2	1	4	0/1
15	1999	NTA	1	1, 3, 4	2	0.12	2/3	4	4	3
16	2003	NTA	1	1, 2	1	0.27	PNA	PNA[1]	0	2
17	1997	NTA	1	3, 4	2	0.49	3	2	2	2
18	2002	NTA	1	3	4	0.34	3	4	3	2
19	1999	NTA	1	−5	1	0.29	2	1	3	0
20	2000	NTA	1	0	0	0.41	3	3	1	1

21	2001	NTA	1	0	0	0.12	3	3	1	1
22	2002	NTA	1	−2, 1, 2	3	0.015	3	5	1	2
23	2003	NTA	1	2, 3	0	2.5	2/3	2	2	0
24	1998	NTA	1	3	3/4	0	2	2/3	3	3
25	1999	NTA	1	1	0	0.075	2	2/3	0	2
26	1998	NTA	1	−5, −4, 3	1	0.14	2	2/3	1	2
27	2002	NTA	2	−5, −3, 2, 1, 4	3	0.125	2/3	5	4	3
28	2000	NTA	2	1	0	0.147	1/2	0/1	0	0
29	2001	NTA	2	1, 2	4	0.0036	3	0	1	0
30	2002	NTA	3	1, 2	4	0.82	2	3	3	2
31	2003	NTA	3	1, 2	4	0.82	3	4	4	3
32	2002	NTA	3	1, 2, 3	3	0.128	3	4	2	0
33	2004	Policy	3	−2, 1, 3, **4, 5**	5	1	5	**5/6**	3	**5**
34	1990	ALRA	4	3	4	**3.05**	5	2	4	**5**
35	1994	QMRA	4	DNA	5	**2.5**	3	4	3	3
36	2001	Policy	4	−4, −2, … −1, 3, 5	3	**2**	3	4	4	**5**
37	1997	Policy	4	2, 3, 4	6	**2.25**	5	3	4	2
38	2000	NTA	4	1	5	**0.4**	4/5	4	4	2/3
39	2006	NTA	4	2	4	**1.5–2**	4	5	5	**5**
40	1979	ALRA	5	DNA	3	**2**	3	1	3	2
41	1982	ALRA	5	3	5	**3.05**	5	3	4	**4**
42	1992	QMRA	5	DNA	6	**3**	5	2	0	2
43	1997	NTA	5	−2, 1, 3, **4, 5**	4	**0.5**	3/4		4	**4**
44	1999	NTA	5	1, 2	5	**2**	5	2	3	2
45	2005	NTA	6	1, 3	5	**1.6–2.5**	4/5	4	4	3

Note

1 PNA = provisions not available, as they were contained in a separate cultural heritage management plan that was not incorporated into the Agreement.

activities, processes and resources applied to securing protection (CHAPR). Abbreviations used in relation to other provisions are self-explanatory.

A number of general points emerge from the analysis. First, the agreements represent a wide range of outcomes, containing provisions that fall along the entire scale for each of the six non-financial indicators. A wide range of outcomes also occurs in relation to financial provisions, ranging from a royalty equivalent of 0 (i.e. no payments) to a royalty equivalent of 3.05 per cent.

Second and very importantly, agreements that display strongly positive outcomes in one area tend to be strong in others; weaker agreements tend to be weaker across the board. This fact emerges very clearly from Table 5.1, where agreements have been ranked according to their scores on the 'environmental management' scale, with outcomes improving as one moves down through the Table from –1 to 6. Scores of 4–6 are regarded as strongly positive on this scale (see Chapter 4). Strongly positive outcomes on this and other issues are indicated by the use of bold print in the matrix.

As Table 5.1 reveals, a high proportion of the total number of strongly positive scores are contained in less than a quarter of the agreements (numbers 34 to 45). The same applies to negative or very low scores, with most clustered in a (different) set of agreements. There are two exceptions to this general picture. The first involves 'outliers', or individual scores for particular agreements on specific criteria that do not fit the overall pattern. In general these are easily explicable in terms of the particular circumstances of the agreements concerned. For instance, agreement 13 is an outlier in having strong financial provisions and level of cultural heritage protection, but weak provisions on environment, employment and business development. This was one of the first agreements negotiated in Australia and it was concluded under severe time pressures, helping to explain its uneven treatment of these issues. Subsequent agreements negotiated in the same jurisdiction score consistently across all of these areas.

The other anomaly relates to activities, processes and resources applied to securing cultural heritage protection (CHAPR), where stronger scores occur in a number of agreements that rate poorly or moderately on other criteria. A possible explanation for this pattern is that all jurisdictions in Australia have cultural heritage legislation with which mining companies must comply. Mining companies that are otherwise unwilling to agree on 'strong' agreement provisions may be prepared to do so in relation to cultural heritage because this involves activities and a commitment of resources that would be required in any case to fulfil their legal obligations.

The picture in relation to interests and rights in land is somewhat blurred by the fact that the issue does not apply to some of the agreements (indicated in Table 5.1 by 'DNA') that achieve strong outcomes on other issues and by the need to allocate multiple scores to agreements. However, in this area also agreements that are strong on other issues and do deal

with land either achieve a number of positive scores (for instance agreements 37, 44 and 45) or have strongly positive outcomes (4, 5) that coun-
teract negative outcomes (agreements 33, 36, 43).

A final general point worth noting is the relatively poor performance of
nearly all agreements on implementation, a point documented in detail
elsewhere in relation to agreements in Canada as well as Australia
(O'Faircheallaigh 2002). However, in this area also the stronger scores are
concentrated among the agreements that perform well on the other issues.

To summarise, Aboriginal groups that achieve strongly positive outcomes on one negotiation issue tend also to achieve strong outcomes on
other issues, while groups that perform poorly tend to do so across the
board. Thus, in some cases, Aboriginal groups are achieving substantial
economic benefits and innovative provisions to minimise the impact of
commercial activities on their traditional lands. In others, the benefits
gained by Aboriginal groups are negligible and impact minimisation provisions are minimal, while in some cases the exercise of rights that Indigenous parties possess under general legislation are restricted. Where
benefits are slight and the exercise of existing rights restricted, the Aboriginal parties may be worse off than in the absence of an agreement.

Explaining agreement outcomes

How can we explain the variation in outcomes illustrated in Table 5.1?
The fact that agreements tend to be weak or strong across the board indicates that it does not reflect deliberate trade offs undertaken by Aboriginal
parties through the negotiation process, for example by choosing a lower
level of financial payments in return for stronger provisions on cultural
heritage, or by trading off the opportunity to influence environmental practices for higher financial payments. If this were occurring, we would expect
to consistently observe a mix of weak and strong provisions in individual
agreements. This does not mean that no trade-offs occur, but they must
generally be at the margin. For instance, Aboriginal people may accept
somewhat less favourable environmental provisions (for example a 5
rather than a 6) in order to secure somewhat more favourable outcomes on
cultural heritage protection (for instance a 5 rather than a 4). However,
there is no indication that strong outcomes on one issue are being traded
off against weak outcomes on another.

Some other possible explanations can also be excluded. Variation in
outcomes does not reflect project scale. For instance, while in absolute
terms the highest figures for financial compensation have certainly been
negotiated for large projects, in relation to the value of project revenues
payments under agreements, some small mines are among the highest indicated in Table 5.1. Certain agreements for smaller projects have some of
the strongest provisions in relation to cultural heritage and environmental
protection, while one agreement for a project with a turnover of less than
A$50 million provides for the establishment of more apprenticeships for

Aboriginal people than almost any other agreement. On the other hand, there are agreements for both large and small projects that appear to offer little benefit to Aboriginal participants. Neither do outcomes reflect the identity, characteristics or policies of the companies entering agreements, as indicated by two findings. First, both small single-project companies and large multinational mining companies are distributed across the entire table. The second finding relates to a large multinational company that is involved in six of the agreements summarised in Table 5.1. If company characteristics or corporate policy were a primary influence on outcomes, agreements in which this company is involved should be grouped in general proximity to each other in Table 5.1. In fact the opposite is the case, with two falling in the group of agreements numbered 1 to 11 (i.e. the 'weakest' agreements in terms of Aboriginal interests), one in the group numbered 12 to 22, one in the group numbered 23 to 34, and two in the group numbered 35 to 45.

Neither does the timing of agreements offer a satisfactory explanation. It could be argued that, after the introduction of the *NTA* in 1994, Aboriginal groups had to undertake a learning process during which they could not be expected to achieve strong outcomes, and that this reflects the uneven outcomes in Table 5.1. However there is little evidence to support such a claim. First, on other occasions agreements reflect a capacity to immediately extract substantial benefits from legislative opportunities. This occurs within a few years of the passage of the *Land Rights Act*, while one of the strongest financial outcomes yet agreed in Australia was achieved through an agreement pursuant to Queensland's *MRA* just three years after its passage. Further, a number of the weaker agreements in Table 5.1 were concluded in 2003, almost a decade after the passage of the *NTA*.

Differences in legislative regimes clearly do explain a significant part of the variation in outcome evident in Table 5.1. A large proportion of the weaker agreements have been negotiated under the *NTA*, while a substantial number of the stronger agreements resulted from the *Land Rights Act* or the *Mineral Resources Act*. As explained in Chapter 3, the *Land Rights Act* confers on Aboriginal owners an effective veto over the grant of mining leases, placing them in a strong negotiating position. The *Mineral Resources Act* does not confer a veto, but under its terms a mining company wishing to obtain a mining lease must seek the consent of Aboriginal landowners and, if that consent is not forthcoming, a decision by the Governor-in-Council (effectively the Queensland Cabinet) is required before a lease can be granted. Achieving such an outcome can be time consuming and is of necessity public, providing Aboriginal landowners with an opportunity to bring political pressure to bear on decision-makers. This situation creates a substantial incentive for the project developer to reach agreement.

The position of Aboriginal groups negotiating under the terms of the *NTA* is quite different. They only have a Right to Negotiate, initially for six months, in relation to the terms on which a project may proceed.

At the end of that period and in the absence of an agreement, the project developer may, if it wishes, apply to the NNTT for a determination that mining leases may be granted and the project proceed. The NNTT can determine that a lease be granted with or without conditions, or that a lease not be granted. The relevant federal or state government minister can overturn the NNTT's decision if it does determine that a lease may not be granted. It can be argued that these legislative provisions place native title parties in a weak negotiating position, because, if a mining company cannot secure an agreement with them, the company can quickly pursue an administrative solution and, if this fails, appeal to government ministers who have, in Australia, historically been strongly supportive of mineral development.

Other provisions of the *NTA* further weaken the bargaining position of Aboriginal groups. Under Section 33 of the Act, agreements reached within the negotiation period can include payments to native title parties worked out by reference to the amount of profits made, any income derived or any things produced by the grantee party as a result of the proposed 'act'. However, under Section 38(2), if an agreement is not reached within the negotiation period and the matter is referred to the NNTT, the tribunal must not determine a condition that entitles native title parties to payments worked out by reference to the amount of profits made, any income derived or any things produced by the grantee party. This places native title parties under considerable pressure to conclude an agreement within the negotiation period. For them, negotiated outcomes 'will invariably be preferable to arbitration [by the NNTT] from a financial perspective owing to the existence of a no rent-sharing proviso at Section 38(2)' (Altman 1995: 6).

In theory, this pressure on the native title holders to reach agreement is balanced by the pressure created on developers to do the same by the additional time which would elapse if a matter is referred to the NNTT for arbitration, and by the uncertainty that arbitration creates given that the tribunal might not approve the grant of a mining lease or might attach stringent conditions to a lease. Thus *both* sides would be under pressure to do a deal, helping to ensure that the agreements reached would be equitable to both parties (Corbett and O'Faircheallaigh 2006: 158). However, this assumes there is a real possibility that the NNTT will not allow all mining leases to be granted, or that, in a significant proportion of cases where approval is given to the grant of leases, stringent conditions will be attached. Only if these assumptions hold will mining companies feel that going to arbitration involves a significant risk that their proposed activities will be halted or delayed or subjected to conditions more onerous than those likely to apply under a negotiated agreement.

In fact it has become increasingly obvious that the NNTT is most unlikely to reject an application for a mining lease or to impose substantial conditions on its grant. A detailed analysis covering the period 1996–2006 indicates that, in every one of the 17 cases where agreement was not reached and the matter was referred to the tribunal for arbitration, the mining lease was granted. In addition, the tribunal has been very reluctant to impose substantive conditions on the grant of leases, rejecting conditions proposed by native title parties and imposing only conditions of a minor and/or procedural nature, such as a requirement that the mining company inform the native title parties when it is about to commence operations or if it sells its mining lease (Corbett and O'Faircheallaigh 2006).

Thus the Aboriginal parties are under considerable pressure to settle during the Right to Negotiate period, while mining companies are under no such pressure, knowing that if they do not achieve an agreement that suits them, they can go to the Tribunal and obtain the interests they need to proceed with their project. To express this situation in negotiation parlance, for the Aboriginal parties their Best Alternative To a Negotiated Agreement (BATNA) is very poor indeed, while mining companies have a positive and low-risk BATNA. The negotiation literature suggests that in this situation one can expect outcomes highly unfavourable to the Aboriginal parties, and it can be argued that this reality is only too clearly reflected in the outcomes summarised in Table 5.1.

However, inequities in bargaining power created by the *NTA* do not provide an adequate explanation for these outcomes, for three reasons. First, a number of the strongest agreements summarised in Table 5.1 *were* negotiated under the *NTA* (agreements 38, and 42 to 45). Clearly, in these cases, Aboriginal communities and their negotiators have found ways to overcome the disadvantage the Act potentially creates for their bargaining positions. Second, while the legal and procedural rights conferred by the *NTA* may be limited, a number of groups have achieved positive outcomes from policy-based agreements, that is in situations where they brought *no* legal or procedural rights to the negotiation table (agreements 36 and 37). Finally, while many agreements negotiated under the *NTA* are not in the strongest group, the variation among these agreements is itself very substantial and needs to be explained. There is a marked difference in outcomes, for instance, between agreement 30, which contains a royalty equivalent of 0.8 per cent and achieves moderate scores on most other issues, and agreements (for example, numbers 2 to 5) that contain no or minimal cash payments and score poorly on other issues.

Figures 5.1 and 5.2 provide an important insight into other key explanatory variables by introducing a spatial dimension to the data in Table 5.1. Figure 5.1 shows the approximate location of all the projects dealt with by the agreements summarised in Table 5.1. Figure 5.2 indicates the location of 12 agreements that represent a strong outcome overall, as judged by the fact that they achieve a 'strongly positive' score on at least 5 of the 7 negotiation issues dealt with in Table 5.1. The geographical concentration of the 'strong' agreements in the far north of Queensland, the Northern Territory and northern Western Australia is striking. This pattern partly reflects the application in far north Queensland and the Northern Territory

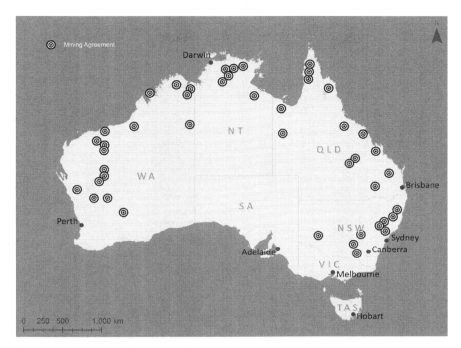

Figure 5.1 Location of 45 Australian agreements.

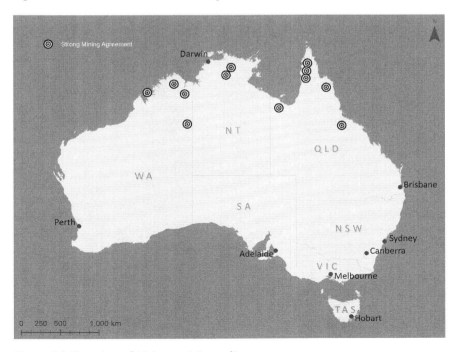

Figure 5.2 Location of 12 'strong' Australian agreements.

of particular legislation that confers a strong bargaining position on Aboriginal people. However, the operation of this legislation cannot provide the only explanation, given that three of the strong agreements occur in Western Australia, where it does not apply, and more generally that, as mentioned earlier, a number of the strongest agreements were negotiated under the *NTA* or in the absence of any legislative requirements.

Two general explanations suggest themselves. First, the regions in which these agreements occur are characterised by well-established, politically active Aboriginal regional organisations, such as the Cape York Land Council, the Northern Land Council and the Kimberley Land Council. These bodies have, in the context of Aboriginal Australia, access to significant technical and financial resources and their senior office holders (chairman, chief executive officer) have been recognised as part of Australia's national political leadership and have had substantial political profiles. The existence of these organisations reflects, in turn, the fact that in far north Australia Aboriginal people have generally been better placed to maintain a strong land base and, related to this, a high degree of social and cultural vitality and prominent political profiles. In all 12 'strong' agreements, regional organisations played a major role in supporting local Aboriginal groups in their negotiations with mining companies. It appears that, in cases where negotiations occurred pursuant to the *NTA*, the political strength of regional organisations allowed the weakness inherent in the Act to be overcome. The political strength of local and regional Aboriginal organisation could also explain the occurrence of strong 'policy based' agreements in these regions, reflecting the desire of mining companies to develop positive relationships with local communities even in the absence of any legal requirement to negotiate.

Differences in organisational capacity and support and in the political vitality of individual Aboriginal communities may also help to explain the important variations in outcomes that occur among *NTA* agreements other than those included in the group of 'strong' agreements.

The second possible explanation involves the fact that many of the 12 agreements are accounted for by 'clusters' of negotiations occurring close together not only in space but also in time. Most of the 'strong' Northern Territory agreements were negotiated in the early 1980s, the Cape York agreements between 1992 and 2001 and the Western Australian agreements between 2004 and 2006. In each case, the same regional organisation was involved in each negotiation in the 'cluster'. It seems likely that important learning processes have occurred within individual regional organisations, with a succession of negotiations within a relatively short time period allowing an accumulation of relevant skills and experience. This again highlights the apparent importance of regional organisation, since such an accumulation of expertise would be considerably more difficult to achieve if individual Aboriginal communities were undertaking negotiations separately and alone.

Conclusion

The development of evaluative criteria in Chapter 4 has allowed me to document, in a systematic way, outcomes from 45 negotiations between Aboriginal people and mining companies in Australia. The agreements analysed cover a substantial time frame, a wide geographical distribution (as illustrated by Figure 5.1), a range of jurisdictions, mining projects of different scales and mining companies of different sizes and types, and a variety of legislative and policy contexts.

Outcomes from negotiations vary greatly, with the agreements containing outcomes matching every point, from the most negative to the most positive, on each of the scales formulated in Chapter 4. With the partial exception of activities, processes and resources applied to cultural heritage protection, outcomes from agreements tended to be generally consistent across the range of key negotiation issues, with individual agreements delivering either strong or weak outcomes across the board. This indicates that the variation in outcomes so evident from Table 5.1 do not reflect intra-agreement trade-offs between outcomes on different issues effected by Aboriginal negotiators. Neither do outcomes reflect differences in project scale, in the type of mining company involved, or in the timing of negotiations.

Prevailing legislative regimes clearly have a significant impact on outcomes. In particular, the *NTA* places Aboriginal people in a weak negotiating position, helping to explain why a substantial proportion of agreements negotiated under the Act contain relatively poor outcomes. However, legislative differences do not offer a full explanation, given that some *NTA* agreements represent very strong outcomes and that strong agreements have been achieved in some situations where mining companies face no legislative requirement to negotiate. Mapping the geographical distribution of the 45 agreements indicates that positive outcomes are clearly and closely associated with the presence of strong Aboriginal political organisation, related in turn to a strong land base and Aboriginal social and cultural vitality. In particular, a strong relationship exists between positive outcomes and the involvement in successive negotiations of regional land organisations.

This analysis highlights the key role of broader, structural factors, such as legislative frameworks and the distribution of political influence at the regional level, in determining negotiation outcomes. It appears to indicate that more specific, 'micro' factors relating to the behaviour of negotiators and conduct of individual negotiations are of less importance. If this is not the case, it is difficult to explain why not a single 'strong' agreement is found outside jurisdictions where legislation confers substantial bargaining power on Aboriginal landowners and/or outside the sphere of operations of powerful regional land organisations. This is not to say that 'micro' level processes do not count and they could help explain, for instance, the significant variation in outcomes that occur within broad categories of agreements.

The findings suggest that, if Aboriginal groups wish to substantially improve their negotiation outcomes, they cannot do so solely by focusing on the performance of negotiators or the detail of negotiation processes. They must also seek to address the wider structural constraints on their negotiation power represented, for instance, by the *NTA* and the operations of the NNTT. The development of substantial regional organisational capacity appears critical to any such initiative.

While the examination of negotiation outcomes presented in this chapter is based on a large number of negotiations across a wide range of contexts, it is limited both in focusing on one country, and on a 'macro' level of analysis. As noted in Chapter 2, a comparative, case study analysis of individual negotiations is also important in assessing whether alternative or additional explanatory factors must also be taken into account, and in particular in focusing on the way in which 'internal' and 'external' factors interact to shape negotiation outcomes. Against this background, we now turn to the case study negotiations in Canada and Australia.

References

Altman, J. (1995) *Native Title Act 1993: Implementation Issues for Resource Developers*, Canberra: Centre for Aboriginal Economic Research, Australian National University.

Corbett, T. and O'Faircheallaigh, C. (2006) 'Unmasking Native Title: The National Native Title Tribunal's Application of the *NTA*'s Arbitration Provisions', *University of Western Australia Law Review*, 33(1): 153–77.

O'Faircheallaigh, C. (2002) 'Implementation: The Forgotten Dimension of Agreement-Making in Australia and Canada', *Indigenous Law Bulletin*, 5: 14–17.

6   Bauxite mining, Western Cape York, Queensland

Introduction

In the mid-1990s, Comalco Ltd, a Rio Tinto subsidiary which is now part of Rio Tinto Alcan, Rio's bauxite and alumina group, operated one of the world's largest bauxite mines at Weipa on the western coast of Cape York Peninsula (Figure 6.1). Comalco's project was established in the late 1950s and early 1960s on what had previously been Aboriginal reserve land at a time when no legal recognition was afforded the rights or interests of Aboriginal landowners in Australia. In 1995, after the High Court's *Mabo* decision and after a change in Rio Tinto's corporate policies towards

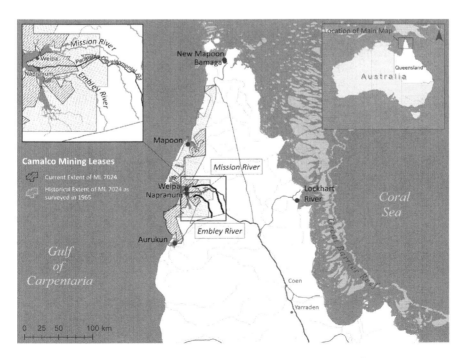

Figure 6.1 Location map, Weipa bauxite mine, Western Cape York.

Aboriginal peoples, Comalco initiated discussions with the Aboriginal traditional owners[1] of its mining lease and Aboriginal communities affected by its operations. The negotiations that followed were protracted, difficult and at times appeared likely to fail, but eventually yielded what is regarded in Australia as a benchmark for agreements between mining companies and Aboriginal peoples.

This chapter traces the history and outcome of the negotiations between Comalco Ltd and the Aboriginal Community of Western Cape York. Comalco's operations had a long history which had a major bearing on the course and outcomes of the negotiations, and particular attention is paid to that history in the opening sections on Comalco and on the Aboriginal groups. Because negotiations were protracted and highly complex, the narrative describing them is broken into three sections: preparations for negotiations; an initial phase of negotiations that failed to yield an agreement (1996–1999); and a second phase that resulted in the signing of the Western Cape Communities Co-existence Agreement (WCCCA) between Comalco, the Queensland government and the Aboriginal Community in March 2001. The final sections summarise the content of the WCCCA and evaluate and explain the outcome of the negotiations.

Comalco and Weipa bauxite

In 1955, the exploration arm of the Melbourne-based company Consolidated Zinc was issued Authorities to Prospect to explore for bauxite over an area of 2,585 square miles of Western Cape York in far north Queensland (see Figure 6.1). Extensive bauxite deposits were located south of the Embley River, on the Weipa Peninsula, and north of the Mission River. In 1956, Comalco Ltd was established as the vehicle that would develop these deposits. Shortly afterwards, Consolidated Zinc merged with Rio-Tinto Mining, and Conzinc Rio Tinto of Australia Ltd (CRA) become the Australian component of the new entity, with the London-based Rio Tinto-Zinc Corporation as its major shareholder.

Authorities to Prospect allowed the mining companies that held them to negotiate Special Bauxite Mining Leases (SBMLs), each covered by dedicated legislation. Under the *Comalco Act 1957*, the Queensland government awarded Comalco a mining lease in Western Cape York (SBML 1, later ML 7024) covering an area of 2,380 square miles. Its term extended to January 2042, with an option to renew for a further 21 years. Progressive relinquishment of areas not needed for mining was to reduce this area to 1,000 square miles by 1977. The area of Comalco's lease had previously been an Aboriginal Reserve set aside for the exclusive use of its Aboriginal inhabitants, with the lease constituting 93 per cent of the area of the Reserve. Comalco's SBML was excised from the Reserve without any reference to the wishes or interests of its Aboriginal inhabitants. This action was consistent with a general policy and legislative regime in Queensland and Australia which at this time failed to recognise the fundamental human, democratic and property rights of Aboriginal people (see Chapter 3).

Over the period 1961–1964, Comalco developed large-scale mining operations, power and transport infrastructure and a port to ship its bauxite on the Weipa peninsula. It also established the Weipa township, complete with new shops, hospital, schools, and recreational and sporting facilities, to house non-Aboriginal workers and associated service personnel such as teachers, medical staff and police. Weipa was established as a 'closed' town administered by Comalco, with access to housing tied to employment with Comalco, its contractors or public agencies delivering services. Over the years a range of tenures including freehold, leasehold and Special Purpose Mining Perpetual Leases (SPMPLs) were issued to allow the establishment and ongoing development of Weipa.

By the early 1970s, Comalco was producing ten million tonnes of bauxite per annum, had built a railway bridge over the Mission River and had extended mining to areas north of the river. The Weipa bauxite operations provided the platform for Comalco to develop as a fully integrated producer of aluminium metal and manufactures. In 1963, Comalco and a number of other international aluminium companies, including the Canadian-based Alcan Ltd, established Queensland Alumina Limited (QAL), which constructed an alumina refinery at Gladstone on Queensland's east coast. Its partner companies entered 25-year contracts with Comalco to purchase bauxite equivalent to their shareholding in QAL on a take-or-pay basis. This provided Comalco with a major and secure market for its Weipa bauxite.

In 1970, Comalco became a public company, with CRA as its major shareholder. Expansion continued over the following decades, and by 1995 Comalco had a 25 per cent stake in a second alumina refinery in Sardinia and interests in three aluminium smelters. In 1995, its total assets were A$2.9 billion, sales revenue was A$2.2 billion, and net profit A$274 million (Comalco Ltd 1998: 37).

In 1995, Comalco's parent company, CRA Ltd, merged with its largest shareholder, Rio Tinto, to create a dual-listed entity with headquarters in London and Melbourne. Comalco Ltd remained a publicly listed company until 2000, at which point Rio Tinto bought out the minority shareholders and it became a wholly owned subsidiary of Rio.

The Aboriginal groups

The archaeological evidence indicates that Aboriginal people have lived in Cape York for some 30,000 years. The arrival of Europeans brought fundamental change to all Aboriginal people in the region, but the contact history of different groups varied significantly. Towards the southern end of Comalco's lease, the Wik and Wik Waya peoples were left largely undisturbed in possession of their traditional lands, though the presence of Christian missions, in particular, had major impacts on their culture,

economy and family structures. Further north, the impact of white settlement was more severe and extensive, with depopulation occurring in some
areas and with large numbers of Aboriginal people being brought from
outside the region, particularly to the large 'industrial' mission established
at Mapoon in the 1890s. By the early 1960s most Aboriginal people in the
area were resident at mission settlements at Aurukun, Napranum and
Mapoon for at least part of the year. Many still continued to hunt, fish and
gather on their traditional country, in some cases spending a part of each
year on small family-based settlements called outstations.

Over the period 1957–1963, the Queensland government sought to
close the Mapoon mission, according to Mapoon people in order to make
way for construction of a second port for Comalco at nearby Port Mus-
grave (Holden 1996a). In 1963, the Queensland government forcibly
moved the remaining Mapoon residents to a location hundreds of kilo-
metres away at the tip of Cape York, called New Mapoon (see Figure 6.1).
In 1974, some former residents returned to Mapoon and over the following two decades re-established the community.

The Queensland government's actions severely disrupted the social, cultural and economic lives of Mapoon residents (Holden 1996a, 1996b).
Comalco's operations had negative cultural and social effects on Napranum, the community nearest to its mine (Howitt 1996), and less direct but
still significant effects on Aurukun, further to the south (O'Faircheallaigh
1996). At the same time, Aboriginal people received only a small share of
the economic benefits generated by Comalco. As Howitt notes, their exclusion from the benefits and opportunities of mineral development was particularly obvious to Aboriginal people living at Napranum, only 10 km
south of the prosperous and well-serviced Weipa community (Howitt
1996).

After the *Mabo* decision in 1992, a number of Aboriginal groups lodged
common law native title claims in the courts. One of these, lodged on
behalf of the Wik Peoples, included the southern portion of Comalco's
mining lease. The claim challenged the validity of the Comalco interests
and the *Comalco Act*, and asserted native title to the Wik lands, the subject
of Mining Lease 7024. Other claims were lodged by the Alngith, Taepa-
dhigi, Thaayorre, Tjungundji, Yurpungath, Thanikwith and Waranggu
peoples. None of the claims had been settled by the time negotiations commenced with Comalco. As discussed in Chapter 3, the *Mabo* decision and
the *NTA* protected existing commercial interests, so these legal actions did
not represent any clear threat to Comalco's operations. However, their resolution would remove a source of uncertainty for the company, especially
in relation to the grant of any future interests it might require to further
develop its mining and related activities in Western Cape York.

The Aboriginal interests affected by Comalco's operations were diverse,
reflecting both the large area covered by its lease and the complex contact
history of the region. Anthropological work undertaken as part of preparations for negotiations showed that eleven separate groups of traditional

owners held primary interests in areas covered by Comalco's mining lease, the Weipa township and Comalco's port. Most, though not all, traditional owners lived in Aurukun, Mapoon, Napranum and New Mapoon. By the mid 1990s, each of these communities was governed by an elected community council, whose constituents included people, among them descendants of former mission residents, who were not traditional owners of Comalco's lease but as community members were affected by its operations. I use the term 'traditional owners' when referring to the Aboriginal owners of land covered by Comalco's leases; the term 'the Aboriginal communities' to refer specifically to Aurukun, Mapoon, Napranum and New Mapoon; and the term 'Aboriginal Community' to encompass the traditional owners, other Aboriginal residents of the four settlements and the four community councils.

The Aboriginal Community was supported in the negotiations by the Cape York Land Council (CYLC), a regional land organisation based in Cairns. The CYLC had been established as a grass roots organisation in 1989 to fight a proposed space base in Cape York, and it was successful in doing so. Initially the CYLC operated on a shoestring, but by 1995 it had built an organisation that, though still small, had successfully supported communities in negotiating a number of agreements with mining companies and with the Queensland government. A key component of its success in negotiations with mining companies was the preparation of clear negotiating positions strongly endorsed by the Aboriginal communities concerned, based on extensive information gathering and community consultations (O'Faircheallaigh 2000). After the passage of the *NTA*, the CYLC became the Native Title Representative Body for Cape York and assumed relevant statutory responsibilities under the Act.

Preparing for negotiations

In March 1995, Leon Davis, CEO of the newly-merged Rio Tinto, publicly declared that, unlike much of Australia's mining industry at the time, Rio Tinto accepted the *Mabo* decision and the reality of native title and stated his determination to establish positive relationships with Aboriginal communities adjacent to its major mining operations (Davis 1995). Shortly after Davis's announcement, Comalco approached the CYLC and asked it to facilitate discussions with the Aboriginal Community.

However, the CYLC was unsure whether the Aboriginal Community would agree to negotiate with Comalco, given its history on western Cape York and given that a number of landowner groups had initiated legal action involving the company. In addition, because the negotiations would be based on a policy initiative by Comalco rather than on the future act provisions of the *NTA*, the CYLC would not be performing a statutory role in any negotiations and the Aboriginal Community would have to decide if it wished CYLC to support it in the negotiations. In November 1995, a series of community meetings was held, approval was given for negotiations with Comalco, and the CYLC received instructions to represent the Aboriginal Community.

The CYLC established four steering committees to provide overall direction for the negotiations, one for Aurukun, one for Napranum, a third for Mapoon and New Mapoon and a fourth for the traditional owners of the Weipa peninsula. The latter were recognised as having specific interests and issues to address because of the presence on their land of the Weipa township and Comalco's port and other facilities. The CYLC insisted as a condition for being involved in the negotiations that each steering committee should be broadly representative of the interests affected by Comalco's operations, and not just of the traditional owners of the company's leases. However it was not prescriptive about how the steering committees should be established or about their membership, and each community or group made its own arrangements in this regard. It was accepted that the membership of steering committees was provisional and might have to be revisited once anthropological studies were complete. In the event, the Napranum Steering Committee was substantially restructured when anthropological work indicated that not all groups whose lands were affected by Comalco's operations were represented on the original committee.

During the remainder of 1995 and 1996, consultants retained by the CYLC worked with the Aboriginal Community to undertake a range of studies and reports to help prepare for negotiations. These included anthropological studies to ensure that all the Aboriginal groups affected by Comalco's operations were correctly and fully identified; a report on the requirements for effective protection of Aboriginal cultural heritage; an assessment of the efficacy of Comalco's environmental management systems; and three economic and social impact assessments focused on Aurukun, Napranum/Weipa Peninsula and Mapoon/New Mapoon. Drawing on extensive community consultations over a period of six months, the economic and social impact assessments documented the effects of Comalco's presence in Western Cape York, including the impact of associated government actions and policies, on the Aboriginal Community. They established Community aspirations and goals in relation to Comalco's future operations, and identified strategies to help achieve these goals and address the impacts of mining.

In the meantime, the CYLC and Comalco negotiated a Memorandum of Understanding to create a framework within which the preparations for negotiations and the negotiations themselves would occur. Issues it addressed included the preparatory studies, funding arrangements, confidentiality provisions, communication protocols and membership of negotiating teams. The CYLC's nominated negotiating team consisted of its CEO Noel Pearson, who was on the way to becoming one of Australia's most high-profile Aboriginal leaders, the author, who was supervising the preparatory studies and the CYLC's Principal Legal Officer. The CYLC expected that this group would conduct initial negotiations, and that it would support the Aboriginal Community throughout. However, it assumed that senior traditional owners and other community leaders nominated by the steering committees would later join the negotiations, as only they would have the authority to finalise a draft agreement, which would then be approved or rejected by the Aboriginal Community.

In relation to communication, CYLC's position was that all communication about the negotiations should be channelled through the Land Council rather than occur directly between Comalco and the Aboriginal Community. This issue was to prove contentious throughout the negotiations. The CYLC was concerned that Comalco, which had a substantial presence on the ground in Western Cape York, might employ 'divide and rule' tactics in the community when negotiations reached a critical phase. Negotiations regarding the MoU proved acrimonious, particularly in relation to issues of confidentiality, communication and funding. It was May 1996 before agreement was reached, by which time the preparatory studies were well under way.

As the preparatory studies were completed, draft reports were discussed with each steering committee, further work was undertaken if this was required, draft reports were amended and final reports signed off by the steering committees. Once the studies were largely completed, the CYLC turned its attention to establishing an Aboriginal negotiating position. The author, working with senior CYLC staff, developed a draft negotiating position addressing the major issues that had emerged from the various reports and the community consultations. This was then canvassed with each steering committee, further developed, approved by the steering committees meeting jointly, and then approved by a large public meeting involving all four communities in November 1996.

On 28 November 1996, the Aboriginal Negotiating Position was handed to Comalco, along with copies of the reports used in its preparation, with the exception of the review of Comalco's environmental management system that was yet to be completed. The Aboriginal Negotiating Position was a brief but comprehensive document setting forward what the Aboriginal Community wished to achieve from negotiations with Comalco, across 14 major areas. In relation to financial compensation, it demanded ongoing payments based on a percentage of Comalco's revenues, on the principle that a portion of the wealth extracted by Comalco from their country should accrue to the traditional owners and that the amounts involved should increase if Comalco's production increased. It also demanded a one-off payment to compensate for the past impacts of Comalco's operations, regarded by the Aboriginal Community as critical, given the history of Comalco's operations and associated government actions in Western Cape York. The Aboriginal Negotiating Position sought recognition of Aboriginal title to the land underlying Comalco's interests, surrender of parts of Comalco's mining leases to their Aboriginal owners, recognition and respect for Aboriginal traditional owners, cultural heritage protection, controls over use of land and sea by non-Aboriginal people and an active role for traditional owners in environmental management and decision-making. It also sought Aboriginal participation in employment and business development opportunities associated with Comalco's operations and enhanced access to education, housing and other services. Some of the issues raised in the document could only be addressed with the participation of the Queensland government, reflecting the CYLC's assumption (shared at this time by Comalco) that Queensland would play an active role in negotiations and any subsequent agreement.

The course of negotiations: 1996–1999

Comalco presented its initial reply to the Aboriginal Negotiating Position just three weeks later, at a meeting at Aurukun. This was in the form of a draft agreement, which did not in fact respond in any detail to many aspects of the Aboriginal Negotiating Position. To the extent that it did, in all but a few cases it indicated a large gap between the positions of Comalco and the Aboriginal Community. On financial compensation, Comalco rejected in principle the concept of a royalty payment, and offered instead a fixed amount of less than $1 million (indexed). It did not accept the proposal for general compensation for past impacts of its operations, but was prepared to consider a one-off benefits package for those community members who had been permanently deprived of the ability to enjoy areas of significance to them because of the construction of the Weipa township and mine processing facilities.

Comalco's response to the Aboriginal Negotiating Position may have been premature, particularly since the company was involved in a serious industrial dispute that required the attention of a number of senior personnel involved in the discussions with the Aboriginal Community. The company had very little time to absorb the Aboriginal Negotiating Position and the supporting documentation, to consider how that position related to its own core interests, or to assess how it might respond in a way that protected and promoted those interests while offering substantial gains to the Aboriginal Community. There may also have been an issue regarding the *ability* of Comalco negotiators to respond in such a manner at this time. It was one matter for CEO Leon Davis to set a new direction for Rio Tinto group companies in their relations with Aboriginal communities, and another for this new approach to be internalised by key staff in operating companies. This was perhaps especially so for a long-established enterprise such as Comalco, many of whose employees had an understanding of the development and impact of the company's operations at Weipa very different to that of the Aboriginal Community (Howitt 1996: 2).

On 23 December 1996, the High Court of Australia ruled on key matters of law relating to the native title claim of the Wik peoples. It found in favour if the Wik on a number of points, but also unanimously confirmed the validity of Comalco's interests and of the *Comalco Act*.

As 1996 had progressed, the CYLC leadership reached the conclusion, on the basis of its interactions with Comalco and a number of informal meetings between the two negotiating teams, that the company was unlikely to accept the Aboriginal Community's position on major issues in the normal course of negotiations. The CYLC sought ways of enhancing the community's bargaining position. At this time, another aluminium company, the Canadian-based Alcan, announced plans to develop the Ely bauxite lease, which Alcan had been allocated in 1965 but had never developed. The terms of Alcan's 'take-or-pay' bauxite contracts with Comalco, under which Alcan obtained bauxite to provide its share of the feedstock for the QAL alumina refinery, had become increasingly onerous on Alcan as time passed. The contracts were due to expire in January 2000. Alcan announced that it would commence development of Ely to allow it to provide its own bauxite to QAL. It was essential that Alcan move quickly to develop Ely given that its contracts with Comalco would expire in less than four years.

This situation seemed to offer the CYLC and the Aboriginal Community a valuable opportunity. If they could facilitate the speedy development of Ely, Alcan might be prepared to negotiate an agreement that accepted key Aboriginal negotiating positions. This could establish precedents that Comalco would hopefully then find difficult to reject, especially given that the Aboriginal traditional owners for Ely were also involved in the negotiations with Comalco, that Alcan's lease was adjacent to Comalco's, and that its development would involve mining and shipping operations very similar to Comalco's. The CYLC initiated discussions with Alcan and, during late 1996 and early 1997, developed a negotiating position in a manner similar to that used for Comalco.

A number of the events and developments described above did not augur well for a smooth negotiation process and early agreement between the Aboriginal Community and Comalco. Initial negotiations between the CYLC and Comalco in relation to the MoU had generated tensions between the two; Comalco had responded rapidly to the Aboriginal Negotiating Position in a way that left a very large gap between the parties; and CYLC had embarked on a strategy to enhance the Aboriginal Community's bargaining position which diverted a substantial part of its limited resources to another set of negotiations.

In February 1997, the CYLC negotiators rejected Comalco's initial response as entirely inadequate. In March 1997, Comalco offered a second response to the Aboriginal Negotiating Position. This was considerably more substantial than the first, and put forward proposals in relation to many of the issues raised by the Aboriginal Community. In some cases (surrender of areas from the mining lease, access to mining leases, control of non-Aboriginal use of country) these appeared to be generally consistent with the Aboriginal position. In others (cultural heritage protection, employment and training) Comalco's draft indicated a willingness to negotiate relevant provisions, but substantial discussion would be required to bring the parties to agreement. However, the parties were a long way apart or in fundamental opposition on some key issues. These included:

- recognition of underlying Aboriginal title to Comalco's leases;
- financial compensation, where Comalco was still offering fixed dollar payments, albeit at a somewhat higher level, and still refusing to consider compensation for past impacts;
- recognition of the key place of Aboriginal traditional owners, with Comalco failing to employ the term 'traditional owners' even in discussing protection of Aboriginal cultural heritage and emphasising throughout the role of the Aboriginal communities who, for instance, would be the recipient of compensation payments;
- environmental management, where Comalco indicated a willingness to consult with the communities but not to afford traditional owners an active role in decision-making;
- Comalco's requirement for Aboriginal indemnities against a much wider range of possible legal actions, and Aboriginal consents for a broader range of Comalco interests, including future interests, than the CYLC had contemplated.

In March 1997, the CYLC and traditional owners for the Ely lease reached an 'in principle' agreement with Alcan that included many of the key elements of the Aboriginal Negotiating Position presented to Comalco in November 1996. (A final agreement with Alcan was signed in September 1997.) These elements included Alcan's recognition of native title, subject to the Aboriginal Community accepting the validity of Alcan's interests and approving its mining and related activities, and compensation payments based on a payment for each tonne of bauxite produced and at a level well in excess of that proposed by Comalco when the latter was converted to an 'amount per tonne' basis. The Alcan agreement reinforced the CYLC negotiators in their view that much more favourable terms could be obtained from Comalco and the Alcan agreement became, in effect, a 'bottom line' for the negotiators across a range of key issues.

In April 1997, all four steering committees rejected Comalco's revised offer, and instructed the CYLC to draft a fresh agreement reflecting the Aboriginal negotiating position and to then organise negotiation meetings in Cape York with senior staff from Comalco and from Rio Tinto. However, the CYLC's capacity to develop a draft agreement was in fact constrained, reflecting severe pressures on its limited resources. In addition to the Comalco negotiations, these included dealing with Alcan, a series of other development proposals on the Cape, the Wik and other native title claims and wider political agendas, particularly a national campaign by Aboriginal organisations to fight the federal government's proposed amendments to the *NTA* (see Chapter 3). In addition, at this juncture two members of the CYLC negotiating team left the Cape to take up roles with a Melbourne law firm, and while their involvement continued they were not in a position to maintain their previous level of participation. It was to be March 1998 before the CYLC was able to provide a draft to Comalco.

In May 1997, the environmental consultants finally presented their report. This identified what the consultants regarded as major shortcomings with Comalco's environmental management system. This may have reinforced Comalco in its opposition to according traditional owners an active role in environmental decision-making. However Comalco did undertake a major revision of its key environmental management documents, the Environmental Management Overview Strategy and the Environmental Management Plan, drawing in part on the CYLC consultants' report.

In September 1997, Comalco made a further offer, based on a fixed annual payment somewhat higher than its March offer, but still far removed from the Aboriginal position both in terms of structure (because it would not adjust to increases in Comalco's output) and in the level of proposed payments. The CYLC rejected the offer.

Little progress occurred in the following months, but in November Comalco approached the CYLC about reviving the momentum of negotiations and in early December 1997 Comalco provided a further draft agreement. Over this period Comalco also commenced a number of initiatives on the ground in the areas of employment and training and business development, outside of the framework of the negotiations with the CYLC. This represented a source of significant tension between the parties, as the CYLC saw it as an attempt by Comalco to build an alternative platform on which it could develop a relationship with the Aboriginal Community if it could not achieve an acceptable outcome through the negotiations.

The pace of negotiations picked up substantially in late 1997 and early 1998, with detailed work being undertaken to advance matters on which there was some agreement, such as employment and training and the establishment of an Aboriginal ranger program, and with alternative approaches being canvassed on some difficult issues such as financial compensation. Both parties were hopeful of reaching agreement by April 1998, but the large difference in positions regarding financial compensation was recognised as a fundamental problem in that regard. The CYLC undertook work aimed at quantifying the component of financial compensation relating to past impacts, as no specific figure had been attached to this item in the Aboriginal Negotiating Position. Extensive discussions occurred in relation to the possible transfer of the Sudley pastoral station, operated by Comalco, and of property within the Weipa township to their Aboriginal traditional owners. The CYLC felt that such transfers could constitute part of a settlement in relation to past impacts. It was agreed that both sides would try to identify alternative ways of structuring financial provisions to address Comalco's opposition to a 'payment per tonne' approach, while allowing the Aboriginal Community to benefit from any significant expansion of Comalco's operations.

In addition, Comalco and the CYLC agreed to renew efforts to persuade the Queensland government to contribute to an agreement and so supplement Comalco's financial offer. The CYLC hoped that the government might be persuaded to transfer underlying title to Comalco's leases under the *Aboriginal Land Act 1991 (ALA)*, which would then entitle the traditional owners and possibly also the Aboriginal Communities to a share of the statutory royalties paid by Comalco to the government. Over the next six months the CYLC engaged in extensive discussions with government officers about a possible transfer of title under the *ALA*, and Comalco executives met with relevant government ministers to explore ways in which Queensland might contribute to an agreement. These attempts to obtain a contribution from government were not successful. The National Party Premier, Mr Borbidge, was implacably opposed to use of the *ALA*, whose introduction he had strongly opposed when in Opposition, and objected in principle to the allocation of a share of statutory royalties to Aboriginal interests. One result of this response was that the focus of negotiations in relation to recognition of Aboriginal title shifted to the possible recognition by Comalco of underlying native title to Comalco's leases. Native title was to prove a highly complex and contentious issue in the negotiations (see below).

In March 1998, the CYLC provided Comalco with the agreement it had drafted that reflected the Aboriginal Negotiating Position. In addition it addressed the question of native title, which the Aboriginal Negotiation Position had not specifically discussed, proposing provisions which mirrored what the CYLC described as the 'live and let live' approach of the Alcan agreement. Comalco would recognise the existence of native title underlying its leases, and the Aboriginal Community would recognise the validity of Comalco's interests and not attempt to use their native title in a manner that would interfere with Comalco's mining and related activities.

Comalco replied in April, not with a detailed response to the CYLC Draft Agreement but with a further and revised offer expressed in general terms. The offer reiterated positions on issues where there had been significant agreement and also Comalco's position on environmental management, where the company still proposed that traditional owners would only have a right to be consulted. Comalco indicated in-principle willingness to agree to a determination of native title, on specific terms to be agreed in subsequent negotiations. It made a further financial offer that was higher than Comalco's September 1997 offer but was still based on a fixed annual amount and, on the CLYC's calculation, fell far short of being equivalent to the Alcan agreement when converted to an 'amount per tonne' basis.

By this point, funding for Aboriginal participation in the negotiations had reached a critical stage. Comalco's funding was exhausted and, while the CYLC had committed resources from its general organisational budgets, there were serious limits on its ability to continue doing so. The Land Council approached the federal government's ATSIC and secured substantial funding to support the negotiations. This funding was indispensable in allowing the Aboriginal Community to maintain its positions during a critical phase of the negotiations.

The CYLC replied to Comalco's offer by requesting a detailed response to its draft of March 1998, and stated that once this was received negotiations should, as requested by the steering committees, move to Cape York and involve the traditional owners and senior officials of Comalco and Rio Tinto. Comalco responded that it would only engage with the Aboriginal Community in relation to a proposal that had the support of Comalco and CYLC negotiators and that both negotiating teams should focus on concluding such a proposal.

At this point, it appeared that negotiations might become deadlocked, particularly on the matter of financial compensation, and in May 1998 the CYLC canvassed a new proposal aimed at finding a way to supplement Comalco's existing financial offer. This followed the announcement by Alcan and Comalco in January 1998 that they had negotiated a Bauxite Mining and Exchange Agreement (BMEA) and that as a result construction of the Ely project would not proceed. Rather, Alcan would continue to obtain bauxite from Comalco under new contractual arrangements, and at a later date Comalco would mine Ely and would be 'repaid' the bauxite it had supplied to Alcan from its Weipa operation. Alcan continued to have responsibilities to the Aboriginal Community under the Ely Agreement, but it would not now conduct a separate mining operation. The CYLC suggested that if those responsibilities could be 'rolled into' a single tripartite agreement involving Alcan, Comalco and the Aboriginal Community the companies could achieve considerable rationalisation of expenditures, and the savings could be used to enhance the financial compensation being offered under Comalco's existing offer. The CYLC's proposal was that under a tripartite agreement a single royalty based on the rate used in the Alcan agreement would be applied to all bauxite extracted from both Comalco's lease and Ely.

Considerable effort was devoted to pursuing a tripartite agreement in the following months. In October 1998, Alcan and Comalco submitted a proposal to the CYLC in relation to the financial provisions of such an agreement. This was not based on an 'amount per tonne' approach, but rather again proposed a fixed amount per annum, at a higher level than Comalco's previous offer. The CYLC determined that the revised offer would leave the Aboriginal Community in a considerably less favourable position than would a combination of the Alcan 'stand alone' agreement and the latest Comalco offer. After Alcan and Comalco tabled a draft tripartite agreement in December 1998 that the CYLC saw as seriously diluting aspects of the original Alcan agreement, the CYLC indicated its wish to revert to bilateral negotiations.

The December 1998 draft did provide important insights into Comalco's thinking on native title. Its proposal was that all native title in the Weipa township would be extinguished as would native title in any areas of its leases where third parties held an interest; that traditional owners would give their consent to future grants of interest to Comalco without having the benefit of the Right to Negotiate; and that native title applications could only be made on terms specified in the proposed agreement. This was a long way from the CYLC's 'live and let live' principle that formed the basis for the Alcan agreement.

The CYLC focused once more on trying to improve the benefits available from a separate agreement with Comalco. Jointly with Comalco, it initiated further approaches to the (now Labor) Queensland Government to pursue the possibility of accessing the components of statutory royalties provided for under the *ALA*. Comalco, as a response to the Aboriginal Community's insistence that payments should increase if Comalco's bauxite production rose, proposed a mechanism that it argued would allow the 'base' or starting payment to increase if the scale of the company's operations increased. Comalco also indicated that it wished to discuss the manner in which amounts paid under an agreement would be distributed to and managed by the Aboriginal Communities and traditional owners. The CYLC's analysis indicated that the revised approach did not represent any improvement because in effect the mechanism for adjusting payments would not come into effect over a wide a range of increases in output. Comalco's latest financial proposal was rejected a few days before Christmas 1998.

The course of negotiations 1999–2001

In early 1999, the pace of negotiations intensified once again. Issues for negotiation were broken down into a number of groups and particular negotiators from each side assigned to each group of issues. Provisional agreement was reached on draft clauses dealing with many aspects of cultural heritage protection, employment and training and business development. In January the CYLC submitted a financial proposal it regarded as representing significant movement by the Aboriginal Community and hoped could form the basis of an agreement. This involved converting the whole of Comalco's December 1998 offer (i.e. cash plus identified expenditure on programs and activities such as employment and training and cultural heritage protection) into an 'amount per tonne equivalent' at the existing level of bauxite output. Comalco would pay this amount, indexed for inflation, on each tonne of bauxite produced into the future, and the Aboriginal Community would take responsibility for funding the various activities and programs out of its income.

Comalco rejected this offer, and responded with a proposal under which the Aboriginal Community could choose either (i) its offer of December 1998. (ii) an alternative based on a lower amount per tonne that would not be indexed for inflation, but would be subject to a minimum guaranteed payment per annum, half of which would be indexed. The CYLC in its turn rejected this proposal, on the basis that its previous offer already reflected a substantial element of compromise by the Aboriginal Community and that a less favourable outcome could not be accepted. It was especially concerned about the lack of indexation that, over a period of years, could seriously erode the real value of the offer, especially given the expected longevity of Comalco's Weipa operations.

Despite the fact that significant progress had been made on a range of issues, the negotiations were now at an impasse. The CYLC was determined that financial compensation should rise with Comalco's output, and that the real value of any offer be maintained. This meant combining an 'amount per tonne' approach with indexation, a combination to which Comalco was in principle opposed. Comalco's response to this situation was to ask that the CYLC to communicate the company's offer to the Aboriginal Community. CYLC was unwilling to do this on the basis that the gap between Comalco's proposal and the Aboriginal Negotiating Position was so wide as to preclude the community's acceptance of the proposal. There followed a period of some months when communication between Comalco and CYLC was virtually non-existent. CYLC was deeply concerned about this lack of engagement, fearing that Comalco's desire to present its offer to the Aboriginal Community indicated its intention to deal directly with elements of the Community and to walk away from centralised negotiations coordinated by the CYLC. However when discussions resumed in August 1999, other explanations for the break in negotiations emerged.

First, significant personnel changes had occurred within Comalco, with the executive who had led its negotiating team leaving the company and another executive, who had initially become involved because of the tripartite proposal with Alcan, taking over this leadership role.

Second, when meetings resumed in August, Comalco commenced discussions by presenting a statement of its 'stated needs' and of its understanding (based largely on the Aboriginal Negotiating Position) of the Aboriginal Community's stated needs. In subsequent meetings, Comalco indicated its willingness to address a number of issues critical to the Aboriginal Community, including the issue of indexation; the CYLC's major outstanding concern in relation to employment and training, which involved the need to include specific goals in an agreement and to ensure appropriate responses if these were not being met; and the need to obtain a financial contribution from Queensland. For its part, Comalco placed greater emphasis on the issue of how funds flowing to the Aboriginal Community under an agreement would be managed, and on its desire to have an agreement with the Community registered as an Indigenous Land Use Agreement (ILUA), an opportunity created as a result of the 1998 amendments to the *NTA* and which provided a more robust and comprehensive mechanism for binding all the members of native title groups to agreements signed on their behalf. In addition, Comalco wished to resolve a series of matters relating to native title as part of the agreement itself, rather than establishing core principles in the agreement and resolving specific native title issues subsequently. Comalco also raised some new issues, including resolution of an overlap between the Napranum Deed of Grant in Trust, held by the Napranum Community Council, and a lease

(ML 6024) granted to the company to provide a corridor for bridge access to areas south of the Embley River; and the role it would play in management of payments to the Aboriginal Community under an agreement. It also reopened for discussion a number of issues that had provisionally been agreed.

It appears that Comalco had in fact engaged in an extensive review of its approach to the negotiations, re-evaluating its key objectives and establishing points on which it was willing to move in order to achieve those objectives.

As the year progressed, negotiations again developed momentum, with more meetings occurring in Cape York and fewer in Brisbane, and with the CYLC arranging for the chairs of community councils and senior traditional owners to participate in some meetings in the hope that this would assist in resolving issues. While substantial progress was made on a number of issues including employment and training, the ML 6024 'overlap', and a specific package for the traditional owners of Weipa, the goal of both parties to reach a rapid conclusion to negotiations was again not achieved. This was because of the re-opening of issues the CYLC had considered settled and the introduction of new issues onto the agenda, and because important differences still remained between the parties on the key issues of financial compensation and native title.

In December 1999, Comalco tabled a further proposal on financial compensation including amended provisions on a 'base' payment and on indexation. The proposal also contained a specific suggestion for distributing financial compensation payments, with set proportions being allocated to long-term investment and to projects nominated by the Aboriginal Communities and by traditional owners. The CYLC rejected Comalco's financial proposal yet again. In March 2000, Comalco tabled a further draft agreement and detailed negotiations continued across a range of issues, including the way in which indexes would be constructed for the financial package. Native title remained a major source of difference between Comalco and CYLC. The Land Council wished the agreement to spell out general principles similar to those contained in the Ely agreement, with specific issues relating the impact of particular tenures on native title, or to the exact nature of any native title determination, to be resolved as those issues arose. Comalco wished the nature of native title determinations, and the precise effect of a range of Comalco interests and third party tenures on native title, to be resolved as part of the agreement.

Against this background, complex, time-consuming and at times contentious negotiations occurred in relation to native title throughout the remainder of 2000, further complicated by the fact that when the Queensland Government joined the negotiations later in the year, it introduced its own specific interests and positions in relation to native title (see below).

Substantial differences also remained in relation to environmental management. Comalco took the view that it would fulfil its legal obligations in this area and that in relation to any proposal to exceed those obligations it would listen to the views of traditional owners but would not be bound by them. However, the company did agree to fund a review by the CYLC's environmental consultants of changes to its environmental management system subsequent to the consultants' initial 1997 report.

In mid-2000, financial provisions were finally resolved through the use of a composite index that took into account both the influence of international markets on Comalco's operations and the desire of the Aboriginal Community to protect the real value of its entitlement to compensation. The other critical component in reaching agreement on financial matters involved the Queensland Government. Its contribution was essential if the overall package was to reach a level the CYLC would feel comfortable in recommending to the Aboriginal Community, and if Comalco was to be reassured that Queensland would not recover any contribution it made to an agreement by increasing the statutory royalty on Comalco. The Queensland Government's involvement was also critical in relation to other aspects of the agreement, including the resolution of native title issues, the property transfers proposed for the Weipa traditional owners and the surrender of areas from Comalco's mining lease and their transfer to traditional owners.

As outlined earlier, successive attempts had been made to engage the Government, with little success. However political circumstances were now more favourable. The Government was keen to see Weipa develop as a growth centre for regional development. For this to occur, processes would need to be in place for the orderly expansion of the township and the issue of interests in land, and native title issues would have to be addressed if this was to occur. The Government also wished to ensure secure access for Comalco to areas south of the Embley, which required the resolution of the ML 6024 overlap issue; to ensure that the Weipa port could expand as required; and that an additional port could be constructed on Comalco's leases if this was needed for further development.

At a broader level, the Government was increasingly concerned about alcohol abuse, violence and other social issues in Cape York Aboriginal Communities. It had established a commission of inquiry into these matters and was engaged in discussions on them with Cape York leaders, and in particular with Noel Pearson who, as Executive Director of the CYLC, had led the team negotiating with Comalco. In mid 2000, Pearson suggested to the Premier Peter Beattie that Queensland could make a positive and concrete contribution to economic and social development in Western Cape York communities by participating in the agreement between Comalco and the Aboriginal Communities and in particular by contributing a portion of the statutory royalty paid by Comalco on its bauxite production. Thus Queensland had both a series of specific objectives it wished to achieve and a broader political imperative, and against this background the Government agreed to join the negotiations, to make a financial contribution and to become a party to the proposed agreement.

By October 2000, most substantial issues had been resolved, though there was still a need to address many matters of detail and drafting.

Native title issues were agreed on the following basis. Comalco's principle that issues regarding the content of native title determinations and the effect of Comalco interests on native title should be resolved as part of the agreement was accepted. The traditional owners would recognise the validity of Comalco's interests, and agree that their exercise of native title rights would be suppressed to the extent required to allow Comalco to exercise its interests. Once Comalco's operations were complete, native title rights would re-assert themselves to the maximum extent permitted at common law. Comalco would recognise the underlying native title rights of the traditional owners.

In October 2000, the CYLC brought members of the four steering committees to Cairns for three days to work through with them every aspect of the proposed agreement. This meeting indicated general approval for the proposed agreement. In relation to distribution and management of agreements moneys, a consensus existed between Comalco and the CYLC. This reflected shared assumptions that substantial amounts should be invested to create a capital base for the Aboriginal Community over the long term and that immediate expenditure should focus on the economic and social development of the Community rather than on distribution of money for individual consumption. The Cairns meeting of steering committees strongly endorsed this approach, and indicated that a higher proportion of funds should be directed to long term investment than Comalco had originally suggested.

The time frame for reaching final agreement was extended because of the need to undertake additional anthropological work to meet the requirements for registering the agreement as an ILUA under the *NTA*, and of the need for the CYLC to seek approval from the wider Aboriginal Community for the proposed agreement, including proposals for distribution and use of agreement moneys. Consensus was achieved in the Aboriginal Community on the allocation of moneys between long-term investment, community-initiated projects and traditional owner-initiated projects, but more time was needed to reach agreement on mechanisms for accessing funds and on the distribution of traditional owner funds between the various groups. A process for resolving these issues was written into the agreement. Final drafting work continued until 11 March 2001, and on the following day 11 traditional owner groups, the CYLC, Comalco, the Queensland government and the four community councils signed the Western Cape York Communities Co-Existence Agreement at Weipa.

The Western Cape York communities co-existence agreement

Under the WCCCA, the Aboriginal Community provides its support for the continuation and expansion of Comalco's mining and related activities, including support for the grant of any new rights and interests obtained by Comalco in order to support its business. The community also undertakes not to interfere with Comalco's mining operations.

In particular, the Aboriginal Community agrees:

- to do whatever is required to have the WCCCA registered as an ILUA;
- that all of Comalco's rights and interests are valid;
- that where there is a conflict between any native title rights and Comalco's interests and activities, the native title rights must yield;
- that native title has been extinguished by earlier grants of SPMPLs and by any new grants of SPMPLs that are made in the Weipa township areas, and that any native title in bauxite and kaolin minerals has been extinguished;
- that land in any part of Comalco's leases can be granted to the Queensland Ports Corporation;
- to seek only a particular sort of determination of native title which is supported by Comalco and is in line with the Agreement;
- to drop any existing legal actions which they had started against Comalco in the courts and not to start any new court actions;
- Not to start off any native title claims which do not comply with the WCCCA;
- to the grant of rights over areas within the ILUA which Comalco might need for a gas pipeline to Weipa, subject to the payment of additional compensation to be negotiated between Comalco and the Co-ordinating Committee established under the WCCCA.

Comalco and the State Government undertake to make quarterly payments to a Trust Fund that will be used for the benefit of the Aboriginal Community. Payments will vary depending on bauxite production and the price of aluminium in Comalco's case, though there is a 'floor' below which payments cannot drop and about half of this amount is indexed for changes in the CPI. Payments by the Queensland Government vary with the value of Comalco's bauxite production. Under the WCCCA, Comalco will do the following:

- Support native title claims that are consistent with the terms of the WCCCA, and accept that, once it surrenders its interests, the traditional owners will again enjoy any native title rights which have survived the effects of Comalco's operations;
- Spend at least A$500,000 a year on employment and training programs to help increase Aboriginal employment in its operations and to ensure that Aboriginal workers can move into better paid and more responsible jobs (Comalco also undertakes to do a number of things to try to ensure that the work environment is conducive to recruitment and retention of Aboriginal workers, such as to eliminate racist behaviour by non-Aboriginal workers. Targets are set for levels of Aboriginal employment over specified time periods and, if these are not achieved, Comalco will increase its spending on employment and training, subject to the Aboriginal communities showing improvements in educational outcomes during the relevant period);

- Help the Aboriginal communities set up businesses which will supply Comalco with goods and services;
- Immediately surrender from its mining leases certain areas of land not required for bauxite mining, surrender mining areas once mining is finished and the land has been rehabilitated and hand over to their traditional owners areas within the Weipa township which contain significant sites;
- Pay recognition and respect to Aboriginal traditional owners of the country on which Comalco mines, in part by implementing an Aboriginal relations policy based on such recognition and respect and requiring all employees of Comalco and its contractors to undertake a cross-cultural awareness program;
- Establish with the Aboriginal Community, and meet travel, accommodation and meeting costs for, a Co-ordinating Committee that will monitor and evaluate progress of the WCCCA and perform specific tasks required for its implementation (The Co-ordinating Committee is made up of representatives of the traditional owner groups, the Aboriginal Communities, Comalco, CYLC and the Queensland Government, and a large majority of its members are Aboriginal);
- Meet the environmental standards applied to the Weipa Operations. This undertaking allows the Aboriginal parties to take legal action if they believe that a breach of environmental standards has occurred, because such a breach constitutes breach of the agreement. Comalco also undertakes to respond to the issues raised in the second report submitted by the CYLC's environmental consultants;
- Consult with the Aboriginal Community through the Co-ordinating Committee about the way in which it carries on its mining operations, to ensure that country is damaged as little as possible when mining is happening and that country is properly rehabilitated after mining is finished. More specifically, consultation must occur in relation to development of criteria for rehabilitation of mined land, major changes to the Weipa project that have a significant effect on the environment, reviews of key environmental management documents, material changes in areas proposed for mining and decommissioning and environmental remediation. Comalco must provide a draft of any environmental application it intends to lodge with a government agency to the Committee, take into account any comments by the Committee on draft applications and include any such comments with the applications when they are submitted;
- Agree with the traditional owners of particular areas on ways to protect significant Aboriginal sites to make sure they are not damaged by mining;
- Do a number of things to help traditional owners enjoy their country and to make sure that non-Aboriginal residents of Weipa and tourists do not damage country. These include allowing members of the Communities to access mining lease areas for traditional purposes, and for

business purposes agreed with Comalco, supporting a Ranger Program and outstation development, closing or rehabilitating tracks that the traditional owners do not want to be used and implementing a permit system regulating the use of the mining lease areas by non-Aboriginal people;

• Give the Aboriginal communities A$150,000 per year to spend on supporting cultural heritage protection, a ranger program and scholarships for Aboriginal students.

Queensland will pay to the WCCCA Trust a proportion of the statutory royalties it receives from Comalco, calculated on the basis that would apply if the underlying title to Comalco's leases were transferred to Aboriginal ownership under the *Aboriginal Land Act 1991*. Queensland will use its best endeavours to transfer to their Aboriginal traditional owners, within specified time frames, areas surrendered by Comalco from its leases and relevant areas within the Weipa township.

Assessing and explaining outcomes

The outcomes described above are strongly positive for the Aboriginal Community of Western Cape York in a number of respects, and substantially address many aspects of the Aboriginal Negotiating Position. On the basis of publicly available figures, payments into the WCCCA Trust by Comalco and the Queensland Government amounted to about 2 per cent of Comalco's revenue in the year after the Agreement was signed (Comalco/CYLC 2001). This is considerably larger than the equivalent figure under the Canadian agreements discussed in Chapter 8, and substantially larger than most agreements negotiated during recent years in Australia (see Chapter 5). Payments under the WCCCA are linked to Comalco's output, a core objective for the Aboriginal Community and one whose achievement has proved to be of enormous significance, because Comalco's production of bauxite increased from about 11 million tonnes in the year before the Agreement to 17 million tonnes in 2005.

The Aboriginal Community did not succeed in its bid to obtain a one-off payment to provide compensation for the earlier impact of Comalco's operations and related government actions. However, specific recognition has been afforded to the situation of the traditional owners of the Weipa Peninsula who have felt and will feel those impacts with particular intensity because of the permanent presence on their land of the Weipa township and Comalco's facilities.

The Aboriginal Community also achieved another of its core goals in winning recognition of underlying Aboriginal title to Comalco's leases, and of the capacity of native titleholders to exercise their rights on Comalco's leases. That recognition is circumscribed in important ways. In particular, it does not extend to title in bauxite and kaolin, and the Aboriginal Community has recognised that certain categories of tenure extinguish native title and that native title must yield to the extent required to facilitate Comalco's operations. The community has also recognised the validity of Comalco's interests; given its consent to future interests that Comalco requires to continue and expand its operations; and agreed to the grant of rights for the construction of a gas pipeline on the ILUA area.

These undertakings and commitments are clearly of considerable value to Comalco because of their effect in reducing uncertainly in relation to its future ability to utilise a critical resource. However it can be argued that practical effect in further constraining the rights of the Aboriginal Community are limited. This is because of the fact that the *Wik* decision had confirmed the validity of Comalco's interests and the *Comalco Act*; that the *NTA* generally operates to validate existing interests; that the 1998 amendments to the Act removed the right to negotiate in relation to renewals of mining leases; and that in 2002 Australia's High Court ruled in the *Ward* case that native title does not exist in minerals and that mining leases can extinguish native title.

The Aboriginal Community achieved a number of other important goals. Comalco undertook to commit substantial funding to an employment and training program that includes specific targets and a mechanism for ensuring that Comalco commits additional resources if those targets are not being met. Comalco undertook to immediately release some areas of land that are of substantial significance to traditional owners from its leases. Traditional owners are guaranteed access to Comalco's lease areas subject to operational and safety requirements, and a system is in place that will allow traditional owners to ensure protection of Aboriginal cultural heritage. Comalco has also committed funds to assist in supporting cultural heritage work. A series of initiatives are included in the WCCCA designed to control use of country by non-Aboriginal people and to afford recognition and respect to Aboriginal traditional owners.

One area in which the Aboriginal Community's success was limited relates to environmental management, where it wished to achieve an active role with Comalco in making decisions with major environmental consequences. The community had instead to accept only a right to be consulted, though that right does extend to a range of key environmental issues and areas and includes a right to have comments on Comalco's environmental applications submitted to government agencies. In addition, the agreement involves a commitment by Comalco to the Aboriginal Community to comply with environmental standards; and the process of negotiations with Comalco did lead to a review of the company's environmental management system and contributed to improvements in that system, increasing the prospects of achieving improved environmental outcomes.

How do we explain these outcomes? To the extent that they are positive for the Aboriginal Community, the following factors appear of central importance.

The first is the extensive preparation undertaken by CYLC and the Aboriginal Community during 1995 and 1996. This resulted in a clear and

comprehensive articulation of the Community's position on key negotiation issues. It also resulted in the creation of the steering committee structure that subsequently provided critical support for the CYLC negotiators
and a vital link between the negotiators and the community, and facilitated
communication between the components of what is a diverse and geo-
graphically dispersed Aboriginal Community, building understanding and
solidarity.

This last point leads to the second critical factor. It would be incorrect
to suggest that no differences emerged within the Aboriginal Community
over the period 1995–2001. Differences did emerge, for example, regarding
the advisability of continuing to reject successive financial offers from
Comalco, and regarding the best way of distributing and managing payments that would flow into the WCCCA trust. However, as a whole the
Aboriginal Community displayed an impressive level of solidarity, particularly given its diversity and the long period of time over which negotiations
occurred. Its ability to do so is critical in explaining the outcomes described
above.

Third, the Aboriginal Community had access to substantial resources
and expertise provided by the CYLC. Financial resources were obtained
through arrangements negotiated with Comalco, from the Land Council's
own budget and from ATSIC. The CYLC's ability to secure funding from
ATSIC was of particular importance in allowing the CYLC and the Aboriginal Community to maintain their negotiating positions at a time when
initial Comalco funding was exhausted. Absence of this funding would
have placed the CYLC and the Aboriginal Community under enormous
pressure to accept outcomes less favourable than those eventually achieved.
The CYLC also had the benefit of experience gained in negotiating earlier
mining agreements; had access to technical expertise that was essential in
formulating positions and in analysing the large number of proposals and
draft agreements generated by Comalco; and its political leaders had access
to government decision-makers that was very important in achieving
Queensland's commitment to the Agreement.

Fourth, the fortuitous decision by Alcan to start developing its Ely lease,
and the time pressures it faced in doing so, allowed the CYLC and the
Aboriginal Community to negotiate an agreement with Alcan incorporating key components of the Aboriginal Negotiating Position, creating a
precedent that CYLC negotiators sought to apply to Comalco. The proximity of the Ely lease, the similarity of the Weipa operation with the
planned Ely project, and the fact that (after the signing of the BMEA)
Comalco would mine Ely strengthened the CYLC's hand in arguing that it
could not accept from Comalco terms inferior to those agreed with Alcan.

Also critical in explaining outcomes was the change in Comalco's
approach to negotiations in mid-1999. This may have in part been a
question of personnel, with a change in negotiators allowing a reassess-
ment of positions and approaches. It also apparently involved a more systematic assessment by Comalco of its fundamental interests and priorities

in undertaking the negotiations. This led Comalco to introduce some new issues for discussion and to adopt strong positions on certain issues, particularly native title, that may have resulted in the Aboriginal Community being required to make concessions it would prefer to have avoided. However it also provided a basis for Comalco to alter its position on some key issues, especially the structure of financial payments, and as a result pave the way for the Aboriginal Community to achieve core objectives. It should also be noted that, in at least one case, a position pushed by Comalco as part of its 'new' approach, that a portion of payments should be earmarked for long-term investment, resonated with the CYLC and the Aboriginal Community and that consensus around this issue facilitated a positive outcome to the negotiations.

What explains the Aboriginal Community's failure to achieve some key negotiating goals, in particular a stronger role in environmental management and payment of 'retrospective' compensation, and the necessity for it to accept significant limitations on the recognition of Aboriginal title? A key part of the explanation lies in its weak legal position. Comalco did not face a legal requirement to negotiate with the Aboriginal Community. While it was keen to remove any uncertainty regarding its future freedom to develop its interests in Western Cape York, the *NTA* and the *Wik* case had confirmed the validity of its interests and the company could continue to operate into the foreseeable future in the absence of an agreement with the Aboriginal Community. It is not the case that Comalco did not face any pressure to reach an agreement. Corporate policy called for it to do so, and, once the negotiations were under way, they generated their own momentum and an expectation within the company that its negotiators should secure a deal. However, that pressure was considerably less than would exist for a company seeking to get a new project off the ground or requiring new leases to expand an existing project.

Another issue was the fact that, while the CYLC brought important resources to bear on the negotiations, the resources available to it were also quite limited. This became evident in 1997 when a number of key personnel left the Land Council and it was faced with a series of competing priorities. One result was the considerable delay before it could produce a draft agreement based on the Aboriginal Negotiating Position, with the result that Comalco's proposals continued to provide the major focus for discussion of specific agreement provisions. The Land Council was also limited in the resources it could deploy in order to maintain its day-to-day engagement with the Aboriginal Community, a fact that helps to explain its sensitivity on the matter of Comalco's interactions with the Aboriginal Community.

On the specific issue of environmental management, Comalco's consistent refusal to move on the issue indicates that it regarded an active role for traditional owners in environmental decision-making as incompatible with its freedom of action in managing its Weipa operations. Its position in this regard may have been reinforced when the consultants retained by the

CYLC submitted a report calling for basic changes in Comalco's environmental management system. Ironically, in this case the thoroughness of the Community's preparation may have inadvertently created an obstacle to achieving its goals, though as mentioned above the consultants' work did inform Comalco's enhancement of its environmental management system.

The long duration of the negotiations affected outcomes for both parties. For the Aboriginal Community, it delayed the point at which benefits began to accrue to the Community under an agreement. This involved not only a deferral of revenues, but also for example of employment opportunities and the recognition of the Aboriginal traditional owners. The latter was of some significance, given that a number of senior traditional owners passed away during the negotiations and did not benefit from the recognition they had strove so long to achieve. For the organisations involved, the length of the negotiations created a substantial financial burden, while for individuals directly involved it brought significant emotional and personal costs. To make these points is not to suggest that the Aboriginal Community should have conceded ground sooner in order to achieve agreement. For instance, especially given the rapid increase in Comalco's bauxite production after 2001, the additional revenues accruing to the Community as a result of having payments linked to bauxite production far exceed any loss of revenue due to reaching agreement in 2001 rather than in 1998, given the terms on offer in 1998. Rather, the question is why it took so long to reach an *acceptable* agreement.

The first point to note is that the negotiations were never likely to be simple or brief, given the history of Comalco's presence in Western Cape York and of associated government actions, and the complexity of the issue arising from this history. Reflecting the extent of Comalco's interests, the size and diversity of the Aboriginal Community affected by its operations introduced further complexities. However the following factors were also important.

First, the CYLC and the Aboriginal Community devoted considerable time and resources to establishing, and ensuring Community ownership of, a comprehensive negotiating position. The Community was unlikely to easily move from this position, especially after Alcan signed an agreement containing many of its key components. This approach had proved effective for the CYLC in other negotiations, but in previous cases the companies concerned had been developing new projects or requiring new leases to maintain existing projects. Facing significant time pressures, they had been prepared to quickly (in each case within 12 months) negotiate agreements acceptable to the Aboriginal Community. However Comalco faced no such time pressures. The result was a protracted negotiation, given Comalco's unwillingness to accept key elements of the Aboriginal Negotiating Position and the Community's reluctance to move away from it. Reinforcing this situation, Comalco had operated at Weipa for over four decades. It had strongly entrenched corporate values, worldviews and operational procedures that would be difficult to change and were not readily compatible with some elements of the Aboriginal Negotiating Position.

Second, one of the CYLC's responses to Comalco's initial resistance to key elements of the Aboriginal Negotiating Position was to pursue negotiations with Alcan and, especially given the Land Council's limited resources, this absorbed a significant amount of time. Third, the initial phase of negotiations between the CYLC and Comalco was characterised by tension and in some cases conflict, and this did not create a solid foundation on which to advance the negotiations. Tensions over Comalco's activities 'on the ground' helped maintain a climate of suspicion that negotiators then had to work hard and take time to overcome. Finally, Comalco's apparent re-appraisal of its approach to negotiations during 1999 also took time, though it seems clear that this re-appraisal was essential for an agreement to be achieved.

Note

1 The term 'traditional owners' is used in Australia to describe those Indigenous people who have primary affiliations with, and responsibility for, areas of land and water and the cultural and spiritual sites they contain.

References

Comalco/Cape York Land Council (2001) *A Way Forward Together*, Press Release, Cairns, 11 March 2001.

Comalco Ltd (1998) *Annual Report 1998*, Brisbane: Comalco.

Davis, L. (1995) *New Direction for CRA*, Address to Securities Institute of Australia, 20 March.

Holden, A. (1996a) 'Mapoon: "Home to Stay"', *The Economic and Social Impact of Bauxite Mining and Related Activities on the West Coast of Cape York Peninsula*, CYLC Confidential Report, November.

Holden, A. (1996b) 'New Mapoon: "Out of Sight, Out of Mind"', *The Economic and Social Impact of Bauxite Mining and Related Activities on the West Coast of Cape York Peninsula*, CYLC Confidential Report, November.

Howitt, R. (1996) 'Napranum: Part of the damage or part of the healing?' *The Economic and Social Impact of Bauxite Mining and Related Activities on the West Coast of Cape York Peninsula*, CYLC Confidential Report, November.

O'Faircheallaigh, C. (1996) 'Arukun: Mining Is Here *Already*', *The Economic and Social Impact of Bauxite Mining and Related Activities on the West Coast of Cape York Peninsula*, CYLC Confidential Report, November.

O'Faircheallaigh, C. (2000) 'The Cape York Model of Project Negotiation', *Discussion Paper No 11*, Canberra: AIATSIS.

7 Silica sand mining, North Stradbroke Island

Introduction

This chapter deals with a negotiation between the Quandamooka Native Title Group (QNTG), represented by the Quandamooka Land Council (QLC), ACI Industrial Minerals (ACI) and the State of Queensland ('Queensland'). The negotiation involved the proposed grant of a mining lease to enable the continuation and expansion of a long-established silica sand mining operation on North Stradbroke Island (NSI) or Minjeribah, located some 30 minutes by boat from Brisbane, the capital of Queensland (see Figure 7.1). This negotiation differs from the other case studies in that

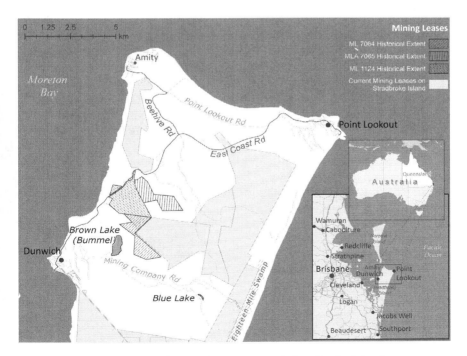

Figure 7.1 Location map, Silica sand mining, North Stradbroke Island.

government played a direct and substantial role in the conduct of negotiations and in shaping the negotiation approaches and strategies of both the Aboriginal community and the mining company. Reflecting this fact, background material is provided on the Queensland government as well as on ACI and the QNTG/QLC. The course of negotiations is then outlined, and the agreement that emerged from them is described and evaluated.

Negotiation outcomes for the Aboriginal community were in this case strongly negative, not only because of the content of the agreement with ACI and Queensland. The negotiation process resulted in or sharpened community divisions, and had negative ramifications for the wider efforts of the QNTG to secure legal recognition of its native title rights and to win a share of the economic benefits generated by other mining activity on NSI. The chapter concludes with an analysis of the reasons for these outcomes.

ACI and North Stradbroke Island

ACI is a private company that mines silica sand on NSI. Silica is trucked to Dunwich (see Figure 7.1) and then barged to Brisbane for use in a glass manufacturing plant owned by a related company, or for export. At the time of the negotiations, ACI was owned by the US glass and packaging producer Owens Illinois.

ACI commenced mining on NSI in 1971 and held two mining licences. The first, ML 1124, located just north of Dunwich, had been extensively mined and by 1997 was, according to the company, approaching exhaustion. ACI had not undertaken any mining on the second lease, ML 1132, situated in the north-west of the island (see Figure 7.1). In the late 1980s, Queensland approached ACI with a proposal that ML 1132, which it regarded as having high environmental values and which lay within a larger area that the government wished to declare as a national park, should not be developed. ACI would instead be offered alternative sources of silica sand on NSI. Accordingly ACI lodged two additional mining leases applications (MLAs), MLA 7065 (which ACI was to abandon in 1997 for environmental and operational reasons) and MLA 7064. The southern part of MLA 7064 lies close to Brown Lake or *Bummel* (see Figure 7.1), a place of great cultural and spiritual significance to Quandamooka people. The Government and ACI agreed that the new leases would be granted to ACI, subject to environmental conditions being met and, assuming the leases held reserves equivalent to those in ML 1132, the company would surrender the latter. In December 1992, the Queensland Cabinet approved the proposed arrangement. The QNTG was not consulted about Queensland's decision nor asked for its assessment of the relative ecological, cultural or spiritual significance of the different areas involved.

ACI's annual silica production remained steady at around 175,000 tonnes until the late 1980s, before rising rapidly to 665,000 tonnes in 1993, in part to support the company's growing involvement in export markets. The company planned to continue to expand its exports, which would require construction of a new ship loader at Dunwich (see below). ACI's mining operation was small by Queensland and Australian standards, with output valued at just under $5 million in 1993–1994 and a workforce of some 40 employees and contractors (QLC 1999: 16). However, its economic significance to Queensland was substantially enhanced by its role as a supplier of a critical raw material to a glass manufacturing facility that employed over 200 people in Brisbane. This was especially so since no alternative sources of silica existed in the Brisbane region.

Few Quandamooka people were employed by ACI, in contrast to the other NSI based mining company, Consolidated Rutile Ltd (CRL), whose operations were much larger and which had employed substantial numbers of Aboriginal people throughout its history. More generally, ACI had little experience of dealing with Aboriginal communities, and had limited resources at its disposal in this regard given its small size and the localised nature of its operations.

Aboriginal groups

The term 'Quandamooka' refers to the waters and islands of southern Moreton Bay and adjacent parts of the mainland (see inset map, Figure 7.1). Archaeological evidence reveals continual Aboriginal occupation within Quandamooka for at least 20,000 years, with a more intense period of occupation and use commencing some 3,000 years ago. The Aboriginal traditional owners of Quandamooka are descended from three language groups (commonly referred to as 'clans'), the Ngugi, Nunukul and Koenpul. Much inter-marriage has occurred between the three groups. Within this broad structure is a set of 11 descent groups described as 'families' and identified by surnames (QLC 1999: 74). In 1991, the QLC was established as a vehicle for pursuing legal recognition of the rights of the traditional owners of Quandamooka and more generally for ensuring them a say in developments affecting their ancestral lands. In January 1995, the QLC lodged a native title claim covering part of the Quandamooka lands, including ACI's MLAs 7064 and 7065. The NNTT accepted the claim in September 1995.

While the territorial areas associated with the three clans are 'in a broad sense fairly well defined' (QLC 1999: 74), the Quandamooka native title claim was made on behalf of the entire group of traditional owners including descendants from the Ngugi, Nunukul, and Koenpul clans, reflecting the contemporary organisation of the Quandamooka community and the manner in which native title rights are exercised. This group is referred to here as the 'Quandamooka Native Title Group' (QNTG) or the 'Quandamooka people'. Any rights determined as a result of the native title claim would be in favour of the Group as a whole, as opposed to three clans asserting distinct territorial estates.

Quandamooka people live mainly on NSI, in the bayside suburb of Cleveland and elsewhere in Brisbane. They have felt the impact of white settlement for longer than many other groups in Australia, with regular contact with settlers well established by the late 1820s. That impact has been similar in important ways to that felt by other Aboriginal groups. For example Quandamooka people suffered the ill effects of introduced diseases and settler violence and were denied recognition of their rights in the land and the sea. However, most were able, unlike many other Aboriginal peoples in settled Australia, to remain on or close to their ancestral lands, for three main reasons. The first was the absence of agricultural activity on the islands which would have resulted in large-scale alienation and freeholding of land. The second involved their ability to secure employment in the commercial fishery, in a benevolent asylum established at Dunwich in 1865, and in the initial labour-intensive phase of sand mining that commenced after World War II. The third was their continued ability to exploit food and other resources on their traditional country, particularly marine resources. Historical accounts spanning the whole of the period since the 1820s stress the absolute importance of marine resources in providing people with sustenance and the necessities of life (QLC 1999: 12–15).

Continuity in ties to land and sea, and in use and management of resources, has also meant the continuation of cultural forms which, though developed and adapted over the years in response to changing circumstances, remain both vibrant and distinctive. In particular, the QNTG continues to display distinctive forms of social structure and social interaction, cultural norms and activities, and spiritual beliefs and practices. One of the strongest norms is that Quandamooka people have a responsibility to protect and manage the land and its resources for the benefit of future generations.

Quandamooka people resident on NSI display demographic, social and economic characteristics that are typical of Aboriginal Australia (see Chapter 3). Their economic status is relatively low, with average incomes well below those of non-indigenous residents, high unemployment rates and under-representation in more highly skilled and highly paid occupational categories (QLC 1999: 14–15). Against this background, it could be expected that Quandamooka people would be keen to utilise available opportunities to increase their income levels and their access to educational and employment opportunities. In the context of mining on NSI, these goals could clearly come into conflict with norms regarding protection of the land and its resources.

The QLC was the registered native title claimant on the Quandamooka native claim, but was replaced by two individual members of the QNTG following the 1998 amendments to the NTA. Membership of the QLC is open to all members of the QNTG, and it is governed by a board elected by members at annual general meetings. By 1997, the QLC, though small in size, had developed significant organisational capacity. It was involved in pursuing the Quandamooka native title claim, in part through negotiations with Queensland and the local government authority for NSI, the

Redland Shire Council. It had initiated negotiations with CRL, played an active role in statutory planning processes and developed and implemented cultural heritage management strategies. The QLC had a small full-time staff, supported by specialist consultants. Native title and other negotiations were conducted by teams that comprised board members, staff and consultants. QLC's core funding for native title and related work was provided by the Native Title Representative Body (NTRB) for South East Queensland, until 2000 the Brisbane-based Foundation for Aboriginal and Islander Research Action (FAIRA). A number of FAIRA Board members were Quandamooka people and FAIRA and the QLC worked closely together, with the QLC exercising substantial autonomy in pursuing the Quandamooka native title claim and other initiatives. In 2000 FAIRA was not reappointed as an NTRB and it was replaced by the Toowoomba-based Queensland South Representative Body, which became the NTRB for a large area of southern Queensland.

In 1987, a 'break away' organisation, referred to here as the Cultural Heritage Corporation (CHC) (not its actual name), was formed by members of certain Quandamooka families. The membership of this organisation overlapped with that of the QLC, and one of its office holders was Chairman of the QLC in 1998–1999. Not all members of the families involved in establishing the CHC supported the organisation, including a senior elder who was Chairman of the QLC during the key phase of negotiations with ACI and Queensland. The CHC had few resources and no full time staff, but for reasons that will become apparent people associated with it were to have a profound impact on the negotiations with ACI and Queensland.

The Queensland Government

Historically, Queensland governments have shown scant regard for the political rights or economic interests of their Aboriginal citizens (Chesterman and Galligan 1997; Kidd 1997). In more recent decades, some recognition has been afforded to Aboriginal interests, for instance through the establishment of elected councils in Aboriginal communities in the 1980s and passage of an ALA in 1991 which created, at least in principle, the possibility of legal recognition of Aboriginal land rights. However initially the ALA could apply to a maximum of only 3 per cent of Queensland, and in effect was not implemented. More generally, in a state whose economy depends heavily on mining and agricultural production and with a strongly conservative political culture, the Queensland government's priority has remained to ensure that resource development proceeds without interruption. It has often seen this goal as incompatible with recognition of Aboriginal interests (Holden and Pearson 1993; O'Faircheallaigh 2005).

After the election of the Beattie Labor government in 1998, Queensland was regarded as more willing than some other state governments in Australia to use negotiation as a basis for resolving conflicts between developer and Aboriginal interests. It contributed substantially to the package of benefits offered to Aboriginal landowners under agreements in which it had a strong interest, for instance that allowing development of the Century zinc mine in Queensland's Gulf region in 1997, and the Western Cape York Communities Co-existence Agreement (discussed in Chapter 6). More generally, the Beattie Labor government was seen as supportive of negotiated outcomes and as fostering a positive atmosphere for agreement making (ATSISJC 2004; French 2003: 514–15). However, its position in this regard must be placed in context. For example, the first legislative enactment of the newly elected government in 1998 was to pass a *Confirmation and Validation Act* that extinguished any surviving native title over, and therefore removed the Right to Negotiate in relation to, some 13 per cent of the state. In addition, the Queensland Government's involvement in a negotiated resolution to the conflict over the Century project came after repeated attempts to override Aboriginal opposition to the project had failed (Cowell 1996; O'Faircheallaigh 2005, 2006).

For reasons that will become clear, one other point should be made in relation to the Queensland Government's role in the Century negotiations. In that case, the government attempted to use the wider aspirations of the native title group (the Waanyi people) as a bargaining chip to secure its support for a mining project that faced widespread community opposition. The Waanyi wished to secure title to the Lawn Hill National Park, a key part of their ancestral lands, by having it gazetted under the ALA. Despite having publicly committed themselves to gazetting the Park, Government ministers and senior Government officials made it clear to the Waanyi that this would occur only if the Waanyi supported the Century development (Howlett 2006).

Three specific Queensland government agencies played a major role in the negotiations involving the QLC and ACI. The Department of Mines and Energy (DME) was the line agency with primary responsibility for both regulation and promotion of the mining industry in Queensland, and was responsible for coordinating environmental impact assessment and regulatory approval processes for ACI's proposed new mining lease and ship loader. The Department of State Development (DSD) was charged with promotion of industrial development in the state, and in particular had a coordinating role in ensuring that governmental processes worked to support major new industrial projects. The Department of Premier and Cabinet (DPC) played a 'whole of government' coordinating role to ensure that Queensland agencies worked in concert to advance the Government's policy priorities. At the time of the negotiations, the DPC also held portfolio responsibility for native title issues through its Native Title Services branch.

Chronology of the negotiations

The SIA and community consultations

Though its existing reserves of silica sand were apparently limited, ACI was slow to undertake the regulatory approval processes required so that the Queensland Government could decide whether the company would be granted MLA 7064. It was 1998 before arrangements were in place to undertake the Environmental Impact Statements (EISs) required for mining leases under the *Mineral Resources Act* and for ACI's proposed new ship loader under the *State Development and Public Works Organisations Act*. The company had initially planned to undertake the EISs itself, including their social and cultural impact components. However the QLC insisted that, as traditional owners and native title claimants, Quandamooka people had a particular and special interest in the outcome and that the social and cultural components of ACI's EISs should be conducted through the QLC. After a series of meetings and negotiations between the QLC, ACI and the Queensland Government, terms of reference were agreed for the QLC to undertake these components. ACI provided the funding for it to do so.

During these exchanges the company indicated its interest in undertaking negotiations with the QLC aimed at securing the QNTG's support for development of MLA 7064. ACI indicated a willingness to discuss measures relating to cultural heritage issues and protection of significant sites, royalty payments, employment and training opportunities and environmental monitoring. The QLC's position was that a Right to Negotiate (RTN) process would have to occur under the NTA if the Minister for Mines and Energy decided to issue a new mining lease to ACI, but that any discussion of negotiations was premature given that the environmental assessment of ACI's proposals, including consultations with the Quandamooka community, had yet to occur. The Queensland Government's position was that the grant of MLA 7064 could proceed pursuant to the 'past act' provisions of the NTA and so without the need for an RTN process. It did not indicate the basis on which it took this view, but presumably it was relying on the December 1992 Cabinet decision approving the proposed 'exchange' of MLA 7064 and MLA 7065 for ML 1132. The Government also informed the QLC that, if ACI did not obtain alternative silica sources, the company could proceed to mine ML 1132, as a granted lease, without the need to undertake an EIS or have any negotiations with the QLC.

In late 1998 and early 1999, the QLC undertook a Social Impact Assessment (SIA) to disseminate information about ACI's planned mining operation on MLA 7064 and the new ship loader and to establish community concerns and aspirations in relation to the proposals. The SIA involved extensive and varied community consultations, including general public meetings; public meetings for specific groups such as women, mineworkers, elders, community members living in Brisbane; small group and one-on-one discussions with community members; and a survey mailed to

Quandamooka community members. The consultations revealed over-whelming opposition to ACI's proposals for MLA 7064 and the ship loader. During face-to-face consultations, no person argued in favour of the proposals, while many articulated strong opposition to them. In the survey of community members, 87 per cent stated that MLA 7064 should not be approved, and 85 per cent that the ship loader should not be approved (QLC 1999). The SIA report noted that the lack of ambiguity in the community's response to ACI's proposals was significant given that 'the general issue of mining on Minjeribah [NSI] raises complex and indeed contentious issues, and generally speaking attitudes to mining are both varied and at times ambiguous' (QLC 1999: 6). Many of those consulted asked that the QLC immediately begin to lobby the Queensland govern-ment to reject ACI's proposals, including a meeting of Quandamooka elders which passed a unanimous resolution to this effect.

Community opposition was based on extensive concerns (also expressed in anthropological studies undertaken as part of the EIS) regarding the cul-tural, social, health and environmental impact of ACI's existing operations and the likely negative impact of ACI's proposals for MLA 7064 and the ship loader. These concerns related in particular to: impacts on areas of spiritual and cultural importance, and especially on Brown Lake which, as noted above, is of special significance to Quandamooka people (see Figure 7.1); negative effects on landscapes, flora and fauna, ground and surface waters; noise and dust problems associated with mining of silica and its transport through Dunwich, particularly given the higher truck traffic expected to result from expansion of ACI's activities; and anticipated restrictions on the ability of Quandamooka people to utilise parts of their traditional estate (QLC 1999). Community members also expressed dissat-isfaction at the lack of economic benefits flowing to the Aboriginal com-munity from ACI's existing operations, a situation they did not expect to change if MLA 7064 were approved.

Against this background, most of those consulted were unsympathetic to ACI's desire to establish a resource base that would support its opera-tions in the long term. A small minority of community members did indi-cate their support for ACI to continue operating if it could secure alternative resources to both MLA 7064 and ML 1132, for instance in the Pines area to the east of Dunwich (QLC 1999: 60). The Pines, where ACI and the company that barged ACI's silica sand held a number of MLAs, was already degraded due to the spread of introduced pine trees and to bush fires, and its location would allow sand to be moved to the new ship loader without trucking it through Dunwich.

At the conclusion of the SIA process, a community meeting of QLC members, by unanimous resolution, instructed the QLC to oppose ACI's MLA 7064 and ship loader.

In August 1999, ACI submitted its draft EIS. The DME established an Advisory Group, consisting of government departments and stakeholder groups, to provide a preliminary environmental assessment report that would help ACI complete a final EIS. The Advisory Group, including representatives of a number of government agencies as well as the QLC and environmental groups, found serious deficiencies with the draft EIS. Against this background, and given the strong opposition expressed in the community consultations, the QLC took the view that MLA 7064 should not proceed and that the preferred course of action was for ACI to quickly investigate the possibility of moving its operations to the Pines area or to a mining lease adjacent to MLA 7064 and held by CRL, which had no plans to mine the silica sand contained in the lease. In late August, the QLC indicated to government its willingness to facilitate a community consultation process in relation to such alternative proposals.

Mining options for ACI and the Quandamooka native title claim

In November 1999, the Minister for Mines and Energy met the QLC and Quandamooka elders in Dunwich to discuss the future of ACI's operations. The Minister stressed the importance to the Government of ensuring that ACI had a reliable source of silica sand over the long term; offered to facilitate the QLC's involvement in discussions about ACI's future operations; and indicated that the QLC's participation would assist in facilitating a determination of the Quandamooka native title claim. The QLC in response stressed the need for the QNTG to be adequately consulted about any future proposals, and rejected the suggestion of a link between discussions about those proposals and the native title determination, arguing strongly that the two were entirely separate. By this time, the QLC had been involved in negotiations about its native title claim with the Queensland Government's Native Title Services (NTS) and the Redland Shire Council for over three years and substantial progress had been made towards achieving a consent determination of native title through the Federal Court. For example, NTS had accepted the QLC's 'connection report' for the claim, a critical step towards a determination, and agreement had been reached on the effect on native title of 125 of the 130 dealings in land (other than grants of mining leases) on the island. The QLC was preparing to engage in negotiations at the political level to resolve key matters that could not be addressed by the Federal Court, including compensation for past impacts on native title rights, grant of freehold title to certain areas of land, and implementation funding. The QLC did not want potentially contentious issues relating to ACI to undermine its efforts to achieve a satisfactory resolution of the QNTG's claim.

During late 1999, the QLC pressed the Quandamooka community's opposition to mining of MLA 7064 at a number of meetings with Government officers and politicians. In early December 1999, the QLC believed it had achieved some success when it was briefed by NTS officials on the outcome of a Cabinet decision dealing with ACI's future operations. The QLC was informed that the Government intended that, when ML 1124 was exhausted, ACI would be permitted to mine for a maximum of two years in the least environmentally sensitive areas of ML 1132, rather than commence mining on MLA 7064. In the meantime, the company could investigate options for securing a longer-term resource base.

In late December 1999, the Queensland Government assured ACI that it would progress the grant of mining leases to meet the company's long-term resource needs, and the QLC assumed that this would involve implementing the recent Cabinet decision. However, the DME pursued a course that would in fact involve mining on MLA 7064 in the short term. It encouraged ACI to relinquish the southern portion of MLA 7064, closest to Brown Lake, which the company did in February 2000 (see Figure 7.1). The company then took the view that its EIS should be accepted and that it should be allowed to submit a draft Environmental Management Overview Strategy (EMOS) as the next step towards obtaining approval for mining on MLA 7064. The DME concurred, determining that the mining of MLA 7064 would now represent an extension of ACI's existing operations and that the social and cultural impacts of mining on MLA 7064 would be similar to those of the company's existing operation. It therefore concluded that the deficiencies in ACI's EIS were cured by the abandonment of the southern portion of MLA 7064 and allowed ACI to proceed to the preparation of an EMOS.

The QLC strongly objected to this course of action, on the grounds that it ran contrary to the December 1999 Cabinet decision and that major environmental, cultural and social issues identified in the QLC's SIA and in the EIS but not addressed by ACI would still arise from mining of the northern portion of MLA 7064.

At this point it is necessary to set out the remaining steps in the regulatory approval process for the grant of MLA 7064. These would depend on whether or not MLA 7064 was a 'past act' under the provisions of the NTA. If it were a 'past act', those steps would be as follows. The company would lodge its EIS and EMOS with the DME, which would complete an assessment report of the documents and forward them to the Assistant Mining Registrar in Brisbane, who would set a date for public objections to the EIS/EMOS to close two months after the receipt of the documents. At the end of this period, the Assistant Mining Registrar would set a date for the hearing of ACI's application for MLA 7064 by Queensland's Land and Resources Tribunal (LRT). The Tribunal would hear ACI's application and the objections to it and make a recommendation to the Minister to grant or reject the application. The Minister would then either reject the application, or recommend its approval to the Governor in Council (in effect, approve the application).

If the grant of MLA 7064 was not a 'past act', the LRT would not finalise its hearing of the application until the Right to Negotiate process under the NTA had been undertaken. This could take well in excess of six months if ACI and the QLC were unable to reach agreement.

In July 2000, the DME accepted ACI's EIS and EMOS, and the Mining Registrar set 25 September 2000 as the closing date for objections. The

QLC lodged an objection, and in August 2000 also wrote to the Mining Registrar asking that he exercise his discretion to deny ACI's application for MLA 7064 on the grounds that the EIS had not complied with the guidelines issued by the Minister for Minerals and Energy and that ACI had failed to give notice of its application to the native title claimants. The Mining Registrar rejected this suggestion, and in subsequent correspondence stated as part of the grounds for doing so that MLA 7064 constituted a 'past act' under the *NTA* and so that there was no obligations on ACI to notify the native title claimants. The Registrar failed to provide any grounds on which MLA 7064 should be regarded as a 'past act', despite the significance of this decision for the QLC's legal position.

In September 2000, the Director General or Head of the DSD wrote to the Director General of the DPC regarding ACI's future operations, and in doing so provided important insights into the Government's strategy. He identified the Government's two key aims as securing ACI's long-term future on NSI, and ensuring that mining not occur on ML 1132, maintaining the environmental value of the area and protecting the Government from public criticism for allowing them to be compromised. He stated that the Government's preferred strategy was to secure the QLC's approval for ACI to mine the northern portion of MLA 7064 for some five years, allowing time for ACI to establish alternative long-term silica reserves. Given the QLC's reluctance to engage in mediation with ACI, his preferred course of action was to use negotiations on the QLC's native title claim to secure its cooperation. He recommended that the Government reject the QLC's position that the native title claim and ACI's proposals be dealt with separately, and not agree to some key elements of QLC's proposed native title determination until the QLC supported the grant of MLA 7064. In his view it was 'critical that any determination of the QLC native title claim should include resolution of issues related to the ACI matter...'.

In the light of the widespread community opposition to ACI's original proposal, he suggested offering the QLC limited funding (about 15 per cent of the budget available for the SIA conducted in 1998–1999) to consult with the QNTG about ACI's revised proposal for MLA 7064. He hoped that this would allay community concerns and allow the QLC to support the grant of MLA 7064. The possibility of further community consultations was raised with the QLC, which indicated its willingness to facilitate consultations on appropriate terms relating to matters such as timing, provision of funding and clear terms of reference. The QLC subsequently indicated that a budget of $50,000 and a time frame of six months would be required, and that the consultations should remain entirely separate from the native title claim process.

In late September 2000, the QLC complained to the Director General of DPC that officers of the DME and DSD, including one individual who was a member of the Quandamooka community, had inappropriately approached individual members of the QNTG, including one of the registered native title claimants, to canvass a proposal about allowing

MLA 7064 to proceed. Such an approach would contravene a protocol signed by the State and the QLC in 1998 to govern conduct of negotiations on the native title claim. The QLC was to regularly repeat claims about similar behaviour by government officers over the following nine months (see below).

In October, the Premier appointed the Director General of DSD and his Senior Economic Advisor to take charge of negotiations both in relation to ACI's proposals and the Quandamooka native title claim. At a meeting with the QLC on 11 October, the two indicated that the ACI issue would have to be resolved as part of the claim process and that ACI required a decision on the MLA 7064 proposal by February 2001, a time frame inconsistent with the QLC's demand for a six month consultation period. In response, the QLC indicated its willingness to initiate a process of information dissemination in relation to the options being considered for ACI; to enter negotiations with the government in relation to those options; and to hold a meeting with the QNTG early in 2001 to decide on a preferred option. On 21 November, the QLC provided Queensland with a detailed proposal for the consultation processes that would be required to obtain approval for a resolution to the native title claim and the ACI issue, which it planned would take place over the period December 2000–March 2001. As the QLC noted, a critical obstacle to completion of consultations involved the absence of detailed information regarding the Government's proposals in relation to the claim and ACI, information that would have to be available before the QNTG could be consulted. Indeed at this point the government had not made any written proposal to the QLC, and had not responded to numerous requests by the QLC to indicate the basis on which the State believed that MLA 7064 was a 'past act'. Queensland did not respond to QLC's funding proposal until March 2001.

In December 2000, hearings in relation to ACI's MLA 7064 commenced in the LRT. The tribunal's President decided that the tribunal would determine whether or not MLA 7064 constituted a 'past act', and in the meantime referred the dispute between ACI and QLC regarding MLA 7064 to mediation. In January 2001, ACI appealed against these decisions in Queensland's Court of Appeal on technical and legal grounds, and sought orders that they be set aside and that the tribunal proceed to hear the objections to MLA 7064. In lodging its appeal, ACI informed the court that if it was not to gain access to MLA 7064, then in order to ensure continuity in its supply of silica sand it would have to begin preparatory work on ML 1132 by April, commit to moving its operations to ML 1132 by July, and commence mining there in September. Thus, to prevent the disturbance associated with preparatory work, MLA 7064 would have to be granted by April 2001, and to prevent mining of ML 1132 it would have to be granted by July. The QLC was anxious to ensure that the 'past act' issue would be resolved if ACI's appeal was successful, and in February 2001 it lodged an Application to Review in Queensland's Supreme Court and sought an order directing the Mining Registrar to issue the notices that would initiate the RTN.

In mid-January 2001, the QLC reiterated its position in relation to the requirements for community consultations; demanded that the Queensland Government communicate with native title claimants only through the QLC; and stated that, while it was willing to enter negotiations regarding the grant of MLA 7064, it was only prepared to do this on the basis that the grant would constitute a 'future act'. It did not receive a response, according to officials because a state election had been called for 8 February and it was therefore not possible for the Government to present proposals to the QLC until the election outcome was determined. In the event, the election returned the Beattie Labor Government to office.

Negotiation and community conflict

By late 2000, considerable internal tension had developed within the QNTG. This reflected, in part, wider political and personal tensions between Quandamooka families or parts of families, but it also reflected differences in attitude towards mining in general and ACI's proposals in particular. Those differences had not emerged in relation to ACI's original application for MLA 7064 because of the scale of ACI's proposal and in particular because of overwhelming community opposition to mining near Brown Lake. However, now that ACI had surrendered the southern portion of MLA 7064, at least some community members were more favourably disposed, some because of economic benefits they hoped to secure from ACI's operations, others because they did not wish ACI to mine ML 1132 and considered the mining of the northern portion of MLA 7064 a preferable alternative. More generally, certain sections of the community that supported mining on the Island perceived the QLC as being dominated by Quandamooka people who were 'anti-mining' and so unlikely to deliver the economic benefits that could be achieved through negotiations with ACI. Some people saw the QLC's lodgement of objections to MLA 7064 as evidence of the QLC's 'anti-mining bias'.

As mentioned earlier, Queensland officials had approached a number of community members to canvass obtaining approval for ACI's application. In December 2000, the Director General of DSD informed the QLC that he had agreed to meet a number of community members, separate from the negotiation process between the Government and the QLC, who had approached him and expressed concerns about the way the QLC was dealing MLA 7064. On 16 January 2001, a number of people associated with the break-away CHC organisation (referred to here as the 'CHC group') who were not authorised to speak on behalf of the QLC or the QNTG attended and sought to disrupt a meeting organised between the QLC and the DSD to discuss a proposal by the government to allow MLA 7064 to be treated as a 'past act'. As the QLC had not informed the people involved about the meeting, it could only conclude that Government officials had done so. The QLC abandoned the meeting. On 27 January, some of the same community members met ACI's General Manager, who reportedly canvassed certain benefits ACI might be prepared to provide if MLA 7064 was approved. On the same day, a number of community members wrote to the QLC claiming a lack of community input into negotiations with ACI. They asked that a Special General Meeting of the QLC be convened to discuss the matter; that State Government representatives be asked to attend to inform members about developments in the negotiations; and claimed that the board of the QLC did not adequately represent the Quandamooka families. The letter was copied to the Director General of DSD.

The Special General Meeting of the QLC was held on 24 February 2001 and State Government representatives presented broad principles for an agreement in relation to MLA 7064. Under this proposal, the QLC would facilitate the grant of MLA 7064 and, assuming the grant occurred before 1 July 2001 or other mutually agreed date, the Queensland Government would:

- recommend to the Governor in Council that an unmined portion of ACI's existing ML 1124 be granted to a Trust under the *Aboriginal Land Act*;
- following completion of mining on MLA 7064, recommend the freehold grant of 53 hectares of land to the Trust;
- make an annual payment of $90,000 for each year of mining on MLA 7064, to a maximum of five years, to a Trust established to assist with development of Quandamooka businesses or community infrastructure.

According to the State, the issue of whether or not the grant of MLA 7064 was a 'past act' would remain unresolved, but the Government's offer would constitute full compensation under the NTA for either scenario. ACI would develop a training program for Quandamooka members, and leave certain infrastructure on ML 1132 when mining finished for use by the Quandamooka community. The company would gradually surrender ML 1132, as equivalent alternative resources were made available to it, initially from MLA 7064. In making their presentation, state officials stressed that, given the time constraints facing ACI, there was insufficient time to undertake the RTN process in relation to MLA 7064. Either agreement would be reached on the basis of the State's proposal, or ACI would proceed to mine ML 1132, in which case MLA 7064 would become irrelevant.

In early March, the CHC group provided the QLC with a statement setting out its position. This stated that, despite opposition from some community members, mining could be expected to continue for decades, and that traditional owners should derive economic benefits from it. The group's view was that the proposals from ACI and the State deserved to be taken seriously, especially since in its opinion ACI's revised MLA 7064 would pose no threat to Brown Lake and would have minimal impact on native title and cultural heritage. It stated that if the QLC did reject the proposals 'without good reason' and failed to carry out what the group regarded as satisfactory consultation processes, it would challenge the QLC native title claim, pursue its own claim, oppose funding applications by the QLC to the NTRB, and challenge any agreements entered into by the QLC. At the same time the CHC Group approached the Queensland South Representative Body (QSRB) complaining about the QLC's conduct of matters in relation to MLA 7064. The CHC asserted that one of the Quandamooka clans held primary responsibility for the land on which MLA 7064 was located; stated that the QLC should cease to represent the clan; and asked the QSRB to act on their behalf in negotiations with ACI and the State Government. The QSRB forwarded these demands to the QLC and insisted that the QLC provide it with a range of information regarding the native title claim and the negotiations so that the QSRB could determine what action it should take.

Subsequent to the QLC's Special General Meeting, ACI informed QLC staff that the company would also be prepared to make royalty payments as part of a negotiated agreement. Also subsequent to the meeting, Queensland rejected the QLC's November 2000 proposal for consulting with the Quandamooka community, on the grounds that it would not allow the grant of MLA 7064 within the time frame required by ACI. Instead, the Government offered the QLC $5,000 to consult with the community about its ACI proposals. Government officials also offered to meet the QLC and provide details regarding Queensland's proposals that, as the QLC had noted, contained scant detail as to how they would be put into effect. The QLC declined the offer of a meeting when it learned that members of the CHC group had been informed of the meeting (again, the QLC assumed, by State Government officials) and would be in attendance. It rejected the offer of $5,000 to fund community consultations as grossly inadequate, and on 8 March the QLC submitted a revised proposal involving a budget of $30,000 and a time frame that would allow the community to reach a decision on a revised proposal regarding MLA 7064 by end May 2001. The Government rejected this proposal also.

On 15 March 2001, the QLC wrote to Premier Beattie criticising the behaviour of State officials, the Government's delay in responding to the QLC's original funding proposal and the Government's failure to offer what the QLC regarded as adequate funding to undertake community consultations. It sought a commitment from the Government that it would undertake negotiations in good faith, and would provide the resources required for the QLC to consult with the community in a way that would allow an agreement to be reached that would meet the requirements of the NTA. Such a commitment was not forthcoming, and on 22 March another proposed meeting to discuss the QLC's funding proposal was cancelled by the QLC when it learned that members of the CHC group were again planning to attend. On this occasion, the QLC had been careful to ensure that no one other than the QLC representatives were informed of the meeting, and it was thus certain that the information had come from State officials.

On 13 March, the QLC and ACI participated in mediation, and as a result ACI provided more information on what it would be prepared to offer as a basis for negotiations. It listed the infrastructure items that it would leave on ML 1124, and indicated a willingness to discuss trainee-ships, employment and commercial opportunities and annual payments linked to silica production to be spent on community purposes.

On 23 March, the QLC did meet the State to discuss its proposal in relation to MLA 7064 and core issues in relation to the native title claim. Later that day, the Government provided the QLC with a set of principles that could form a resolution to the native title claim. These were very general in nature and did not have Cabinet endorsement. They included a number of proposals of concern to the QLC, including that the benefits offered would constitute full compensation for all future acts, for example the grant of new mining leases, and that a large area of the island (over time, some 90 per cent of the claim area) would be declared national park. On the other hand, national park areas would be managed by a board that included QNTG representatives, rather than by the Queensland Parks and Wildlife Service; and the government would offer the QNTG access to a portion of statutory royalties derived from all mining leases and from camping fees; secure title to two traditional living areas near Dunwich; a portion of land earmarked for expansion of townships; and employment of Quandamooka rangers in national parks. In later discussions, the Government also offered to secure title (ALA land) to 1,000 hectares of land within the claim area. A number of these items had not been included in proposals discussed between the QLC and NTS, and potentially offered benefits that could be achieved only through a political settlement and not a Federal Court determination.

While there would certainly be a need for substantial negotiations on a range of specific issues and for Cabinet endorsement, the QLC hoped the proposed principles might form a basis for a speedy resolution of the native title claim. However a major issue involved how this could be achieved within the time frame required by ACI for approval of MLA 7064. Against this background, the QLC agreed to commence community consultations regarding MLA 7064 and the native title claim despite the fact that the funding available from the State was in its view entirely inadequate for the process. The QLC hoped that if the consultations were proceeding in a positive manner the State would later agree to commit additional funds.

At a separate meeting on 23 March 2001, senior state officials discussed the issue of representation in the negotiations with the QLC chairman and secretary and suggested that the QLC should include a representative of the CHC group in its negotiating team. In the last week of March, a community workshop resolved to offer the group representation on the negotiating team (an initiative viewed with disquiet by some QLC office holders), and also to ask the QSRB to assist in establishing a mediation process between the QLC and the CHC. A meeting between the QLC and CHC was held on 3 April 2001, and it was agreed that the latter could nominate three members to join the QLC negotiating team.

At a second mediation meeting on 29 March, ACI specified 26 April as the date by which it would require a legally binding agreement that QLC would withdraw its objection to MLA 7064 if ACI were to avoid starting work on ML 1132. The company indicated that, if agreement was not reached by that date, its proposal for an agreement would be withdrawn and it would focus on legal proceedings in the LRT. At this meeting and a further mediation meeting with the State on 30 March, it was also confirmed that the QLC and the Queensland Government would work to develop enforceable principles for a native title determination by the time any agreement with ACI was to be executed. These developments were followed by a period of intense negotiations relating to an agreement between ACI and the QLC, an agreement between the QLC and the State in relation to the grant of MLA 7064, and the development of agreed principles for settling the Quandamooka native title claim. The State Government's proposal in relation to the grant of MLA 7064 and that in relation to the native title claim were discussed with the QLC on 3 April. Queensland officials indicated that the mechanism to manage the claim negotiations would involve an agreement on principles, and written commitment to these by the Premier, by the time an agreement was executed with ACI; and subsequently the incorporation of these principles and commitments, combined with the detail necessary for their realisation, in a legally binding ILUA under the NTA.

On 30 March, the Court of Appeal ruled in favour of ACI and instructed the LRT to hear the objections to MLA 7064. This left the QLC with only one avenue (its judicial review action in the Supreme Court) to challenge Queensland's assertion that the grant of MLA 7064 would constitute a 'past act' and, if the QLC succeeded, trigger the RNR. However the QLC had very limited funding with which to pursue Supreme Court litigation.

Any hopes that inclusion of CHC group in the negotiating team would allow a 'united front' to be presented were dashed at a meeting on 5 April. In the presence of Government and ACI officials, some of the CHC group attacked the QLC negotiators, actions that were to be repeated in subsequent meetings. Indeed, during one meeting, a senior Government official felt compelled to try and defend QLC staff against such an attack. On other occasions, company negotiators turned the behaviour of CHC group members to their advantage, using their criticisms to undermine positions presented by QLC negotiators. Further difficulties were created by the fact that some CHC group members did not attend preparatory meetings before negotiating sessions, with the result that their interventions in meetings were at times at cross purposes with the positions and strategies agreed by the QLC negotiating team. After a meeting between the QLC and the CHC group on 12 April, agreement was reached on a number of measures to address these issues, including a commitment by the group that its nominees would participate as representatives of the QLC and the QNTG rather than of the CHC group and would attend preparatory meetings.

However, problems continued to arise as a result of the non-attendance of CHC group members at preparatory sessions. Other group members pressed the QLC to accept whatever ACI and Queensland were prepared to offer, and strongly resisted any procedural or substantive proposals by the QLC that might have the effect of pushing back the date of an agreement past April 26, in case ACI followed through on its threat to withdraw its offer if agreement were not reached by that date. QLC negotiators took the view that neither ACI or the Government had provided convincing reasons why agreement had to be reached by that specific date and were engaging in brinkmanship to put pressure on the QNTG. They argued that it was essential that the QLC maintain a firm position on issues of key interest to the QNTG and push hard to improve the ACI and Queensland offers in relation to MLA 7064 and to secure a binding commitment from Queensland in relation to settlement of the native title claim. They pointed out that, if negotiations with other mining companies were a guide, ACI would improve on its first offer if the QNTG held firm.

In mid April, the QLC provided ACI with an alternative set of proposals in relation to MLA 7064. These included:

- a royalty set at twice the level offered by ACI;
- more extensive provisions in relation to Aboriginal employment, training and business development;
- provisions to ensure a collaborative approach by ACI and the QNTG to environmental management;
- measures to minimise the impact of truck traffic on Dunwich;
- development of a cultural heritage management plan to ensure the protection of significant sites.

However, in subsequent meetings between ACI and the QLC the company refused to change its position on these issues.

On 5 May, a community meeting was held at Dunwich to consider ACI's offer in relation to MLA 7064, the Government's offer in relation to MLA 7064 and the proposed principles for settlement of the native title claim, which had now been endorsed by the Queensland Cabinet. By a majority of a single vote, the meeting resolved to accept the proposals in relation to MLA 7064 but determined that more time was required to consider the Government's proposals in relation to the native title claim.

On 8 May 2001, the QLC signed a Deed of Agreement, which anticipated that the QNTG would authorise the ILUA by 5 June, and, on the same day, the QLC withdrew its objection in the LRT to the grant of ML 7064. On 26 May, a community meeting was held to consider the ILUA attached to the Deed of Agreement. The meeting was called off after only a few minutes when a male member of the QNTG, who supported the grant of ML 7064, assaulted a woman member with a different viewpoint. On 2 June, a further meeting was convened, and the ILUA was authorised. However one of the two registered native title applicants, who would have to sign the ILUA before it could be registered, refused to do so. Attempts were subsequently made to have the Federal Court remove this individual as an applicant, but the relevant proceedings were not completed. As a result, the ILUA has not been registered to date. In the meantime ACI was granted ML 7064, and has been mining there for a number of years.

In the aftermath of the conflict surrounding MLA 7064, a number of QNTG members ended their involvement with the QLC, and the staff and consultants who had been involved in the negotiations, including key QLC personnel, resigned. Attempts had been made in the weeks after the 5 May meeting to develop a counter-proposal to the Government's offer for settlement of the native title claim, but these lapsed. The QLC no longer had the capacity to effectively pursue the Quandamooka native title claim, in part because of loss of staff and community support, in part because the QSRB did not maintain previous levels of funding for the Council because of federal Government changes to funding guidelines applied to NTRBs.

The Quandamooka agreements

Under the Deed of Agreement, the QLC undertakes to withdraw its objection to MLA 7064, and the QNTG undertakes to consent to the grant of MLA 7064 and not to challenge its validity. In return, ACI and Queensland make a number of commitments, some of which come into effect on removal of the objection and some on the registration of an ILUA pursuant to the terms of the Deed.

On removal of the objection, ACI and the QNTG will establish a Quandamooka and ACI Operations Committee ('the Committee'), comprised of two representatives of each party. The Committee's functions are to deal with issues concerning ACI's operations on NSI; consider employment, training and business development opportunities that may arise for QNTG members from ACI's operations; and make provision for the QNTG's involvement in environmental management and planning for ACI's operations including management of surface and sub-surface waters, flora and fauna and rehabilitation of mined areas. ACI undertakes to employ two trainees nominated by the QNTG and to offer them permanent positions if ACI is satisfied with their performance, and ACI and the QNTG will cooperate through the Committee in identifying and maximising employment, training and commercial opportunities for Quandamooka people. ACI will apply its procedures, as reviewed by the Committee, to report and protect any possible occurrences of Aboriginal cultural significance on ML 7064, and implement a cultural awareness training program for employees and contractors at its NSI operations.

Upon registration of the ILUA, QLC would withdraw its action in the Supreme Court. (This did not occur because the ILUA was not registered, but the action effectively lapsed.) ACI would pay into a Quandamooka Community Trust the amount of 15 cents per tonne for silica sold from MLA 7064. Upon completion of silica sand processing at the plant located on ML 1132, ACI would offer to transfer to the QNTG ownership of infrastructure located on the lease, including sheds, roads, water bores and power supply. ACI agreed to surrender as soon as practicable an unmined area of 13 hectares from ML 1132, and, on completion of processing on ML 1132, to surrender the balance of the lease and the mined area of ML 7064.

When ACI surrendered land from ML 1132, Queensland undertook to make its best endeavours to transfer to the QNTG the 13 hectares of unmined land from ML 1132 under the *Aboriginal Land Act*, and the remaining area eventually surrendered by ACI from the lease as freehold land. Queensland would pay the QNTG $100,000 on each anniversary of the ILUA registration date for five years, and provide business development assistance to the QTNG by facilitating its access to relevant government programs. As the ILUA was not registered, many of the provisions described did not come into effect.

Evaluating and explaining outcomes

The QLC and the QNTG succeeded in stopping ACI's original MLA 7064 proposal, which it strongly opposed. However, this success did not result from negotiations. Rather it resulted from the QLC's use of opportunities provided by the regulatory approval process to disseminate information about the proposal and to canvass community reaction to it; from its subsequent use of administrative and political channels to oppose the proposal; and from opposition to or concerns about the proposal expressed by certain government agencies and by environmental groups.

The Quandamooka agreements and the process that led to them generated few benefits and substantial costs for the QNTG. Because the ILUA was not registered, those benefits have been restricted to the employment and training, environmental management and cultural heritage protection initiatives associated with the establishment of the joint ACI–QNTG Committee. In the case of cultural heritage protection, the relevant initiatives were already in place. These would be reviewed by the Committee, but the Agreement contains no commitment by ACI that it would implement any changes resulting from that review. ACI's only specific commitment in relation to employment and training was to hire two Quandamooka trainees, but it is at the company's discretion whether or not the trainees would subsequently obtain employment. There are no ongoing commitments in relation to creation of employment or training positions for Aboriginal people. In relation to environmental management, the Deed of Agreement requires ACI to involve the QNTG, but provides no specific indication as to how this will occur or any resources to support it.

The ACI negotiation process imposed significant costs on the QNTG. It resulted in serious divisions within the community. Combined with the federal government changes in funding guidelines for NTRBs mentioned earlier, it undermined the QNTG's pursuit of its native title claim in a number of ways. First, it damaged the solidarity of the QNTG and so its ability to successfully pursue the claim. Second, it resulted in a decline in the organisational capacity of the QLC and so in its ability to support the QNTG. Third, and following on from the first two points, the opportunity to achieve a rapid resolution to the claim provided by the ACI negotiations was not realised. Yet, at the same time, the existing negotiation process in relation to the claim was sidelined and the progress achieved through that process was dissipated.[1] Significant costs also arose because of the impact of the ACI process on other negotiations in which the QNTG was involved, for example with CRL, whose operations were much larger than ACI's both in economic terms and in terms of their impact on the island. The QLC had been working since 1995 to engage CRL in negotiations, and by early 2001 these were well advanced and substantial components of an agreement had been drafted. After the loss of personnel and organisational capacity that followed the ACI process the negotiations with CRL faltered and an agreement was not concluded.

What explains these outcomes? A fundamental issue involves the disunity that characterised the QNTG during the negotiations, both the conflict between the CHC group and QLC's negotiating team and the wider conflict that characterised community interactions in late 2000 and 2001. The first made it extremely difficult for QLC negotiators to make gains at the negotiating table, as indicated for example by their inability to get ACI to accept any of the substantive positions expressed in the QLC's counter-proposal of 17 April 2001. Wider community conflict undermined the QLC's strategic position and made it easier for ACI and Queensland to insist that their preferred position on the future of ACI's operations became the basis for the negotiations. In March 2001, the QLC Chairman, in requesting the assistance of the QSRB to resolve the dispute between the QLC and the CHC group, made what proved to be a prophetic statement:

> The present instability caused by the dispute with the [CHC] group not only detracts from the ability of the QLC to achieve the best outcome possible for the QNTG, it also jeopardises negotiations with the Queensland government concerning the QNTG native title determination application.

The lack of unity within the QNTG may have resulted in part from fundamental factors such its structure and history and differences of philosophy within the QNTG regarding the acceptability of mining. Such factors frequently exist within Aboriginal groups and have been noted in case studies presented in other chapters. The critical issue is whether such differences can be managed so that they do not intrude into negotiations with companies and governments, and in this case they clearly could not. Apart from any personal issues that may have affected the behaviour of individuals, four factors explain this failure.

The first was ACI's strategy of amending its proposal to exclude the southern portion of MLA 7064. This strategy was suggested to the company by State officials, and appeared to run counter to the Queensland Cabinet Decision of December 1999 that had followed extensive political lobbying by the QLC against the proposal to mine MLA 7064. ACI's strategy undermined the strong sense of unity felt by the QNTG in response to ACI's original proposal and the threat it posed to Brown Lake.

The second factor was the QNTG's knowledge that the alternative to mining of MLA 7064 was that ACI would mine ML 1132, and that the Quandamooka community would have no ability to negotiate about how mining would happen or to gain any benefit from it, given that ML 1132 was a granted lease. To some community members, mining of the northern portion of MLA 7064 on the basis of a negotiated agreement appeared preferable. This factor also had wider political ramifications in terms of the potential for the QLC to obtain support from environmental groups. A number of environmental organisations had publicly supported the QNTG's stance in opposing ACI's original MLA 7064, and had joined in the QLC's criticisms of ACI's EIS. However they supported the proposed inclusion of ML 1132 in a national park and were keen to protect the environmental values of the area. When ACI revised its proposal for MLA 7064, some environmental groups preferred this to the prospect of mining on ML 1132 and in March 2001 a number of them wrote to the Queensland Premier expressed the view that, in the short term, mining of MLA 7064 represented the best available option.

The third factor affecting the unity of the QNTG was the role of State Government officials and ACI in giving legitimacy to and encouraging the CHC group in its opposition to the QLC. As the QLC Chairman noted when complaining about their role to the Premier, the alleged behaviour of officials indicated either that the Government was not negotiating in good faith, or that it had lost control of its officials. In either case, the impact on the negotiations was considerable both as a result of the interruption and cancellation of negotiation meetings, the undermining of QLC negotiators and the wider impact on the unity of the QNTG.

The fourth factor involved the inability of the QLC to undertake a community consultation process during late 2000 and early 2001 in relation to ACI's revised proposal and the alternatives to it. This reflected the Government's delays in providing the QLC with concrete proposals in relation to MLA 7064 and the native title claim; its failure to respond to QLC's November 2000 consultation proposal; and the Government's subsequent refusal to provide QLC with other than minimal funding to support a consultation process. Had such a process occurred over a reasonable period and with adequate funding, it would have allowed a thorough discussion of the available options, which in itself could have reduced the level of community conflict, and permitted the QLC to identify a course of action that had broad support within the QNTG.

The QLC's inability to undertake a thorough consultation process helps explain outcomes in another way. In its absence, the QLC had no community-endorsed position to take to the negotiating table, and the only formal instructions it held in relation to MLA 7064 was to oppose it. Neither had the QNTG appointed a community-endorsed negotiating team to deal with ACI as it did for other negotiations, because negotiations with ACI were not envisaged at the time community consultations occurred. When the QLC found itself involved in negotiations, they were initially managed, be default, by some of its native title negotiators and its mining consultant. A negotiating team formally endorsed by the QNTG would have found it easier to deal with the criticisms and attacks of the CHC group.

The QLC did use community meetings to test the response of the QNTG to proposals emanating from ACI and Queensland and used the knowledge it had gained from the ACI SIA and from community consultations for the CRL negotiations to develop the alternative proposal it put to ACI on 17 April. However these were not an adequate substitute for negotiating positions that had emerged from community consultations focused on a specific project proposal and endorsed through the consultation process (see Chapters 6 and 9).

The QLC faced additional obstacles in establishing and maintaining a strong negotiating position. One involved the legal processes relating to whether or not MLA 7064 constituted a 'past act'. Had the QLC been able to establish that it did not, a RTN process would have been required. Faced with the considerable delays this might create, ACI and Queensland might have been willing to offer substantial additional benefits to the QNTG. ACI might of course have immediately decided to move to ML 1132, but this would at least have ended the community conflict regarding MLA 7064 and minimised the collateral impact on the QLC and on other negotiations.

More generally, the reallocation of NTRB functions from FAIRA to QSRB and the changes in federal funding guidelines for NTRBs did not assist the QLC's negotiating effort. The QLC and the QSRB did not enjoy the strong working relationship that had existed between the QLC and FAIRA, and indeed the QSRB appeared more inclined to support the CHC group than the QLC leadership. It certainly made it clear that it was not prepared to support the QLC in the way FAIRA had done, which played a role in the decision of key staff and advisers to leave the QLC.

In the absence of a statutory time frame provided by the RTN process, the negotiations occurred within a time frame largely dictated by ACI's requirement to gain access to MLA 7064 in time to avoid disturbance to ML 1132, and by Queensland's delays in providing concrete proposals endorsed by Cabinet in relation to MLA 7064 and the claim. This placed enormous pressure on the QLC in the months leading up to the Agreements, making it very difficult to properly canvass issues within the QLC leadership and the QNTG and to develop and pursue coherent negotiation strategies.

Another key explanation for the outcomes described above was the Queensland Government's strategy of linking ACI's proposals to a negotiated determination to the Quandamooka native title claim, a strategy similar to that it employed in the Century Zinc negotiations. A negotiated outcome could offer the QNTG benefits not obtainable through a Federal Court determination. As mentioned above, Queensland's proposals for determining the claim did potentially offer substantial benefits, assuming they were made in good faith; and linking settlement of the claim to the ACI proposal offered the prospect of a speedy outcome. On the other hand, if the Government saw the QLC as obstructing a resolution of the ACI issue, it might be much less generous in the claim negotiations or force the QLC into a Federal Court hearing, which would cost hundreds of thousands of dollars and offer uncertain outcomes. A QLC briefing paper summarised the situation:

> The State has shown that it is prepared to negotiate about things that a court cannot order in litigation … but only on condition that the ACI mining proposal is resolved at the same time. It can be expected that if the QLC does not agree to this position, the State will adopt a less generous position in negotiation … or even that the claim could be forced to go to a Federal Court hearing.

In other words, the State government was in a position of considerable power and against this background it was difficult for the QLC to refuse to become involved in negotiations with ACI, despite the fact that its original preconditions for becoming involved (adequate funding and timeframe, adequate resources for community consultation) had not been met. However, to secure the potential benefits available from linking the ACI and native title discussions, the QLC and the QNTG needed to maintain pressure on the State government and ensure that Queensland made binding commitments to agreed principles for a native title determination *as part of the process through which they gave their approval for ML 7064*. As the QLC's solicitor pointed out to the meeting of 5 May, once the QNTG approved the grant of MLA 7064, there was nothing to prevent the Government from walking away from the proposals it had tabled and litigating the native title claim. In the event, and for reasons explained in detail above, the QLC and the QNTG were unable to secure the required commitments from Queensland before concluding an agreement with ACI.

Note

1 The QNTG eventually achieved a determination of native title a decade later, but this did not contain a number of the benefits or potential benefits 'on the table' during the earlier negotiations discussed in this chapter.

References

ATSISJC (Aboriginal and Torres Strait Islander Social Justice Commissioner) (2004) *Native Title Report 2003*, Sydney: Human Rights and Equal Opportunity Commission.

Chesterman, J. and Galligan, B. (1997) *Citizens without Rights: Aborigines and Australian Citizenship*, Melbourne: Cambridge University Press.

Cowell, S. (1996) *Aboriginal Interests and the Century Zinc Proposal: Resource Planning, Development and Impact Assessment in the Gulf of Carpentaria*, Brisbane: Honours Dissertation, Griffith University.

French, R. (2003) 'A Moment of Change – Personal Reflections on the National Native Title Tribunal 1994–98', *Melbourne University Law Review*, 27: 488–522.

Holden, A. and Pearson, N. (1993) 'Time for Leadership: Issues of Importance to Aboriginal and Islander People', in B. Stevens and J. Wanna (eds), *The Goss Government: Promise and Performance in Queensland*, Melbourne: Macmillan, 189–201.

Howlett, C. (2006) *Indigenous Peoples and Mining Negotiations: the Role of the State: a Case Study of Century Zinc Mine in the Gulf of Carpentaria*, Brisbane: PhD Thesis, Griffith University.

Kidd, R. (1997) *The Way we Civilise: Aboriginal Affairs – the Untold Story*, St Lucia: University of Queensland Press.

O'Faircheallaigh, C. (2005) *Creating Opportunities for Positive Engagement: Aboriginal People, Government and Resource Development in Australia*, Paper presented to the International Conference on Engaging Communities, Brisbane, 12–17 August.

O'Faircheallaigh, C. (2006) 'Aborigines, Mining Companies and the State: A New Political Economy or "Business as Usual"', *Australian Journal of Political Science*, 41(1): 1–22.

QLC (Quandamooka Land Council Aboriginal Corporation) (1999) *Impact Assessment Report on Social and Cultural Impacts of ACI Industrial Minerals' Mining Lease Application 7064 and proposed Dunwich Sandloader*, Dunwich: QLC.

8 The Ekati diamond mine, Northwest Territories

Introduction

Five agreements involving Aboriginal peoples have been concluded in relation to BHPBilliton's Ekati diamond mine in the Northwest Territories of Canada. Four of the agreements, referred to as Impact and Benefit Agreements (IBAs), are between BHP and individual Aboriginal groups. Each covers a similar range of issues but their provisions differ in significant ways. The fifth agreement deals with environmental management of Ekati. The parties to the Environmental Agreement are BHP, the Government of Canada ('Canada') and the Government of the Northwest Territories (GNWT). However, Aboriginal representatives were involved in its negotiation and are signatories to an Implementation Protocol to the Environmental Agreement that guarantees Aboriginal groups a say in environmental monitoring of Ekati.

This chapter briefly profiles BHPBilliton and the Aboriginal groups. It then outlines the course of negotiations, focusing on the Dogrib Treaty 11 Council and the Akaitcho Treaty 8 Tribal Council agreements that were concluded in late 1996 before the Ekati project received its final approvals from Canada. It then sets out the content of the agreements that were negotiated, assesses their outcomes for the Aboriginal groups, and seeks to explain those outcomes.

Ekati and BHPBilliton

Ekati, Canada's first major diamond mine, is located in the Lac de Gras area, about 300 km north-west of the capital of the Northwest Territories, Yellowknife (see Figure 8.1). In 1989, a prospector Charles Fipke discovered indicator minerals for diamonds and began staking minerals claims. BHP Ltd gained an 80 per cent share in the project by meeting exploration costs and the bulk of mine construction costs. Following the discovery of Ekati, numerous companies, large and small, staked thousands of claims throughout the surrounding region.

Canada's federal Cabinet approved the project on 1 November 1996, regulatory approvals were finalised in January 1997, and commercial

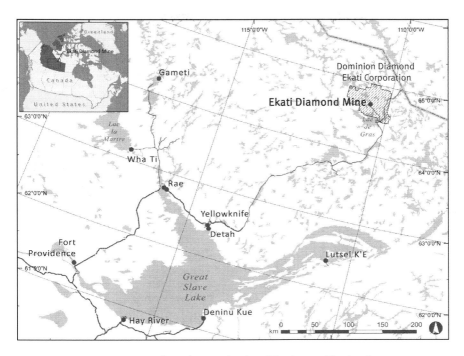

Figure 8.1 Location map, Ekati diamond mine, Northwest Territories.

production commenced in Autumn 1998. Ekati is among the world's largest diamond mines. It had an initial capacity to produce some 3.5 million carats a year over an expected mine life of about 25 years, by processing 133 million tonnes of ore from five Kimberlite pipes, the carrot-shaped volcanic cones that contain diamond bearing ore. A combination of open cut and underground mining methods are used. In January 2003, BHPBilliton, formed in 2001 through a merger of BHP and the London-based Billiton PLC, received authorisation to develop three additional pipes. In 2004, total diamond production from Ekati rose to 6.8 million carats, or nearly twice the initial capacity. Ore reserves are sufficient to support mining until about 2020 (BHPBilliton 2003, 2005). Processing is by mechanical methods that do not involve application of chemicals. There is no year-round road access to the mine site, and vehicle traffic is only possible during a ten-week period each year via a 475 km winter ice road. The project, which cost US$700 million to build, was initially expected to generate $12 billion worth of diamonds (BHPBilliton 2003; Couch 2002).

At the time Ekati was developed (1991–1998), BHP was Australia's largest mining company, with extensive interests in oil and gas, iron ore, steel, coal, bauxite/alumina and base metals. Its international profile was limited, and some of its overseas ventures were less than successful. For example the Ok Tedi copper/gold project in Papua New Guinea incurred significant financial losses and caused major environmental damage due to the disposal of mine waste into the Ok Tedi and Fly Rivers. (BHP withdrew from Ok Tedi in 2001.)

BHP was not under a legal obligation to negotiate agreements with the Aboriginal owners of the land on which Ekati was found, in the absence of settled land claims in the Lac le Gras area and of any general statutory requirement to do so (see below). On the other hand, it wanted to demonstrate its corporate social responsibility, particularly in light of the growing international criticism of its role at Ok Tedi. In addition, the company believed it was essential to obtain Aboriginal support for the project, because of the political climate in Canada generally and the Northwest Territories (NWT) in particular; the emergence of new administrative and regulatory structures in the NWT which would place Aboriginal landowners in a position of considerable influence; and its desire to minimise Aboriginal hostility to the project in the environmental assessment and other regulatory processes Ekati would have to negotiate (Canadian Institute of Resources Law (CIRL) 1997).

BHP had substantial prior experience in dealing with Aboriginal peoples. It was a pioneer in terms of Aboriginal–industry relations in Australia, being the first mining company to pay a negotiated royalty to Aboriginal traditional owners (of its Groote Eylandt manganese mine, developed in the mid 1960s). It also operated a coal mine on Navajo lands in the United States under an agreement with the Tribal Council. BHP's experience at Ok Tedi was much less positive, but possibly no less instructive especially in terms of its approach to Indigenous participation in environmental management. By 1996, the problems associated with the Ok Tedi mine were all too obvious, and were brought into sharper relief when a Papua New Guinea landowner, Alex Munn, testified in front of the Ekati Environmental Assessment Review Panel. Munn described the impact of Ok Tedi on villagers in the Western province, argued that BHP could not be trusted and that it would damage the environment in the NWT as it had in Papua New Guinea. BHP denied any wrong doing in Papua New Guinea and claimed that the experience at Ok Tedi had no relevance to Canada's NWT (Reuters News Service 1996a). However, developments in Papua New Guinea placed the company under greater pressure to respond to Aboriginal concerns about Ekati's potential impact on the environment.

Aboriginal groups

Ekati is located in an area of overlapping land claims outside the boundaries of Treaty 8 and Treaty 11, negotiated in 1899 and 1921 respectively, and south of the Nunavut land claim settlement, finalised in 1993. When the Ekati agreements were negotiated (1996–1998), the area was included both in land claim negotiations being undertaken by the federal government with the Dogrib Treaty 11 Tribal Council and in (separate) treaty entitlement negotiations with the Akaitcho Treaty 8 Tribal Council.

The Dogrib Treaty 11 Tribal Council (now the Tlicho Government)[1] represents some 3000 Tlicho living mainly in four communities located to the west and south-west of Ekati, Behcho Ko (Rae-Edzo), Wha Ti, Gameti, and Wekwiti (Snare Lake, some 180 km from the mine site and the closest community to Ekati) (see Figure 8.1). The Akaitcho Treaty 8 Tribal Council represented a population of some 1,500 people consisting of the Yellowknifes Dene First Nation, focused on Dettah (adjacent to Yellowknife), Lutsel K'e and Deninu Kue. Both groups are Dene, and archaeological evidence indicates they have inhabited the region for between 4,000 and 8,000 years. In the past, they have engaged in warfare, and in the modern era there has been tension between them in relation to disputed land boundaries, use of game, and the appropriate manner for seeking recognition of their interests in land. On the last point, the Dogbib accepted Canada's Comprehensive Land Claims Policy and sought to negotiate a comprehensive land claim settlement. Negotiations commenced in January 1994, a Framework Agreement was signed in August 1996, an Agreement-in-Principle in early 1999 and a Land Claims and Self-Government Agreement in 2003. The Tlicho became 'self-governing' on 4 August 2005. The Akaitcho, unwilling to accept the extinguishment that is an integral part of comprehensive land claim settlements, have sought to negotiate Treaty Land Entitlement under the federal Specific Claims Policy and also to negotiate a 'treaty of co-existence' with Canada, that would provide for co-governance of their traditional territory (Bielawski 2003: 152–3, 191–2, 211–12; CIRL 1997: 5). Treaty entitlement negotiations started in 1992, a Framework Agreement was signed in 2001, and negotiations towards a final agreement are yet (2015) to be concluded.

Both groups had similar political structures at the time of the negotiations. Each community had a band council elected through custom and chaired by a chief. Councils were responsible for community administration and provision of local government services. The Dogrib and Akaitcho Tribal Councils were directed by the chiefs collectively, and were responsible for coordinating land claim or treaty entitlement negotiations. They were also the primary means of interface with BHP and government in relation to Ekati, though each individual community included in an IBA was required to ratify the agreement negotiated by the Tribal Council.

A third claim process that might include Ekati was being sought (but had not been accepted by Canada) by Metis who resided in Yellowknife, in the Dene communities and elsewhere in the Yellowknife area. They were represented by the North Slave Metis Association. Ekati is located on the Coppermine River drainage basin, which flows through land covered by the 1993 Nunavut Land Claims Agreement. Inuit people, particularly those living in the hamlet of Kugluktuk, were concerned about the impact of Ekati on the basin and on their traditional harvesting activities in the Lac le Gras area. They were also interested in employment opportunities at Ekati. They were represented by the Kitikmeot Inuit Association.

The Aboriginal groups had not been consulted about, or had an opportunity to benefit from, earlier large-scale development projects on their ancestral lands. For example, they were not even informed when construction started on the Taltson hydro-electric dam, which flooded large areas of land in the early 1960s, and found out about it only when hunters encountered construction crews dynamiting rock to create a spill way. The dam was built to provide electricity for the Pine Point lead-zinc mine, which commenced operations in 1965. Pine Point paid $176 million in taxes to Canada and $339 million in dividends to its shareholders, and not one cent to the Dene (Bielowski 2003: 59). While Aboriginal people had gained little from earlier resource development projects, they were well aware of the potentially negative effects of mining, because both gold and uranium mines in the Territory had been abandoned leaving serious environmental problems in their wake. This legacy left Aboriginal sceptical of the willingness or ability of government to protect the environment and Aboriginal interests (CIRL 1997: 40).

Aboriginal people in the NWT rely heavily on land, water and wildlife both in economic terms and to sustain cultural, spiritual and emotional values. Throughout the environmental assessment and other regulatory processes for Ekati, Aboriginal people stressed the importance of protecting the long-term capacity of the land-based subsistence economy. At the same time, they were concerned to facilitate economic growth that would generate employment opportunities for a rapidly growing Aboriginal population and provide the resources required to address social needs and problems in Aboriginal communities. They stressed that they were not opposed to development as long as they could share in its benefits, and influence how it occurred (CIRL 1997: 6–7; IEMA 1998).

The course of negotiations

Government policy and environmental assessment

BHP had completed a number of exploration seasons and had established the existence of substantial diamond reserves when discussions with Aboriginal groups commenced in 1994. The Aboriginal groups took the view that the project site and the corridor for the winter road were located on lands for which they had never surrendered title. Their view was that the Federal Government thus had a fiduciary duty to ensure that development of Ekati should not proceed until their land claims had been settled and BHP had negotiated IBAs with them. In the absence of settled land claims, the creation of third party interests for BHP and the numerous other companies involved in the staking rush would remove land and water from claim by the Aboriginal groups, while at the same time denying them the benefits of development (Bielawski 2003: 40–1; CIRL 1997: 5; IEMA 1998: 2).

Canada took a different view. The Federal Government was strongly committed to the Ekati project, as was the GNWT (see below). This reflected not only the extent of economic benefits that Ekati itself was expected to generate, but also the fact that it would be Canada's first diamond mine. Further diamond discoveries had been made and successful development of Ekati would reassure other potential investors and open up a new and lucrative mining sector for Canada. Ekati was expected to employ 830 people directly and a further 640 indirectly, to contribute $2.5 billion each year to the GDP of the NWT and generate annual incomes of $39 million in the Territory through direct and indirect employment. Against this background the Canadian and Territorial Governments would be determined that development of Ekati should not be prevented or substantially delayed. The Aboriginal groups were well aware of this reality (Bennell 1996; O'Reilly 1996: 4).

The Dogrib had been pushing to have the area in which Ekati was located withdrawn from disposition by the Federal Government and included in land claim settlement negotiations, thus ensuring that relevant project approvals would not be granted until land claims had been settled and IBAs negotiated. In Autumn 1994, the federal government announced that this would not happen, noting that its land claims policy did not provide for inclusion of 'advanced exploration properties' such as Ekati in settlement areas. It was to reiterate this position and, along with the GNWT, express its strong support for the Ekati development, during public hearings held as part of the environmental assessment of BHP's project (Damsell 1996a; O'Reilly 1996). Canada's decision not to withdraw lands from disposition and so create a situation in which the Ekati project could be approved before IBAs were concluded significantly weakened the negotiating position of the Aboriginal groups (see below).

The GNWT's priority was to maximise the economic benefits generated by Ekati for the NWT as a whole. The NWT had the highest birth rate in Canada and unemployment levels well above the national average. The gold industry, traditionally a mainstay of the economy, was in decline, and government employment in Yellowknife was expected to fall with the creation of a separate Territory, Nunavut, covering the eastern portion of the NWT. For the GNWT, Ekati represented a rare opportunity to obtain a large boost to employment.

The GNWT did not perceive the negotiation of agreements with the Aboriginal groups as an adequate basis for maximising Ekati's contribution to the NWT economy. In the Government's view, Aboriginal groups would be in a position to take up only a portion of available opportunities in areas such as employment and training and business development. In addition, in its view certain opportunities (for example using mine infrastructure to promote more broadly-based development) could only be exploited on a regional basis. For this reason, its major focus was on maximising gains to the Territory through a Socio-Economic Agreement between the GNWT and BHP, rather than on negotiation of IBAs, which it regarded as 'private' agreements between BHP and individual Aboriginal groups (pers. comm., GNWT officials, 15 August 2000, 14 October 2002).

In December 1994, the federal Minister of the Environment, in response to concerns over potential impacts of the proposed mine on northern eco-systems and communities, established a four-member Environmental Assessment Panel (EAP) to conduct an Environmental Assessment and Review Process, the highest level of review in Canada. The Panel would conduct an independent review of BHP's EIS, which would include public hearings and submissions, and recommend to the Minister whether the project should proceed.

In February 1995, scoping hearings were held in seven communities to consider what concerns the EAP should address, and in May 1995 the Panel issued Guidelines for Preparation of the EIS. In July 1995, BHP sub-mitted an eight-volume final EIS, less than two months after the Guidelines were issued. In November, the Panel concluded that the EIS was sufficient to form a basis for the conduct of public hearings, despite concerns expressed by intervenor groups regarding issues including BHP's corporate record, treatment of traditional knowledge, monitoring, mitigation, environmental provisions, community impacts, and employment policies (O'Reilly 1996; Wismer 1996).

In January 1996, public hearings commenced. Aboriginal communities stated in numerous presentations to the EAP that they were not against mineral development per se, as long as they had adequate control over its timing, pace, and impact and over distribution of benefits. They stated that the Federal Government was failing to uphold its fiduciary obligations to Aboriginal people by proposing to allow the BHP development to go ahead on land that had not been ceded. Aboriginal people were also greatly con-cerned about the environmental impact of BHP's operations (IEMA 1998). Ekati was in an area traversed by the NWT's largest caribou herd, num-bering some 350,000 animals. Caribou play a key role in the economic, social and cultural lives of the local Aboriginal people (Wismer 1996). Aboriginal groups were concerned that BHP's operations might disrupt the spring and fall migration of the caribou and more generally interfere with their capacity to hunt and trap. In addition, BHP would drain five lakes to allow mining to occur, killing all of the fish and other life forms they contained.

Hearings were completed in February 1996. Formal objections were submitted by a number of participants, claiming that the hearing process had been neither fair nor adequately thorough. Other intervenors criticised the handling of issues related to land claims, traditional knowledge and cumulative impacts. Federal officials acknowledged that the Review was affected by tight timelines, narrow scope and limited funding (CARC 1996a, 1996b; O'Reilly 1996; Wismer 1996). Aboriginal representatives joined in these criticisms and raised the possibility of taking legal action to delay Ekati's development (Damsell 1996b; Fennell and Selleck 1996).

In June 1996, the EAP recommended that the Federal Government approve development of Ekati. The Panel Report made 29 recommenda-tions on how to deal with various aspects of the project. A number of the recommendations related to land claims and IBA negotiations. Recommendation 1 advised that 'the Government of Canada and Aboriginal people work toward a quick and equitable settlement of outstanding land claims in the region'. Recommendation 17 advised that 'all parties set the timely negotiation, conclusion and implementation of Impact and Benefits Agreements as a priority. The Panel also encourages BHP and Aboriginal people to conclude the agreement before the operational phase of the Project begins' (Canada 1996).

The Aboriginal groups were particularly disappointed with the Panel for its failure to make settlement of land claims and negotiation of IBAs conditions for approval of the Project; making the commencement of the operational phase the deadline for concluding IBAs, meaning that they could play no role in capturing benefits from or dealing with impacts of project construction; and failing to address the possibility that the parties might not be able to reach agreement. Once again the option of taking legal action to stop the project was canvassed by Aboriginal leaders (Damsell 1996c; O'Reilly 1996; Reuters News Service 1996b).

Negotiation of the IBAs

Negotiations between BHP and Aboriginal groups had been under way since mid-1994. The Dogrib had started to establish access to relevant expertise, retaining a Vancouver-based law firm and an economic adviser. They exchanged drafts with BHP outlining possible provisions of an IBA in broad terms, and negotiations continued throughout the summer of 1995. However by early 1996 little of substance had emerged from discussions between BHP and the Dogrib (or the other Aboriginal groups), and, at the start of Panel hearings in February 1996, Dogrib Grand Chief Joe Rabesca publicly withdrew his support for the mine as a result of what he called the slow pace of talks (Fennel and Selleck 1996). By this time, BHP had extended its ore reserves, undertaken feasibility and environmental studies, and invested an estimated $165 million in Ekati.

During the spring of 1996, BHP had provided the Aboriginal groups with a standard agreement template that it proposed would form the basis of IBAs. BHP's template was to play a critical role in the negotiations, and so it is discussed here in detail.

The document did not make any proposal in relation to financial matters. Apart from definitions and 'boiler plate' clauses dealing with matters such as confidentiality and applicable laws, much of it dealt with employment and training and business development. In relation to employment and training, BHP states its intent to provide Aboriginal people 'with the opportunity to maximise ... employment, recruitment and training that may be obtained during all phases of the Project'. BHP undertakes to 'take all reasonable steps' to employ the greatest number of Aboriginal people in the Project, assuming there are sufficient qualified and interested candidates available. The Aboriginal Parties recognise that BHP will need to employ a substantial number of non-Aboriginal employees to establish and operate the project in an efficient manner. Selection, hiring, promoting or dismissing of employees 'shall be the sole responsibility of BHP'.

BHP commits itself to a number of initiatives to encourage Aboriginal people to apply for positions, including the hiring of an Aboriginal Employment Coordinator; not applying the standard requirement for year 12 schooling for job applicants for the first five years of the Project; taking 'all reasonable steps' to ensure that its contractors employ the greatest number of suitably qualified Aboriginal candidates; and not allowing lack of English to act as a barrier to employment for positions that do not require a second language skill. BHP would 'take all reasonable steps' to employ Aboriginal people throughout the range of job classifications, and 'provide training and apprenticeship programs with the intent of promoting qualified Aboriginal candidates'. BHP undertakes 'where appropriate' to require potential contractors to expressly state their commitment to Aboriginal training, to outline their training programs, and to evaluate tenders 'on the basis of whether or not an appropriate amount was included for Aboriginal training costs'.

BHP committed to undertake training and apprenticeship programs, but the template agreement does not provide for specific levels of expenditure on employment and training programs, or particular numbers of apprenticeships or trainees, or contain target employment levels for Aboriginal peoples.

In relation to business development, BHP undertook to promote the utilisation of 'qualified Indigenous businesses whenever possible in supplying goods and/or services required during all phases of the Project'. Goods and services purchased 'will be those which are most competitive'. BHP agrees to 'take all reasonable steps' to provide local Aboriginal businesses with the opportunity to supply goods and services to the Project. Measures to be taken by BHP in this regard included providing information regarding the goods and services it requires; providing financial institutions with documentation to facilitate Aboriginal groups in securing finance; and requiring potential contractors to indicate Aboriginal content expectations and sub-contracting plans.

The agreement foreshadows the creation of a scholarship fund for Aboriginal students; states that BHP will use 'reasonable efforts' to ensure that mining does not disturb heritage sites; and commits BHP to meet the requirements of environmental permits, laws and regulations.

In return for the benefits offered by the agreement, the Aboriginal parties are required to provide a covenant that they will not 'object to the issuance of any licences, permits, authorisations or approvals to construct the project required by any regulatory body having jurisdiction over the project'.

While the employment and training and business development provisions are wide ranging, a notable feature of the template agreement is the use in relation to almost all of BHP's commitments of terms such as 'take all reasonable steps', 'use reasonable efforts' and 'where appropriate'. These terms introduce an element of vagueness and raise questions regarding the enforceability of the provisions in practice.

By the summer of 1996, the Dogrib had developed their own positions on key issues. Their objectives included financial payments linked to gross revenues from diamond sales; a preferential hiring clause for Dogrib citizens; the appointment of local employment officers in each Dogrib community; provision of additional paid leave to Dogrib workers to participate in traditional pursuits; specification of a range of contracts that would, at a minimum, be available to Dogrib enterprises; and a preference for Dogrib enterprises tendering for contracts. They also wanted funding for a Dogrib Environmental Director and a Dogrib Community Impacts Coordinator who would be involved in assessing, monitoring and responding to BHP's environmental and social and cultural impacts, respectively; and extensive Dogrib participation in the environmental monitoring and management of Ekati, from project design through to closure and rehabilitation. The Dogrib were keen to avoid phrases such as 'use best endeavours' and replace them with terms such as 'BHP shall', designed to minimise BHP's discretion in implementing agreement provisions. They were concerned that the inclusion of 'covenant' clauses indicating that the Aboriginal groups would not take legal proceedings to prevent or delay authorisation of the project should not derogate from any Dogrib aboriginal rights, or prevent the Dogrib from bringing a claim or action for loss or damages arising from Ekati.

On 8 August 1996, the Minister announced his response to the EAP recommendations. He stated that he was conditionally approving the Ekati project, but would not provide major licences required before the project could proceed unless 'satisfactory progress' was made within 60 days on negotiation of a variety of regulatory instruments and several agreements, including IBAs, a legally binding environmental agreement that would ensure Aboriginal participation in environmental management of Ekati, and a socio-economic agreement with the GNWT. In relation to IBAs, the Minister stated that the Government 'will be encouraging all parties to negotiate a fair agreement and is prepared to assist when appropriate to ensure agreements are concluded on a timely basis' (Canada 1996).

It is not clear why the Minister decided to apply a period of 60 days. An obvious rationale relates to BHP's construction schedule. If approval for the project were delayed beyond the end of 1996, it would be too late for BHP to build an ice road and start construction over the winter season. This could delay project development by up to a year, a delay that BHP argued might prevent it from taking advantage of opportunities in the diamond market and possibly threaten the project (Bielawski 2003: 50, 72–3). BHP was certainly pushing hard for a speedy approval for Ekati in the hope of commencing construction in October 1996 (CIRL 1997, 17: Kilburn 1996). However, a source close to the Dogrib suggests another or possibly an additional explanation. Shortly before the Minister released his response to the EAP's recommendations, a teleconference was held involving key Dogrib chiefs and negotiators and the federal ministers for the Environment and for Indian Affairs and Northern Development. The Dogrib informed the Minister that they would not support a decision to proceed with development unless an IBA was either in place or close to completion. The imposition of the 60-day deadline may also have represented an attempt to forestall open Dogrib opposition by assuring them that the Minister was determined to achieve rapid progress on securing IBAs.

The requirement for progress on IBAs and other agreements went beyond the recommendations from the EAP, and the legal basis for the requirement was unclear. The Minister appeared to use his authority to approve the water license BHP would need before it could start operating (see below) as leverage to force these additional items from BHP, in the absence of any clear legal requirement for this to occur (CIRL 1997; O'Reilly 1998: 8). However, according to environmental groups, the effect of any pressure on BHP was reduced when the Department of Indian Affairs and Northern Development (DIAND) announced, in a press release on 8 August 1996, that BHP could proceed with the work required to obtain permits and licences. On 30 August, DIAND issued an amendment to BHP's land-use permit covering its exploration activities and allowing construction of facilities to begin during the 60-day period and before Cabinet approval for the project (Bielawski 2003: 157; O'Reilly 1996: 2). The Northern Environmental Coalition, in a letter to the Minister of Indian Affairs and Northern Development dated 9 September 1996, stated:

> Actions of your officials have seriously compromised the ability of the federal government to negotiate a legally binding environmental agreement. They may also have undermined the efforts of Aboriginal organisations negotiating impact and benefit agreements with the company. There is little incentive for BHP to negotiate seriously, now that their project is proceeding.

On the other hand, BHP still needed to obtain its water licence, which would be the subject of a public hearing, and it was apparent that the issue of a security deposit for land-related impacts would be negotiated as part of the 'legally binding environmental agreement' rather than dealt with in the conventional manner as part of a land-use permit. Thus BHP still faced substantial regulatory hurdles and the Minister had made it clear that progress on IBAs was essential to allow the company to deal with these.

The Minister's demand for 'substantial progress' within a 60-day time frame initiated a period of frenetic activity. Regular meetings commenced between BHP and the Akaitcho and Dogrib. Both groups established negotiating teams comprised largely of non-Aboriginal professional staff, Akaitcho's consisting, for example, of a chief negotiator, legal counsel, and specialists in economic, management and community development issues. The negotiating teams kept in regular contact with the chiefs, who also came to the negotiating table at key points. As far as I can establish, no formal mechanisms (such as the steering committee structure employed by the Cape York Land Council in the Comalco negotiations) were in place to ensure broader community input into setting goals for the negotiators or into the negotiation process.

In the case of the Akaitcho, two immediate sticking points involved BHP's demand that its template agreement form the basis for discussion, and its refusal to make an offer in relation to financial payments until Akaitcho acceded to this demand; and BHP's insistence that one Akaitcho community, Deninu Kue, be excluded from the IBA on the basis that the EAP had not defined it as a community affected by Ekati. As BHP was relating its financial offer to the population of affected communities, this would significantly lower payments to Akaitcho. These fundamental differences precluded progress on substantive matters (Bielawski 2003). The Dogrib and BHP were at odds over the quantum of financial payments; over inclusion in the IBA of provisions dealing with environmental management of Ekati, with BHP opposing their inclusion as a matter of principle; and over the Dogrib's insistence that their IBA should include numerical targets for employment of Dogrib people at Ekati.

On 9 and 10 September 1996, the NWT Water Board, which issues licences for water use and waste deposition into water under federal legislation, commenced its hearings in relation to granting of the BHP's water licences. This would be the last public opportunity for the Aboriginal groups to canvass their views on diamond mining or to shape the regulatory conditions under which it would occur. They sought to have the hearings deferred on the basis that they had not received funding in sufficient time to allow them to prepare adequately – Akaitcho had received its modest allocation of $7,000 on the day the hearings commenced. The chair of the Water Board refused this request.

With the limited resources they could muster, the Aboriginal groups sought to play an active and critical role in the hearings. For example, the Dogrib presented detailed technical evidence regarding what it argued were deficiencies in BHP's application. According to the independent review of the Ekati regulatory process, 'the Dogrib intervention raised significant questions regarding the adequacy of both BHP's application and supporting material, and the government response to that application' (CIRL 1997: 30). The Water Board decided to convene a second phase of hearings on 21 and 22 October and referred a series of technical concerns raised at the first hearings to the Board's Technical Advisory Committee. In O'Reilly's view, 'The Aboriginal organisations clearly used these hearings to put further pressure on BHP towards fair negotiation of impact and benefit agreements while raising significant technical issues' (O'Reilly 1998: 3).

In late September, the IBA negotiations came to a head. At meetings on 30 September and 1 October in Lutsel Ke between the Akaitcho and BHP, the company reiterated its demands that its template form the basis of negotiations and that Denine Kue be excluded. BHP negotiators indicated that unless Akaitcho agreed to use the template, the negotiations could proceed no further. On the morning of 1 October, the BHP negotiators cancelled the remainder of the scheduled meeting and left the community (Bielawski 2003: 114–19).

The Akaitcho were under enormous pressure. They were trying to respond to a Federal Government policy initiative on extinguishing Aboriginal title to traditional lands; to prepare for the second set of Water Board hearings; to respond to the thousands of claims being staked by diamond explorers; and to conduct the negotiations with BHP. They were also concerned at Canada's unwillingness to engage in negotiations on their Treaty entitlements, which had been on hold for some 12 months (Bielawski 2003: 86–7).

Akaitcho was aware that the Dogrib were moving towards an agreement with BHP, but there was no exchange of information between the two groups and the Akaitcho did not know just how close BHP and the Dogrib were to concluding a deal or what terms they might agree to. The Akaitcho were fearful that if the Dogrib, the larger of the two groups and closer to a resolution of its land claim, had signed an agreement and the 60 days had expired, the Minister would allow Ekati to proceed in the absence of an IBA with themselves. According to Bielawski (2003: 100):

> The company *needs* the Dogribs to sign an … agreement. BHP only *wants* Akaitcho Treaty 8 to sign. If BHP can reach agreement with the Dogribs.… Minister Irwin might well decide this is all the 'significant progress' he needs. If Irwin approves the mine because the Dogribs and BHP make a deal, the Akaitcho might not get any benefits from the mine (emphasis in original).

On Friday 4 October, three days before Minister Irwin's deadline was due to expire, the Akaitcho met a representative of the Minister in Yellowknife. They sought assurances that any agreements would deal equitably with the Dogrib and the Akaitcho, and that Minister Irwin would not approve the Ekati project unless IBAs were concluded with both groups. The Minister's representative indicated he could not state that the mine would not be approved if the Dogrib only had signed an agreement. The negotiators subsequently met with the Akaitcho chiefs, and the group decided to accede to BHP's demand that they use the company's template as the basis for an agreement (Bielawski 2003: 124–45).

Negotiations resumed with BHP on the same day. At the first negotiating session, Akaitcho agreed to exclude Denine Kue from the IBA, and later in that day BHP tabled its financial offer. Over the following days, both the Akaitcho and the Dogrib engaged in intensive negotiations with BHP on the substance of financial, employment and training and business development provisions. BHP agreed to include employment targets in the Dogrib IBA, and when it became clear that the Dogrib would have representation on the independent environmental monitoring agency being established for Ekati (see below), the Dogrib dropped their demand for inclusion of environmental management provisions in the IBA. Agreement was reached between BHP and the Dogrib late on 8 October, the day the Minister's deadline for 'significant progress' expired. In the early hours of 9 October, BHP informed the Akaitcho that agreement had been reached with the Dogrib, and at 3.00 a.m. the Akaitcho negotiators also reached agreement with the company (Bielawski 2003: 137–8).

The Dogrib draft IBA was ratified by the Dogrib communities in late October and the final agreement signed on 1 November. The Akaitcho IBA was ratified and signed by the Yellowknives Dene and Lutsel Ke in mid November 1996. In the third week of November, Canada resumed Treaty negotiations with the Akaitcho.

The environmental agreement

An environmental agreement between BHP, Canada and the GNWT was also being negotiated during this period. On 2 September 1996, DIAND convened a workshop to discuss the proposed agreement, and the Aboriginal participants insisted on being involved in the negotiations. The Aboriginal groups did not feel that the environmental impact review process had addressed their environmental concerns. In their view, inadequate time and resources were provided to support a thorough process; the findings of the EAP were flawed and its recommendations were weak, failing to address the issues raised in Aboriginal submissions to the Panel; and Canadian and NWT regulatory bodies had failed to seriously address these issues and, indeed, in some cases had not even taken the trouble to appear in front of the Panel. Aboriginal groups lacked faith in the ability and willingness of government regulators to ensure that their concerns were properly addressed and that BHP would abide by commitments made in its EIS and in regulatory hearings, especially given the strong support of the NWT and federal governments for Ekati (IEMA 1998; O'Reilly 1996; Wismer 1996). In this context, the Aboriginal groups were determined to have a direct role in environmental regulation and monitoring of Ekati.

DIAND agreed to Aboriginal participation in the negotiations, but would not allow the Aboriginal organisations to become signatories to the environmental agreement. The legal counsel for the Dogrib suggested as an alternative that they sign an implementation protocol for the agreement. The Aboriginal groups were subsequently provided with drafts of the agreement as they were developed by DIAND, and, at meetings with Canada on 17 September and during the following weeks, they sought amendments that would enhance their role in environmental management and, in particular, in the Independent Environmental Monitoring Agency that would be established under the agreement (see below). Dogrib and Akaitcho advisors cooperated during this process, for example to delay finalisation of the agreement in an attempt to provide some leverage to their IBA negotiators (Bielawski 2003: 133–4). After what O'Reilly describes as 'several furious rounds of negotiation and drafting' a draft agreement and implementation protocol were signed on 18 October 1996. After a legal and technical review by all parties, the final agreement and implementation protocol were signed on 7 January 1997.

The Water Board hearings resumed on 21 and 22 October 1996, with the Dogrib now indicating they no longer objected to Ekati in the light of their success in concluding an IBA with BHP and the conclusion of a draft Environmental Agreement. A draft water licence was circulated to Aboriginal and environmental groups and the licence finalised after receipt of comments from them. According to the Canadian Institute of Resources Law, the licence that resulted 'is generally recognised as the most comprehensive and detailed ever issued by the Water Board' (CIRL 1997: 32).

By 1 November 1996, the Minister was clearly convinced that 'significant progress' had been achieved, and the Minister and the Premier of the Northwest Territories announced that the Ekati Project had received final approval from federal cabinet. On 7 January 1997, the Minister issued the water licences for the project, and the final regulatory approval requirements for Ekati were completed. BHP concluded further IBAs with the North Slave Metis Alliance in July 1998 and with the hamlet of Kugluktuk and the Kitikmeot Inuit Association in December 1998.

The agreements

The impact and benefit agreements

The IBAs have not been made public and are not identical as they were negotiated separately with each group, which creates obvious difficulties in discussing them. However, all follow closely the structure of the BHP template agreement, outlined earlier, and in addition I have been able to view two of the IBAs and to obtain some information on the remaining two through other sources. Thus it is possible to provide a clear picture of the outcomes of negotiations between BHP and the Aboriginal groups.

All of the financial payments to be made by BHP are expressed in fixed annual dollar amounts rather than, for instance, as a percentage of revenues from diamond sales. The amounts vary from agreement to agreement, with those to the Dogrib and Akaitcho being higher than to the other groups. The payments are modest relative to the value of Ekati's output. Adding together the payments under all four agreements, they amount on average to some 0.6 per cent of the gross annual revenues of about $500 million being predicted for Ekati at the time the IBAs were negotiated (see for example Fennell and Selleck 1996). BHPBilliton does not publish figures for revenue actually generated by sales of Ekati diamonds. However the value of Ekati's production can be derived from figures for the value of diamond production published by the GNWT prior to 2003, when Ekati was the only producing diamond mine in the NWT (Cizek 2003: 22).

In 2001–2002, total payments under the IBAs amounted to about 0.4 per cent of this amount.

Because the payments are expressed as dollar amounts per annum, they do not increase if the volume or value of Ekati's output increases. This not only means that the Aboriginal groups gain no additional benefit if this occurs it also means that if mine life is shortened as a result of higher production, the total revenue flow to the Aboriginal groups from the project declines. The significance of this point became clear in 2002 when BHPBilliton decided to expand production, resulting in a shortening of mine life. Between 2002 and 2004 annual diamond production from Ekati rose by 50 per cent. Revenues increased by a significantly larger amount, given that the prices received per carat rose by 27 per cent in 2004. Relative to BHP's revenues in the latter year, the payments under the IBAs would be modest indeed.

All of the IBAs include covenants under which each group provides an undertaking that they will not take action designed to impede development of Ekati. According to one its negotiators Akaitcho has undertaken that it will 'never protest against or block any of BHP's actions ... no one can sue BHP, and we can't block the ice road to the mine site' (Bielawski 2003: 197; see also Weitzner 2006: 29). In one IBA, the form of words used is that the Aboriginal group 'will recognise and respect the rights granted to BHP ... to develop the Project and conduct Operations [and] shall not engage in any unreasonable action that could either delay or stop the Project'. This IBA also includes a statement that the covenant does not impair rights that the Aboriginal party has under any applicable laws to object to the grant of any licence, permit or authorisation in relation to the Project. Another IBA contains a covenant in identical terms but does not contain this qualification.

Such covenants have been criticised on the basis that they restrict the ability of the signatory groups to utilise rights available to them under general regulatory and judicial regimes, which in turn may make it impossible to oppose company actions or policies that might threaten the environment (CIRL 1997: 91–2; O'Reilly and Eacott 1998: 16; Keeping 1998: 7). The Canadian Institute of Resources Law has commented (1997: 92):

> ... it is not clear why [Aboriginal] groups should be asked to constrain their participation in the regulatory process as a condition for receiving benefits.... Is it appropriate that Aboriginal groups should be confronted with a situation where they may, in effect, be asked to choose between their right to participate freely in regulatory processes and their right to benefit from projects occurring within their territories?

CIRL also raises the question of whether, had IBAs been negotiated earlier, the covenants would have affected the ability of the Aboriginal groups to participate in the EAP and Water Board hearings, and so their capacity to secure improved environmental outcomes through the establishment of the IEMA and the terms of Ekati's Water Licence.

Events in 2002 may indicate that these concerns about the Aboriginal covenants are well founded. In that year, licence hearings were held to consider a proposal by BHP to redefine the scope of the Ekati project to include development of three additional diamond-bearing pipes. I am informed by a source close to the Dogrib that they were very unhappy at this development, but felt unable to push their opposition, in part because of indications to them by BHP officials that the company would be entitled to delay payments under the IBA if the Dogrib persisted in their opposition.

Much of the content of the IBAs is concerned with employment and training and business development, and the content is generally similar to that of BHP's template agreement, discussed in detail above. As in the template, virtually all of BHP's commitments are qualified by use of terms such as 'take all reasonable steps', 'use reasonable efforts' and 'where appropriate'; and no specific expenditures are attached to commitments in relation to employment and training or business development, with the exception of university and high school scholarships where dollar amounts are indicated that vary from one agreement to another. With the exception of one IBA, targets are not established for employment outcomes.

As in the template agreement, BHP undertakes to 'use reasonable efforts' to ensure that its plans for the mine will not disturb any heritage site. Provisions related to environmental protection vary from agreement to agreement, but in general involve a commitment by BHP to mitigate any negative environmental impacts associated with Ekati and to be bound by relevant licences, regulations and laws. One IBA makes provision for mitigation and compensation if BHP's operations are shown to be responsible for damage to the environment, wildlife or harvesting rights.

All of the agreements establish arrangements to facilitate ongoing communication between the parties and implementation of their terms. In each case, the Aboriginal group will appoint a representative to consult with BHP on implementation of the agreement, and the agreements either establish a liaison committee, or require a minimum number of meetings between the parties each year, to review implementation of the agreement. BHP undertakes to make a payment to each group to help offset their costs in implementing the agreements. These payments vary considerably, with the largest being in excess of one million dollars.

The Dogrib agreement includes a number of terms more favourable than the equivalent terms in the other IBAs. These include the specification of targets for employment of Dogrib during construction and operations, targets that are substantial relative to the overall size of the Ekati workforce; a longer time period during which the requirement for completion of Grade 12 schooling is waived for Aboriginal job applicants; and the appointment of local employment officers to facilitate recruitment of Dogrib.

The environmental agreement

The Environmental Agreement is a legally binding document that creates a specific regulatory regime to govern the Ekati mine, to be overseen by an Independent Environmental Monitoring Agency. The board that directs the work of this Agency has seven members, four of whom are nominated by Aboriginal groups. The other three are nominated jointly by Canada, the GNWT, and BHP, in consultation with Aboriginal peoples. Under the Environmental Agreement BHP is required to provide 'adequate' financial resources to the Agency to carry out its responsibilities.

The Agreement contains provisions dealing with archaeological sites, which require BHP to minimise impacts on sites; and to conduct archaeological surveys to 'the highest standards of the day', respecting places of significance to Aboriginal peoples, incorporating traditional knowledge, and 'to the greatest extent possible in partnership with the affected Aboriginal Peoples and communities'. They require BHP to 'take all reasonable precautions necessary' to protect identified sites (*Environmental Agreement*, Article X).

Article XI, which deals with traditional knowledge, requires BHP to undertake a study 'in order to identify categories of traditional knowledge of the Aboriginal Peoples' to be incorporated into environmental plans and programs. BHP also commits itself to incorporate all available traditional knowledge into its environmental plans and programs and 'shall give all available traditional knowledge full consideration along with other scientific knowledge as the environmental plans and programs are developed and revised'.

An important feature of the Agreement is the requirement for BHP to provide to the Minister security deposits to ensure the performance of its obligations under the Agreement. In the past, a number of mining projects in the NWT (and elsewhere in northern Canada) were abandoned by their operators before environmental remediation had occurred, and some had caused extensive environmental damage (Wenig and O'Reilly 2005). Aboriginal and environmental groups were concerned that a similar outcome might occur in relation to Ekati, and regarded it as essential that developers provide security deposits sufficient to cover the cost of any uncompleted environmental rehabilitation. As security for performance of its environmental obligations, BHP undertook to provide security deposits to the value of $11 million and an irrevocable guarantee to the Minister for a further $20 million (Article XIII).

Assessing and explaining outcomes

The benefits provided to Aboriginal groups through the IBAs appear quite limited. The financial component of the agreements is considerably lower, for instance, than those under the Comalco and Voisey's Bay agreements, which were negotiated in a similar legal context (see Chapters 6 and 9 for details). As outlined above, the employment and training and business development components of the agreements are heavily qualified and in many cases are ultimately at BHP's discretion. For this reason, one could argue that any positive outcomes that occur in these areas would have emerged in the absence of IBAs. The Aboriginal groups have accepted constraints on their ability to exercise their rights under general legislation and regulation in return for the benefits they receive under the IBA.

Questions have been raised regarding the legal enforceability of the IBAs, because of the uncertainty regarding the nature and extent of BHP's commitments created by the extensive use of phrases such as 'take all reasonable steps' and 'to the greatest degree reasonably practicable' (Keeping 1998: 27; O'Reilly and Eacott 1998: 17). Another issue relates to equity between the various Aboriginal groups. Because the negotiations occurred separately, there are significant differences in the outcomes for each group that often reflect the dynamic of negotiations rather than, for instance, the priorities of each group or differential impacts on them of Ekati.

On a more positive note, the agreements address implementation issues in a substantive manner, creating arrangements to regularly review implementation of the agreements and providing some implementation funding for Aboriginal groups. Of considerable importance, given Aboriginal concerns about protecting land, water and wildlife and their lack of trust in government regulatory authorities, BHP agreed to help establish and to fund an independent environmental monitoring agency in which Aboriginal representatives play a central role. This agency has the potential to ensure that many Aboriginal concerns regarding the impacts of Ekati and the inadequacy of existing regulatory arrangements are addressed. The Aboriginal groups also ensured that the conditions of BHP's water licence would address a number of their specific environmental concerns.

How can these outcomes be explained?

A fundamental factor is the absence of land claim settlements or of any statutory requirement for BHP to negotiate agreements with Aboriginal landowners. The desire to establish its credentials as a good corporate citizen and help negate criticisms of its environmental record did provide a strong rationale for entering negotiations. In addition, BHP apparently reached a political judgment that it needed the consent and support of the Aboriginal groups directly affected by Ekati in order to secure its investment over the longer term. In the absence of agreements, for instance, the Aboriginal groups could have filed an injunction to halt the project (Damsell 1996c). While such an action might not succeed in the longer term, it could cause significant delays, an outcome both BHP and Government were keen to avoid.

However, BHP was acting on the basis of its political calculation that negotiation was the desirable approach, rather than in response to a legal requirement to negotiate, and this weakened the bargaining power of the

Aboriginal groups. This explains their insistent demands that their land claims should be settled before negotiations with BHP commenced. As Bill Erasmus, Grand Chief of the Dogrib Nation stated: 'How can we talk benefits and jobs when we're not on solid ground, when we have no long-term security?' (Damsell 1996d).

Government policy was another key influence on the outcome of negotiations. As noted earlier, Aboriginal groups argued that the Federal Government failed to uphold its fiduciary duty to them by proposing to allow BHP to develop a project on land that had not been ceded for development purposes through land claim or treaty negotiations. The Government argued that claims negotiations and project approval processes were separate issues and that it was not necessary to wait until claims were settled before the project could proceed. The Government's position reflected its strong support for the Ekati project, and it had a major bearing on the relative bargaining position of BHP and the Aboriginal parties. The latter were convinced that the mine would be allowed to proceed regardless of their position on the issue. As one community member later commented, 'I don't think we had a choice. The government had already decided it [Ekati] was going to come in anyway regardless of what we said' (cited in Weitzner 2006: 11). Given this reality, the only option was to negotiate as best they could from a weak position (Bielawski 2003: 49, 136). On a number of occasions the Aboriginal groups did threaten to take legal action designed to improve that position, by halting the project and compelling the government to settle their claims before Ekati proceeded (Damsell 1996c; 1996d). However legal action did not eventuate.

Another critical aspect of the federal government's approach was the pressure exerted by the Minister of Indian Affairs in August 1996 to quickly progress negotiation of IBAs. Aboriginal leaders saw the need to negotiate agreements under time pressure as placing them at a disadvantage (pers. comm. Yellowknives Dene Chief, 15 August 2000; Catholique 2006: iii; Weitzner 2006: 9, 13). It certainly made it difficult to develop coherent negotiating positions. The Akaitcho, for instance, apparently developed their positions by reviewing other IBAs and using this to establish a 'wish list' and on the basis of ad hoc discussions with individual community members (Bielawski 2003: 88–92, 98–9). On Day 27 of the Minister's 60 days, the Akaitcho held a day-long strategy meeting about the IBA negotiations. According to Bielawski, at the end of the meeting 'we are unclear about how to proceed with negotiations. We want to present a clear position to the company, not simply react to formulaic offers that BHP sets out. At the end of the day, we still lack clarity' (2003: 58). A source close to the Dogrib indicated that while the Dogrib chiefs met with their advisors, legal counsel and key community people on several occasions during 1996 to discuss the IBA, the participation of the Dogrib communities was limited. Certainly neither of the Aboriginal groups undertook the sort of thoroughgoing exercise that was involved in establishing Aboriginal negotiating positions in the Comalco and Voisey's Bay negotiations (see Chapters 6 and 9). In the view of one Lutsel K'e community member 'With this first mine ... it happened so fast for us. So it wasn't very much consulting ... so that's why we screwed up.... You've got to have lots of public consultations' (cited in Weitzner 2006: 9).

Not all of the Aboriginal groups were equally affected by the 60-day deadline. The Dogrib had started their preparations earlier and had submitted counter proposals in response to BHP's template before Minister Irwin made his announcement. As a result they were not under as much pressure as the deadline approached. However, in general 'there is little doubt ... that the 60-day time limit put those groups whose IBA negotiations were not well advanced at a significant disadvantage' and that the combination of tight time frames and the occurrence of simultaneous processes in relation to the IBAs, the Environmental Agreement and the Water Licence significantly reduced their bargaining power (CIRL 1997: 85–7).

Time constraints also made it difficult for the Aboriginal groups to resist BHP's pressure to utilise its template as the basis for negotiations, because of the fear that the government might allow the project (already approved by the EAP) to proceed in the absence of IBAs if the deadline was not met.

The 60-day time frame also put pressure on BHP because, if the company could not reach agreement with the Aboriginal groups, Ekati might be delayed (CIRL 1997: 18; Couch 2002: 277). However BHP had three advantages in comparison to the Aboriginal groups. The first was DIAND's amendment to its land use permit, which allowed some development work to continue during the negotiations. The second was its use of the template agreement. It did not have to develop negotiating positions, but simply hold fast and demand that the Aboriginal groups adopt its template. Having reminded the Aboriginal groups of the inherent weakness in their negotiating position (see next paragraph), it could wait and allow the pressure to build on them. Third, BHP did not face the severe resource constraints that affected the Aboriginal groups, in particular the Akaitcho.

Overall, BHP's approach to negotiations appears to have been highly effective, perhaps reflecting its substantial experience in negotiations with Indigenous peoples. Despite the absence of any legal obligation to do so, it committed itself to negotiating agreements with the Aboriginal groups from the start and did not resile from that position at any stage during the regulatory and negotiation processes. This allowed the company to establish a principled position and underpin its credentials as a good corporate citizen. At the same time the company stressed (and has continued to stress since the agreements were concluded) that it was involved in negotiations not because of any legal obligations to do so but on a voluntary basis as a result of its commitment to corporate social responsibility (BHP 1999; BHPBilliton 2003: 2, 7). To emphasise this point, it reportedly fought hard to avoid any language in the IBAs that might indicate that they reflected the exercise of Aboriginal rights. The company determined exactly what it was prepared to agree to, enshrined this in the template agreement, and moved from that position only when absolutely necessary. It made some concessions to individual groups to secure agreement, but the maintenance of separate negotiations with the different groups meant that any concession could be limited to the particular group that extracted it. BHP appears to have achieved a very favourable outcome from the IBA negotiations: Aboriginal support for Ekati, or at least lack of Aboriginal opposition to the project; covenants that diminish the prospects of open Aboriginal opposition in the future; a modest financial commitment; and employment and training and business development provisions that allow the company considerable discretion.

The nature of relations and communications between the Aboriginal groups certainly affected the outcome. With four distinct organisations involved in negotiations and three of the groups engaged in overlapping land claims negotiations, there were significant barriers to coordination and obvious potential for conflict. The paucity of communication between the Dogrib and Akaitcho and the suspicion and tension that existed between them militated against success in the negotiations. The Akaitcho did not know, for instance, what terms BHP had offered the Dogrib or how negotiations between them were progressing. As Bielawski (2003: 131–2) notes, at a critical point of the negotiations the Akaitcho learned 'through various channels ... that the Dogrib met with BHP last night.... We still don't know how much money BHP are offering the Dogrib. Our efforts to find out are going nowhere'. Presumably the Dogrib were in a similar position in relation to the Akaitcho. The lack of communication also meant that the Aboriginal groups were not in a position to benefit from favourable terms negotiated by each other. For instance the more favourable terms extracted by the Dogrib in relation to employment and training did not find their way into the other agreements.

The ability of the Dogrib to win concessions in some areas seems to have reflected three factors. The first is indicated by Bielawski, who suggests that BHP regarded an agreement with the Dogrib as a first priority (see above). Second, the Dogrib had started their preparations earlier and as a result were, for example, able to table an alternative approach to BHP's template in June 1996. Third, the Dogrib appeared to have better access to financial and other resources than did the Akaitcho. However the impact of these factors on the outcome was limited. This is indicated by the fact that the overall structure and content of all four IBAs is similar, and that little of the Dogrib draft agreement found its way into the group's IBA.

The resources available to the Aboriginal groups also affected the outcome. The federal government did provide funding to support the IBA negotiations, but according to Bielawski federal funding was unstable, unpredictable and not nearly sufficient to meet the requirements of a successful negotiation effort. Akaitcho had 'to apply to DIAND for specific, small pots of money.... Scientific experts, much less legal counsel, are way beyond the scope of this piecemeal funding'. It 'cobbled together ... bits of money' for staff and elders to consult and negotiate during the period after the Minister set his deadline (Bielawski 2003: 169; see also Catholique 2006: iii). While the Dogrib were apparently in a better position, the general paucity of available resources is emphasised by O'Reilly, a non-Aboriginal participant in the EAP and Water Board hearings and in discussions surrounding the environmental agreement. O'Reilly also emphasises Canada's support for BHP:

> During the negotiations for the [IBAs] the government neglected its responsibility and seemed to side with the company. The government should have given Aboriginal organisations access to funding so they could properly participate in the negotiations with BHP. Lutsel K'e First Nation received only $7,500 from the government. Lutsel K'e was constantly under pressure to get the resources to hire the appropriate people...
>
> (O'Reilly and Eacott 1998: 25)

A number of participants have suggested (pers. comm. Yellowknives Dene Chief 15 August 2000; pers. Comm. former Dogrib Adviser, 12 October 2002; Weitzner 2006: 9–10) that the relative inexperience of the Aboriginal groups in negotiations may have played an important part in the outcome and that this may explain, for instance, the use of fixed dollar amounts as opposed to royalty-type payments and the use of BHP's template as a basis for negotiations. However the Dogrib and the Akaitcho both proposed royalty-based payments, indicating that they were aware of the advantages of such an approach. The Akaitcho were certainly aware of the drawbacks associated with using BHP's template as a basis for negotiations, as they strongly resisted its use and only accepted it when they believed a refusal to do so might result in a failure to secure any agreement.

Thus while inexperience may have played some role in explaining outcomes, it appears that outcomes essentially reflected fundamental weaknesses in the bargaining position of the Aboriginal groups, associated in particular with their inability to insist that conclusion of IBAs precede project approval; the time constraints imposed by the Minister; the strong support of government for Ekati and its unwillingness to consider any course of action that might delay its development; the limited resources available to the Aboriginal groups; and the paucity of communication and cooperation among them.

The Aboriginal groups had greater success in the area of environmental management, where the establishment of the IEMA and the conditions attached to BHP's Water Licence represented important outcomes. In this case they managed to create sufficient public pressure so that BHP and the Federal and NWT Governments felt compelled to agree to their demands for an independent agency. That pressure could not have been maintained had the Aboriginal groups not had access to Federal Government funding, inadequate as this was in their view. Once again this highlights the critical role of access to resources in shaping the outcomes of negotiations.

In addition, in this area there was closer coordination between the Aboriginal groups. While making separate submissions to regulatory inquiries, the groups did develop a cohesive approach and support each other in representations to the EAP, they pushed together for the Environmental Agreement and they cooperated in the Water Board hearings. They also enjoyed the active support of environmental organisations, in particular the Canadian Arctic Resources Committee (CARC) but also the World Wildlife Fund, illustrating the significance of wider political alliances in enhancing the negotiating position of Aboriginal groups. CARC considered that a close working relationship with the Aboriginal groups was essential in terms of pursuing its environmental goals. It worked hard to establish good relationships with them and attempted to act as a resource for the groups and support positions they adopted in relation, for instance, to the IBAs (CARC 1996b; pers. comm. Research Director, CARC, 15 August 2000).

Why was the same level of cooperation between the Aboriginal groups not possible in relation to the IBAs? Whereas the IBA negotiations were confidential, the environmental assessment and regulatory processes were public. This of itself facilitated exchange of information and cooperation on environmental issues, and also diminished any tendency for distrust to develop between the groups. In addition, all of the Aboriginal groups shared a common interest in ensuring favourable environmental outcomes. On the other hand a competitive element may have existed in relation to the IBA negotiations, with groups believing that allocation of benefits such as financial payments, employment and business opportunities to one group would diminish the opportunities available to others. The final element was time. The IBA negotiations were so hurried that little opportunity exited for cooperation to develop or common positions to be constructed. However, given the strong underlying tensions that existed, it may be that a longer time frame for negotiations would not have resulted in a more cohesive approach among the Aboriginal groups.

Note

1 The term 'Dogrib' is used in the remainder of the case study as it was in common use during the negotiations and figures in documents and other sources on the negotiations. In using it I recognise that the term has since been superseded.

References

BHP (1999) *Aboriginal Groups*, Yellowknife: BHP.

BHPBilliton (2003) *Ekati Diamond Mine TM Facts*, Issue 6, Yellowknife: BHP.

BHPBilliton (2005) BHPBilliton Group Securities and Exchanges Commission Form 20-F, Part A, Description of Business. Online. Available www.bhpbilliton. com/home/investors/reports/Documents/2004/2004Form20FDescriptionofBusiness PartA.pdf.

Bennell, B. (1996) 'Diamonds in the rough', *Globe and Mail*, 27 April.

Bielawski, E. (2003) *Rogue Diamonds: Northern Riches on Dene Land*, Vancouver/Toronto: Douglas and McIntyre.

Canada (1996) *Federal Response to Panel Recommendations: Canada's Diamond Mine Project Backgrounder #8*, Ottawa: Canadian Government.

CARC (Canadian Arctic Resources Committee) 1996a. Letter to Hon. Sergio Marchi, Minister of Environment, 21 June 1996.

CARC 1996b. Letter to Hon. Sergio Marchi, Minister of Environment, 1 August 1996.

Canadian Institute of Resources Law (1997) *Independent Review of the BHP Diamond Mine Process*, Calgary: University of Calgary.

Catholique, F. (2006) 'Forward', in V. Weitzner, *'Dealing Full Force': Lutsel K'e Dene First Nation's Experience Negotiating with Mining Companies*, Ottawa: The North–South Institute and Lutsel K'e Dene First Nation.

Cizek, P. (2003) 'Bankrupting the North with Resource Extraction: A Royal Rip-Off', *Far North Oil and Gas*, 5(3): 22–4.

Couch, W. J. (2002) 'Strategic Resolution of Policy, Environmental and Socio-economic Impacts in Canadian Arctic Diamond Mining: BHP's NWT Diamond Project', *Impact Assessment and Project Appraisal*, 24(4): 65–78.

Damsell, K. (1996a) 'Land Claims Threaten NWT Diamond Mine', *National Post*, 15 February.

Damsell, K. (1996b) 'DiaMet, Natives End Hearings at Loggerheads', *National Post*, 24 February.

Damsell, K. (1996c) '$1.2B diamond mine wins environmental approval', *National Post*, 22–24 June.

Damsell, K. (1996d) 'Dene may not back NWT mine', *National Post*, 16 February.

Fennell, T. and Selleck, L. (1996) 'Northern Gems: Natives battle a proposed $12-billion diamond mine', *Maclean's*, 4 March.

IEMA (Independent Environmental Monitoring Agency) (1998) *Aboriginal and Community Issues at Ekati Diamond Mine – A Progress Report*, Yellowknife: IEMA.

Keeping, J. (1998) *Thinking About Benefits Agreements: an Analytical Framework*, Northern Minerals Program Working Paper No. 4, Yellowknife: Canadian Arctic Resources Committee.

Kilburn, J. (1996) 'BHP Minerals – NWT Project gets Nod from Panel', *Northern Miner*, 1 July.

O'Reilly, K. (1996) 'Diamond Mining and the Demise of Environmental Assessment in the North', *Northern Perspectives*, 24(1–4): 1–5. Online. Available www.carc.org/pubs/v24no1-4/mining.htm.

O'Reilly, K. (1998) *The BHP Independent Environmental Monitoring Agency as a Management Tool: Prepared for the Labrador Inuit Association and submitted to Voisey's Bay Environmental Assessment Panel*. Online. Available www.carc.org/rndtable/vbpanels.html.

O'Reilly, K. and Eacott, E. (1998) *Aboriginal People and Impact and Benefit Agreements: Report of a National Workshop*, Northern Minerals Program Working Paper No. 7, Yellowknife: Canadian Arctic Resources Committee.

Reuters News Service (1996a) *BHP PNG Record Raised in Canada Mine Review*, Reuters, 19 February.

Reuters News Service (1996b) *Aboriginal Chiefs Slam BHP Mine Report*, Reuters, 4 July.

Weitzner, V. (2006) *'Dealing Full Force': Lutsel K'e Dene First Nation's Experience Negotiating with Mining Companies*, Ottawa: The North–South Institute and Lutsel K'e Dene First Nation.

Wenig, M. and O'Reilly, K. (2005) *The Mining Reclamation Regime of the Northwest Territories: A Comparison with Selected Canadian and US Jurisdictions*, Calgary: Canadian Institute of Resources Law and Canadian Arctic Resources Committee.

Wismer, S. 1996. 'The Nasty Game: How Environmental Assessment is Failing Aboriginal Communities in Canada's North', *Alternatives Journal* 22(4): 10–17.

9 The Voisey's Bay nickel project, Labrador

Introduction

The Voisey's Bay ore body was discovered in 1993; project construction started in 2002; and production of concentrates containing nickel, copper and cobalt commenced early in 2006. Voisey's Bay is one of the largest-known nickel deposits in the world and is located in an area where the traditional lands of the Innu and Labrador Inuit peoples overlap. The Innu and the Inuit negotiated separate Impact and Benefit Agreements (IBAs) with the project developer; jointly negotiated an Environmental Agreement with the provincial government of Newfoundland and Labrador ('Newfoundland') and with Canada; and negotiated interim land claims measures with Canada and Newfoundland in relation to the Voisey's Bay area. Negotiation of these agreements was affected by separate discussions between Newfoundland and the project developer regarding construction of a smelter to process Voisey's Bay ore in Newfoundland.

Background information is provided on the project and its developer and on the Innu and the Labrador Inuit. The negotiations leading to the conclusion of the IBAs, the Environmental Agreement and the interim measures agreements are outlined, and their content summarised and assessed. The agreements represent a strong outcome in terms of Aboriginal interests, and the chapter concludes with an analysis of the factors that explain this outcome.

Voisey's Bay and Inco Ltd

The Voisey's Bay nickel deposit is located on a peninsula on the north coast of Labrador, some 35 km south-west of the Inuit community of Nain and 80 km north-west of the Innu community of Natuashish, in the province of Newfoundland and Labrador (see Figure 9.1). Voisey's Bay was discovered by accident in 1993 by two prospectors exploring for diamonds on behalf of Diamond Fields Resources Ltd (DFRL). Initial drilling in October 1994 indicated they had discovered what was potentially one of the world's richest nickel deposits, which also contained substantial quantities of copper and cobalt. DFRL formed the Voisey's Bay Nickel Company

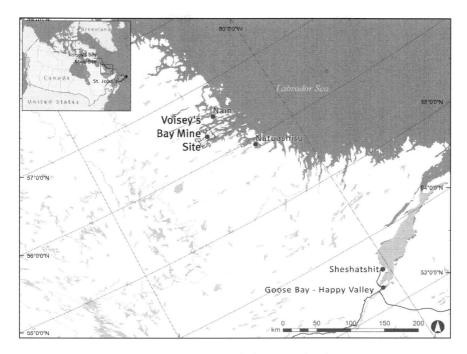

Figure 9.1 Location map, Voisey's Bay nickel mine, Labrador.

(VBNC) to develop the project. The discovery led to one of the largest staking rushes in Canada's history, with thousands of claims staked in a matter of weeks.

In June 1995, Inco Ltd, a Canadian-based multinational and one of the world's largest nickel producers, announced it had purchased a 25 per cent stake in VBNC for $750 million. Early in the following year Inco's major corporate rival, Falconbridge Ltd, moved to acquire the remaining 75 per cent of VBNC. After a bidding war between the two companies Inco emerged in August 1996 as the owner of VBNC. It paid a total of C$4.3 billion, regarded by many observers as a high price for an undeveloped ore body located in an area of overlapping and unresolved Aboriginal land claims (Lowe 1998: 25–30).

Inco's profits had been healthy for much of the post-war period, but by the mid-1990s they were under pressure from low nickel prices and difficulties with some of its overseas investments. In 1994, the company generated a profit of just $30 million on sales of $3.3 billion (Lowe 1998: 14, 143–4; see also Ali 2003: 99). Against this background, Inco would be very determined to achieve a speedy and substantial return on its C$4.3 billion investment in Voisey's Bay, which the company initially hoped would commence production in 1998. Inco had undertaken a major campaign during the early and mid-1990s to improve its corporate image and convince Canadians of its credentials as a model corporate citizen (Ali 2003: 100; Lowe 1998: 13). In pursuing its twin goals of developing Voisey's Bay quickly while promoting a positive public profile, Inco had little relevant experience to draw on in dealing with Aboriginal peoples. It had not developed a new mine in Canada since the 1950s and so had no experience of dealing with Aboriginal groups in a context in which their rights were winning increasing legal, constitutional and political recognition.

The main Voisey's Bay deposit is a bowl-shaped ore body called the Ovoid, containing reserves of 31 million tonnes of ore grading 2.88 per cent nickel, 1.69 per cent copper and 0.14 per cent cobalt. This deposit is being mined by open cast methods, while it is planned to extract other adjacent ore bodies by underground mining. Inco originally intended to construct a mill with a throughput of 15,000–20,000 tonnes of ore a day to process its ore into nickel and copper concentrates, but for reasons explained below this was subsequently reduced to 6,000 tonnes a day. Initial investment in the project was some C$830 million, and it includes a port, storage area, roads, diesel power plant, accommodation and an airport. Copper and nickel concentrates are shipped throughout the year, requiring use of an ice-breaking vessel during winter months. The mine employs about 450 people, who work on a 'fly in–fly out' basis and on a two weeks on/two weeks off schedule, and the mine has an estimated life of about 30 years (VBNC 2005). Subsequent to the events discussed in this chapter, Inco was taken over by the Brazilian multinational mining company, Vale.

Aboriginal groups

The traditional territories of the Innu and the Labrador Inuit overlap in the Voisey's Bay area. Both live at the geographic edges of the traditional lands of the larger Aboriginal groups of which they are a part. The Labrador Inuit are the most southerly of the Inuit nations, while the Innu are the most easterly of the nation of the Algonquin language group. Archaeological evidence indicates that Innu and Inuit have lived in the region for at least 6,000 years. The Innu were nomadic, and followed a seasonal round of harvesting between interior and coastal regions, relying on caribou as a primary source of food. The Inuit were focused on the coast, depending heavily on seals and other species that utilise the sea-ice. The Inuit were in regular contact with Europeans since the late eighteenth century, and established permanent settlements around Moravian mission stations. The Innu visited the coast to trade with Europeans, but had little sustained contact with them until well into the twentieth century.

By the 1960s, the Innu were settled into permanent communities on the Labrador coast. Relocated on a number of occasions forcibly or with minimal consultation and removed from their traditional hunting grounds, the Innu have experienced serious social and economic problems, including absence of employment opportunities, alcohol abuse, family violence and a high incidence of suicide. Innu regard recognition of their Aboriginal rights and protection of their ancestral land and its resource as critical in allowing them to maintain their cultural identity and address the challenges they face (CHRC 2002; Innes 2001; Innu Task Force on Mining Activities 1996).

Newfoundland and Labrador did not become a province of Canada until 1949. The terms of union under which this occurred made no reference to the province's Aboriginal people, and the Innu were not recognised as status Indians and no reserves were created. After 1949 the Federal Government was not active in providing services to the Innu and Inuit of the sort it delivered to Aboriginal peoples elsewhere, instead providing varying levels of financial support for services delivered by Newfoundland. The Innu took legal action to try to force Canada to assume its constitutional responsibilities and in 1992 brought a complaint against Canada to the Canadian Human Rights Commission (CHRC). The Commission found in favour of the Innu, and during the 1990s Canada gradually become more involved in direct service provision. However a further report by the CHRC in 2002 found that Canada had 'not yet provided the Innu with access to all federal funding, programs and services that are available to status, on reserve Indian people in Canada' (CHRC 2002: 3).

Neither the Inuit nor the Innu signed a treaty, nor ceded territory to Canada or to Newfoundland. Both groups filed comprehensive land claims in 1977, but by the time Voisey's Bay was discovered neither claim was close to being finalised. Negotiations with the Inuit were further advanced, and in November 1990 the Federal and provincial Governments and the Labrador Inuit Association (LIA) completed the first stage with the comprehensive land claims process, signing a Framework Agreement that set out the process and subjects for negotiation. An Agreement in Principle was concluded in 1997, and a final agreement initialled by negotiators in 2001. In 2005, the Labrador Inuit Final Agreement was ratified by Canada and Newfoundland and became law. The Innu concluded a Framework Agreement in 1997, but did not sign an Agreement in Principle until 2012.

The Inuit and Innu are represented by the LIA and the Innu Nation respectively, well established organisations set up in the early 1970s. The LIA's 5200 members mainly reside in the coastal communities of Nain, Hopedale, Makkovik, Postville, and Rigolet, with Nain having the largest population of about 1,000. The Innu Nation's 2,400 members live mainly in the communities of Sheshatshui and Natuashish, the latter a recently established community to which people were relocated from Utshimassits (Davies Inlet) (see Figure 9.1). Davies Inlet had in turn resulted from a succession of forced relocations of the Innu by the Catholic Church and the Federal Government.

Historically, relations between the Inuit and the Innu have not been close, and there is 'a long history of Innu and Inuit peoples and organizations pursuing distinct and separate approaches to land claims and political development' (Archibald and Crnkovich 1999: x). However, there is a mutual respect between the two groups and neither has contested the fact that the other has legitimate interests in the Voisey's Bay area. Prior to the discovery of minerals, elders from both groups had met and, in the context of land claim negotiations, reached agreement on the area in which their claims would overlap and that each would recognise the other's interests. While this agreement was not formalised until 2005, it was observed in principle throughout the development of the Voisey's Bay Project, which removed the prospect of open conflict between the groups as a result of attempts by either to establish exclusive control over the Voisey's Bay area. This is an important part of the context for the negotiations described later.

The Innu are generally regarded as being more politically militant than the Inuit. They mounted a protracted high profile campaign against the use of their traditional lands as a location for low flying exercises by aircraft from the NATO air base at Goose Bay. In 1987, they invaded the base and occupied the runway, leading to the arrests of a number of Innu, including mothers who were separated from their children and imprisoned in Newfoundland. Over the following two years they mounted a further 17 incursions into the base, ten of them onto the runway. In 1998 they disrupted a ceremony by the Premiers of Quebec and Newfoundland to mark the initiation of a large hydroelectric project on Innu lands, occupying the press facility and using it to broadcast their opposition to the project (Lowe 1998: 82–3, 171–5). While the Innu did not succeed in stopping low level flying, their obvious willingness to engage in direct action in defence of their interests could create considerable problems for a company wishing to rapidly develop a major mining project. While the Inuit were more inclined to use legal remedies, as we shall see they also were prepared to engage in direct action if they believed the occasion demanded it.

The course of negotiations

Early contacts and preparations for negotiations

As the land claims of the Innu and Inuit were not settled, there was no clear legal obligation on DFRL to seek their consent to develop Voisey's Bay or to negotiate IBAs with them. However, both the Innu Nation and the LIA wrote to DFRL in 1994, informing the company that its discovery lay on unceded Aboriginal land and that it would require their consent before proceeding with the project. In December 1994, the President of DFRL Charlie Russell met Innu and Inuit leaders in Goose Bay. Innu Chief Negotiator Daniel Ashini confronted Russell with the central role he and DFRL's majority shareholder Robert Friedland had played in one of the worst modern mining environmental disasters in the United States, at the Galactic Resources gold mine in Colorado, as a result of which Friedland was under investigation by the Environmental Protection Agency and the FBI. The meeting established the Innu as 'well-informed and politically sophisticated adversaries' (Innes 2001: 13).

Russell promised the Innu and Inuit that DFRL would keep them informed about progress at Voisey's Bay, but in fact it failed to do so when exploration activity intensified in the following year. The Innu Nation issued DFRL with an eviction notice, demanding that drilling cease until an environmental and cultural heritage protection plan was completed, and in February 1995 more than 100 Innu occupied DFRL's exploration camp for 12 days and put a stop to exploration work. This action both established the seriousness of the Innu's demands and helped to solidify a unified Innu response to the project. It also attracted widespread media attention, bringing the Aboriginal perspective on Voisey's Bay to the attention of the Canadian public (Innes 2001: 14, 2002: 5).

Both the Innu and Inuit were concerned that exploration was occurring at Voisey's Bay and on thousands of claims that had been staked by other companies in a context where their Aboriginal rights were not recognised and they were consequently unable to act to protect their traditional lands. They took the position that there should be no development at Voisey's Bay or elsewhere in the region until land claims negotiations with the provincial and Canadian governments were settled, and IBAs were finalised with Inco (Gray 1996; Lowe 1998: 58). Inco and Newfoundland rejected this position, arguing that development of the project could proceed in advance of land claim settlements (VBNC 1998). Inco perceived that it was caught in the middle of a dispute between the government and the aboriginal groups, and that the company 'can't get in the middle of it [the land claims issue]. We're willing to deal with whoever the eventual landlord is' (cited in Innes 2001: 14).

Newfoundland was committed to developing Voisey's Bay as quickly as possible. The province, which historically had high rates of unemployment and an economy vulnerable to the vagaries of seasonal and unstable primary industries, had been dealt a serious blow by the closure of the cod fishery in 1992, which directly affected over 19,000 fishery and processing plant workers. The provincial government believed that the Voisey's Bay project and the revenues it would generate should not be affected by Aboriginal land claims. In January 1997, it unilaterally withdrew the Voisey's Bay area from the land claims negotiations table and indicated that any settlement would not offer the Innu or Inuit mineral rights or access to statutory royalties from Voisey's Bay. The Innu saw this as consistent with a general policy approach that placed the rights of miners ahead of those of Newfoundland's Aboriginal citizens:

> Newfoundland issues exploration permits to the exploration companies without any consultation with the Innu people. They do so in complete disregard to the comprehensive claims negotiations that are supposed to be underway leading to comprehensive rights agreements between the Innu, Newfoundland and Canada and the Labrador Inuit Association...
>
> (Ashini cited in Innes 2001: 14)

In this situation, the Innu and the Inuit decided they had no choice but to negotiate directly with the companies involved. According to Lowe (1998: 59) the Innu 'did not want the Voisey's Bay nickel mine on their land under any circumstances'. However, if the project was going to proceed, they wished to share in its benefits or obtain compensation for its impact and also to minimise the extent of that impact. Thus '(F)or the Innu, the decision to negotiate with the company was not an easy one' (Innes 2001: 14). They had held a position of opposition to the mine, but by mid 1995, they felt they had little choice. Millions of dollars had been invested in the project and exploration results confirmed that the deposit was worth billions. Furthermore, the Inuit had already started negotiations with the company (Gray 1996; Innes 2001: 14).

The Innu did not immediately commence substantive negotiations with DFRL. Instead, they entered an agreement with the company that set out a framework for negotiations and provided the Innu with funding to prepare for discussions. A critical element of this preparation was the establishment of an Innu Task Force on Mining Activities, consisting of three representatives from each of the two Innu communities. The Task Force conducted an extensive process of information dissemination and community consultation, designed to establish Innu aspirations and concerns in relation to mining in general and the Voisey's Bay project in particular. It undertook numerous one-on-one interviews with community members and organised small group discussions, information sessions and open community meetings. Information was provided not only about Voisey's Bay but about how other Aboriginal groups had responded to similar projects on their ancestral lands. For example, a summary document was produced giving an overview of 12 existing IBAs elsewhere in Canada.

The Task Force consultations revealed widespread and deeply felt concerns about the damage mining might cause to land, water and wildlife, and about the negative effects of such damage on the Innu's ability to practice and sustain their culture. That ability was also believed to be under threat by prolonged absences of Innu working at Voisey's Bay. Innu had little faith in the willingness or ability of the company or the Government to prevent environmental damage, and believed that only their own involvement in decisions about the project could protect the land and its resources. Concern was also raised about damage to Innu cultural heritage, especially burial sites; about the inability of Innu to access the Voisey's Bay area; and about the impact on wildlife of hunting by mineworkers. The prospect of additional jobs and business opportunities was widely welcomed. However, many respondents believed that most such opportunities would accrue to people from outside the region and that jobs obtained by Innu would generally be menial and poorly paid. Many Innu expressed fears about the negative social effects of access to alcohol at the mine site, and predicted that alcohol abuse would lead to Innu workers being dismissed. Concerns were raised that the pace of project development was too rapid to allow appropriate Innu involvement in decision-making, and that the absence of sufficient lead time would make it impossible to train Innu for more highly skilled and better paid positions (Innu Nation Task Force on Mining Activities 1996).

The Task Force produced a comprehensive final report, detailing the benefits and costs community members believed would be associated with mining, and identifying strategies for mitigating negative impacts and maximising positive ones (Innu Nation Task Force on Mining Activities 1996). This report was to represent a critical foundation for Innu negotiators in their later discussions with Inco and with Canada and Newfoundland.

The LIA drew on a variety of processes and sources to establish its members' goals and priorities in relation to the IBAs. These included wider consultations and research in relation to development in general (see for example Williamson 1997; LIA n.d.); Inuit submissions and presentations to the Environmental Review Panel for Voisey's Bay (see below); and the LIA's annual general meetings where members received feedback on, and expressed their views on, the negotiations with VNBC. They also included the activities of the Tongamiut Inuit Annait (TIA), the organisation representing Inuit women in northern Labrador. The TIA convened a number of workshops on IBAs, the environmental review process and comprehensive land claims policy and lobbied to ensure that these processes and policies would include a focus on issues of key interest to Inuit women. Many of the aspirations and concerns expressed by the Inuit were identical to those identified by the Innu Nation Task Force (Archibald and Crnkovich 1999: 14).

The Innu and Inuit organised their teams for negotiating with VBNC in a similar manner. They were led by a chief negotiator or negotiators, and consisted of a core group of three or four people with responsibility for major areas of the negotiation, supplemented as required by specialist expertise on particular issues, such as the tax implications of alternative approaches to financial payments. There was a high degree of continuity among the key personnel, with the same small group of negotiators and advisers playing a central role throughout what were to be protracted negotiations. Some change of personnel did occur after the break in negotiations in 2000–2001 (see below), but the new chief negotiators had earlier been involved in land claim negotiations for their respective groups and had a good grasp of key issues and a sense of how the negotiations had developed to date. The negotiations were funded by VBNC, either under provisions of negotiation agreements or through exchanges of letters. Neither negotiating team felt that reliance on company funding affected their capacity to vigorously pursue their objectives (pers. comm. Innu Nation Advisor, 22 April 2005; pers. comm. former LIA Chief Negotiator, 25 April 2005).

While Newfoundland might assert the principle that mineral development should proceed in advance of the settlement of land claims, the political reality was that the cooperation of the Aboriginal groups was essential to facilitate timely development of Voisey's Bay and both Newfoundland

and Canada agreed to 'fast track' land claims negotiations with the LIA and the Innu (Archibald and Crnkovich 1999: 9; Gray 1996). On 5 November 1997, following weeks of intensive negotiations in Ottawa, an Agreement-In-Principle was reached with the LIA. It contained the following key elements.

- Two categories of Inuit land totalling 28,000 square miles were identified in northern Labrador. Labrador Inuit Lands (LIL) provided for surface title to 6,100 square miles, in which Inuit have exclusive harvesting rights and control over new developments. The Labrador Inuit Settlement Area (LISA) covers 21,900 square miles and provide for priority subsistence and the right to participate with government in resource and environmental management.
- A resource royalty sharing arrangement, under which Inuit would receive 25 per cent of provincial resource revenues from mining, oil and gas in LIL.
- The Inuit would receive 3 per cent of provincial resource royalties from the Voisey's Bay project. The LIA agreed to use 'best efforts' to conclude an Inuit IBA with the VBNC.
- IIBAs between developers and Labrador Inuit would be compulsory for developments on LIL and for major developments in LISA.
- Canada would provide the Inuit with $140 million in cash and up to $115 million in dedicated funds to be used for such things as fisheries, economic development and general implementation of the agreement.
- The Inuit were guaranteed political control over their communities.

The LIA membership ratified the Agreement in Principle in July 1998.

Environmental assessment and legal action

Government also responded to Innu and Inuit demands that they should be centrally involved in the environmental assessment of Voisey's Bay, which would require environmental reviews under both federal and provincial legislation. In January 1997, Canada, Newfoundland, the Innu Nation and the LIA signed a Memorandum of Understanding (MoU) outlining the environmental assessment process and providing for the appointment of an Environmental Assessment Panel (EAP), whose membership would be determined jointly by the four parties, to conduct the review. The MoU also set out detailed terms of reference for the Panel, and these included matters of key interest to the Innu and Inuit that went beyond the scope of legislative requirements. For example, the Panel was required to give 'full consideration' to traditional ecological knowledge, to address the relationship between the Voisey's Bay project and land claim negotiations and to identify how the project would affect women differently from men.

Draft guidelines for the environmental impact statement were issued in March 1997, and the Innu and Inuit obtained intervenor funding from

Canada to hire technical experts to review the guidelines. In addressing the draft guidelines, the Innu and Inuit agreed on a division of labour in dealing with environmental issues, with the Innu Nation focusing on terrestrial issues and the LIA looking at marine concerns. This arrangement was to remain in force throughout the environmental review process and subsequent negotiations on environmental issues with government and VBNC.

In the meantime, Inco was coming under increasing pressure from market commentators to demonstrate that a return on its large investment in Voisey's Bay would quickly eventuate. This is indicated by the fact that its timelines for production announced to the stock market seemed consistently and highly optimistic in light of what was actually occurring on the ground (Lowe 1998: 67–75). If VBNC was to have any chance of achieving these optimistic schedules it was essential for it to establish positive relationships with the Innu and Inuit. However, its actions indicated that it was insufficiently aware of this reality, or lacked the capacity or understanding to identify appropriate courses of action.

In May 1997, VBNC announced its intention to construct a 12 km road, an airstrip and a camp facility that it described as 'advanced exploration infrastructure'. If the work was indeed related solely to exploration it would require only provincial approval and would not need to be considered as part of the project environmental review process. The Innu and Inuit believed that in fact the infrastructure would be utilised in mining at Voisey's Bay and that Inco was trying to push ahead with project development before appropriate consideration had been given to potential environmental impacts. They sought a court order to prevent Newfoundland from proceeding with a provincial review, but the trial court found in favour of the province and in August 1997 Newfoundland issued permits to VBNC to proceed with the work. Before work could begin, more than 250 Innu and Inuit protested the court's decision by occupying VBNC's construction site and shutting down work for over a week. Once again, protests at the mine site attracted considerable media coverage. While the protest was under way, the Innu Nation and the LIA were appealing the trial court's decision. In September 1997, the Court of Appeal found the permits invalid and ruled that the company must go through a full environmental review process before developing the infrastructure (Innes 2002: 15; Lowe 1998: 72–5, 96–9).

VBNC officials in St John's had earlier assured the Innu Nation and the LIA that infrastructure work would not proceed without their approval (Lowe 1998: 73). VBNC's decision to proceed confirmed the view held by many Innu and Inuit that the company had little genuine interest in recognising their interests or in developing a positive relationship with them. In mid-1997, the Voisey's Bay Assessment Coordinator for the Innu Nation described the company's attitude to the traditional owners in the following terms: '(t)hey see the Innu and the Inuit as specks of dust to be brushed aside on the way to development' (Lowe 1998: 70). In Lowe's view, the decision to proceed with construction of the infrastructure was 'perhaps the single most damaging decision the company would take in its long struggle to bring Voisey's Bay into production' (1998: 72).

The EAP conducted hearings and received submissions during 1997, taking considerable time and effort to ensure that the Innu and Inuit were able to participate extensively in its deliberations. Both groups committed substantial resources to ensure that their members participated effectively, with attention being paid in particular to bringing to the Panel's notice traditional environmental knowledge and Aboriginal concerns about the project's potential cultural and social impacts. Heavy emphasis was placed on the need for land rights agreements and IBAs to be in place before mining commenced, and on the fact that if Voisey's Bay had a short life there would be little opportunity for Innu and Inuit to share in employment and business opportunities. A mine life of at least 25–30 years would be required for this to occur. This had important implications for the pace and scale of the Voisey's Bay project, because expected mine life would decline as the scale of the project increased (Innes 2002: 13–16).

VBNC submitted its EIS in December 1997 and a statement of Additional Information in June 1998 in response to comments on the EIS by intervenors and by the EAP. The company took the view that its project should not be delayed to allow completion of IBAs, which it regarded as 'discretionary arrangements', or of land claim negotiations, to which it was not a party (VBNC 1998; VBMMEAP 1998: Section 4.1).

VNBC's project proposal was based on a throughput of 20,000 tonnes of ore a day, and it argued that throughput of at least 15,000 tonnes a day was required to achieve economies of scale and make the project competitive (VBNC 1997; Bartek 1998). As part of its response to the EIS, the Innu Nation commissioned independent expert Tom Bartek to review economic-related issues. Bartek argued that the assumptions underlying VBNC's economic modelling were faulty in a number of respects, in particular in that the company did not take into account the downward pressure on nickel prices that would be exerted by a project on the scale it was planning. Bartek claimed that, for this and a number of other reasons, a project on a much smaller scale than that envisaged by VBNC could be economically viable (Bartek 1998).

The Voisey's Bay Mine and Mill Environmental Assessment Panel released its report on 1 April 1999. It included 107 recommendations related to a wide range of environmental, social, economic and cultural issues. It concluded that the project would not 'seriously harm the environment, or country foods and people's ability to harvest them', and should be allowed to proceed as long as its other recommendations were made part of the conditions of approval. Of particular significance in the current context is Recommendation 3, which stated that Canada and Newfoundland should conclude land claims agreements in principle with the Innu and Inuit before issuing project authorisations; and Recommendation 5, that 'Canada and the Province issue no Project authorizations until LIA and the Innu Nation have each concluded Impact and Benefits Agreements with VBNC' (VBMMEAP 1999).

The EAP's recommendations were not binding on Canada and Newfoundland. However, in making them, the Panel emphasised the significance of the Supreme Court of Canada December 1997 judgement in *Delgamuukw* v. *British Columbia*, which it interpreted as meaning that: 'The Crown's traditional position that development can proceed on Aboriginal title land in advance of arrangements for participation, consultation and compensation, if not also consent, is no longer tenable (VCMMEAP 1999: section 4.2.1). Conclusion of IBAs would be of great assistance to the Crown in meeting its obligations to ensure that participation, consultation, compensation and consent had all occurred.

The Panel also addressed Innu and Inuit concerns about project life, recommending that the province include conditions in VBNC's mining lease designed to ensure a mine life of at least 25–30 years.

Conclusion of agreements

In August 1999, both Newfoundland and Canada indicated that they would not accept the Panel recommendations on the requirement to conclude land claims agreements-in-principle and IBAs in advance of project approvals and would release VBNC from the environmental assessment process. On 5 August, Newfoundland issued the Voisey's Bay Nickel Company Limited Mine and Mill Undertaking Order, permitting VBNC to proceed with the project on condition that it abide by all commitments it had made during the environmental assessment process and obtain the licences, permits and other authorisations required by law. However Canada committed itself to the development of 'a project-specific environmental management mechanism for involving affected Aboriginal groups' and indicated that no federal approvals would be forthcoming until 'Canada is certain that appropriate consultation processes are in place and that the environmental management mechanism can be implemented' (cited in Innes 2002: 20).

On 2 September 1999, the Innu Nation initiated legal action in the Federal Court of Canada seeking a declaration that Canada had erred in releasing the project from the environmental assessment process prior to finalisation of land claims and IBAs, and that Canada had acted in bad faith by approving the project without allowing a proper opportunity to consult and negotiate with the Aboriginal groups (Innu Nation 1999).

Separate IBA negotiations between the VBNC and the Innu Nation and LIA had occurred on an intermittent basis over the period 1996–1998. By the end of 1998, 24 negotiating sessions of several days duration had been held with the Innu Nation and 25 sessions with the LIA. Successive negotiation agreements had been signed with both groups outlining issues for discussion, time frames and arrangements for funding the negotiations. By November 1998, many issues had been agreed upon on an 'in principle' basis, pending community ratification, but several substantial matters remained to be settled. For the Innu, these included the relationship between provisions of an IBA and any Innu land rights agreement, the level of funding support VNBC would provide for Innu training and business development programs, compensation for any wildlife and plant harvesting losses, and general financial payments. In relation to the latter, there was in principle agreement that an IBA would provide both fixed payments related to project milestones and variable payments based on economic performance. However, the formula for variable payments was not agreed (Innu Nation and VBNC 1998).

With the LIA, outstanding issues included the LIA's desire to include what VBNC described as 'onerous legal provisions' and inclusion of 'regulatory type matters' (VBNC 1998). The issue of winter shipping was a critical one for both sides. The LIA was opposed to any winter shipping, because of the potential impact of shipping channels on wildlife and on the ability of Inuit to travel safely across and hunt on sea ice. For VBNC, the ability to undertake winter shipping was indispensable to the success of the project.

A key issue for both the Aboriginal groups and VBNC involved the related issues of project scale and mine life. The Innu and Inuit wanted a much smaller mill with a throughput of about 6,000 tonnes a day, compared to VBNC's proposal for 15,000–20,000 tonnes a day. As mentioned above, VBNC argued that the larger scale of operations was essential to the economic viability of the project, a contention the Innu and Inuit did not accept.

On financial provisions, VBNC had reportedly tabled an offer similar in dollar terms to an IBA that Falconbridge had signed for the Raglan nickel mine in northern Quebec in 1995. However that project was much smaller than Voisey's Bay was expected to be, and the Innu and Inuit had rejected VBNC's offer, demanding instead payments to each group equivalent to at least to 3 per cent of Voisey's Bay net revenues (Lowe 1998: 90).

Further progress had been made by the end of 1999, but substantial differences still remained on some key issues, including financial matters, winter shipping and project scale. A major disagreement had also emerged between Newfoundland and Inco, in relation to processing of ore from Voisey's Bay. Convinced that Newfoundland's economic development had suffered in the past from export of its mineral and energy resources in raw form, the Province was adamant that a nickel smelter should be constructed in Newfoundland to process Voisey's Bay output and it refused to issue the final authorisations for the project in the absence of a commitment by Inco to construct a smelter. Inco was adamant that the requirement to build a smelter would render Voisey's Bay uneconomic. In early 2000, the two parties announced they were suspending their negotiations on a project development agreement. Inco shut down the Voisey's Bay project later in 2000, and negotiations on the IBAs and on an environmental agreement were suspended for some 18 months.

By the time they resumed, Newfoundland had reached two decisions that had important implications for the Innu and Inuit. The first, which was not initially made public but was communicated to VBNC, was that project approval would not be forthcoming unless IBAs were concluded with the Innu Nation and the LIA. This position was later formalised in stand-alone land claims agreements between the Province and the Innu and Inuit (see below). The second decision was that Newfoundland would only approve a project with a substantially lower throughput of ore than the 15,000–20,000 tonnes a day planned by VBNC. The precise timing and reasons for these decisions is unclear. It appears that both Newfoundland and Inco finally recognised that negotiation was likely to offer a far better outcome than litigation and protracted project delay.

In early 2001, and after a change in Newfoundland's political leadership, negotiations between Inco and Newfoundland resumed. In June 2001, negotiations resumed for an environmental agreement and for IBAs and negotiations occurred for the first time for land claims provisions dealing directly with Voisey's Bay. Different approaches had to be employed to resolve some key differences in the IBA negotiations. For example, Inuit negotiators were concerned that VBNC might perceive that their unwillingness to budge on the issue of winter shipping was a negotiating ploy, whereas in fact it was an issue on which they had been given no latitude to move. They were equally concerned that their own leadership did not appreciate how critical the issue was for VBNC and that failure to resolve it would threaten the project. They therefore organised a meeting between VBNC's senior executive and the LIA Board, allowing both sets of leaders to gain an appreciation of the absolute importance of the issue to the other and ultimately paving the way for a resolution (see below).

Inco and Newfoundland had hoped that agreements could be finalised in a matter of months, but it was June 2002 before the Innu and Inuit ratified IBAs with Inco and stand-alone land claims provisions dealing with Voisey's Bay. In July 2002, the Environmental Management Agreement was concluded, and in September 2002 a project development agreement was signed between Newfoundland, Inco and VBNC. This included a commitment by Inco/VBNC to build a smelter in Newfoundland by 2011, and to construct a mill at Voisey's Bay with an initial capacity of 6,000 tonnes a day (Newfoundland *et al.* 2002).

The various agreements involving the Innu and Inuit are outlined in the next section.

The agreements

The environmental management agreement

The parties to the Environmental Management Agreement (Newfoundland *et al.* 2002) are Newfoundland, Canada, the LIA and the Innu Nation. It is a legally binding agreement (Part 9.1) whose broad purpose is to provide for 'effective, responsible, comprehensive and coordinated Environmental Management' of the Voisey's Bay project by establishing a Board to give advice to the Parties and establishing the process by which the Board will provide that advice (Part 2).

The Agreement provides for the establishment of an Environmental Management Board consisting of eight members, two appointed by each party, and an independent chair appointed by written agreement of the parties. The Board provides advice to the parties on a wide range of environmental management issues and instruments, including on all applications by VBNC for permits, on its environmental protection plans, financial assurances required for development and closure plans, compliance with approved closure plans and the effectiveness of measures designed to mitigate adverse environmental effects. It also provides advice to the parties on the annual report prepared by VBNC describing its performance in delivering socio-economic benefits to the members of the Innu Nation and the LIA. The Board is required to give 'full consideration to Aboriginal knowledge, scientific information and the precautionary principle' in carrying out its responsibilities (Part 5). Board meetings are open to the public, and members of the public may make submissions to it (Part 7).

Responsible government Ministers shall not make any decision or take any action related to the environmental management of Voisey's Bay without first obtaining and considering a recommendation or report from the Board, except where an unplanned critical environmental situation arises and the delay in obtaining or considering the advice could exacerbate the situation, or where the Board fails to provide a recommendation or report in the relevant time frame (Part 5.9, 5.16–5.19). If they intend to significantly vary or reject a recommendation from the Board, Ministers shall meet the Board before taking a decision, after which they shall accept the recommendation or provide the Board with written reasons why they have rejected or varied it (5.10–5.11). These provisions do not derogate from a Minister's power to issue or refuse to issue a permit or to impose additional or different terms and conditions than those suggested by the Board (Part 5.15). However, they do ensure that the Minister can be made aware of Innu and Inuit concerns and preferences, and they do require the Minister to explain in writing decisions that do not have the support of the Board members nominated by the Aboriginal groups.

The agreement also provides for the establishment of a Technical Environmental Review Committee (TERC) to provide the Board with technical advice and information. Each of the parties may appoint individuals with scientific or technical expertise to the TERC. The Board is supported by a secretariat. Each party bears its own costs in relation to the agreement, but for the first five years Canada and Newfoundland jointly contribute $450,000 annually to the costs of the Board's secretariat and of the participation of the Innu Nation and the LIA (Parts 3.14, 4.8, 8).

Stand-alone land claims agreements

There are differences between the stand-alone land claims agreements negotiated with the LIA and the Innu Nation (Canada *et al.* 2002; Newfoundland and the Innu Nation 2002). However, they are broadly similar in scope and intent. They are legally binding contracts designed to allow the Voisey's Bay project to commence prior to the conclusion of lands claims negotiations between the Innu and Inuit and Canada and Newfoundland, while at the same time providing certain rights or protections to the Aboriginal parties. They provide that the Innu and Inuit will not exercise any aboriginal rights, titles and interests they may have in the Voisey's Bay Area (VBA) or in the Project's shipping zone, against any person (sections 2–4: section references are to the LIA agreement: Canada *et al.* 2002). The Province undertakes not to grant any fee simple or freehold title in the VBA to any person without the consent of the Inuit/Innu, that project infrastructure will not be used by third parties other than VBNC, and that no townsite will be established within the VBA (sections 5–9). The Innu and Inuit may enter and camp temporarily within the VBA to hunt, trap, fish and gather and for social and ceremonial purposes. With the consent of the Innu and Inuit under their IBAs, these activities can be subject to 'reasonable limitations' to ensure the safe and efficient operation of the project (sections 12–13).

The province undertakes not to issue archaeological permits without the consent of the LIA/Innu, and to transfer ownership of archaeological objects and human remains of Innu or Inuit origin discovered as a result of the project to the relevant group. The province also undertakes not to allow any known burial sites or sites of religious or spiritual significance to be disturbed without first consulting the LIA/Innu Nation. Rights under these provisions may not be exercised so as to 'interfere materially with the construction and operation of the Project' (sections 15–17).

Newfoundland agrees that the project shall not be permitted to commence until the Environmental Agreement and contractually binding IBAs have been executed (sections 20–21). It also undertakes to introduce legislation to ensure that 'reasonable' employment and training preferences for Innu/Inuit included in IBAs are lawful (sections 23–4). Canada and the Province undertake to consult with the Innu/Inuit about measures to protect and rehabilitate the environment in the VBA and prior to deciding any application for a permit or attaching any condition or making any amendment to a permit related to the project. Similarly, Canada undertakes to consult the Innu/Inuit in relation to issuance or approvals or other activities related to the project's shipping zone (sections 26–35).

Finally, the agreements provide that the Province will pay to each of the Innu Nation and the LIA 5 per cent of any revenues it receives from the project (section 36).

Impact and benefit agreements

The IBAs are confidential, but it has been possible to gain access to sufficient information to provide a detailed summary of their provisions. The Innu and Inuit agreements are similar in scope and content, and indeed they contain a 'most favoured nation' clause stating that if VBNC/Inco provides any benefits to one group that are, overall, of more value than what has been provided to the other, the second group is entitled to receive the same or equivalent benefits. However, there are some specific differences between the agreements, for example in the timing and structure of financial payments (though not in their overall quantum) and in that the LIA agreement includes provision for negotiation of an agreement on shipping through land-fast ice.

The agreements are legally binding contracts that come into force when ratified by the membership of the LIA/Innu Nation and on conclusion of the Interim Measures Agreements, the Environmental Management Agreement and the Newfoundland-VBNC-Inco Development Agreement. The IBAs are unusual in that they specify the scale of the planned project, which as mentioned earlier was of critical interest to the Innu and Inuit. The mill will process ore initially at a rate of about 6,000 tonnes per day and at a rate of up to 20,000 per day during any later underground phase, and mining is planned to occur over a period of at least 30 years.

The broad objectives of the agreements are to allow the project to proceed, to provide benefits to the Innu and Inuit, and to minimise negative impacts on the environment and on Inuit and Innu.

Economic benefits provided for or envisaged under the agreement fall under three broad categories: financial payments, employment and training opportunities and business opportunities. Financial payments consist of a specific dollar amount payable over the life of the project and, when the price of nickel rises above a specified 'base case' level, an additional amount related to the portion of VBNC's sales attributable to the higher nickel price. If VBNC shuts down the project for economic reasons, the annual payments continue for four years after closure.

Because payment of the specific amounts is structured in ways that take into account taxation and other factors affecting the Innu and Inuit and because of the inclusion of the variable payment related to future nickel prices, it is not possible to calculate future payments as a single *ad valorem* royalty equivalent. However, it is possible to offer a broad assessment of the financial package. Using the 'base case' metal prices employed by VBNC and the Aboriginal groups and expected metal output to calculate gross revenues, assuming an exchange rate of C$1 = US$0.75, and averaging the fixed payments under both agreements over 30 years, the latter are equivalent to a royalty of about 1.35 per cent. This figure is somewhat of an underestimate, as VBNC will not receive payment for all of the metal contained in concentrate and so the fixed payments would amount to a somewhat higher proportion of actual revenues (see Bartek 1998 for a full discussion). As nickel prices rise, the royalty equivalent figure rises substantially. I estimate, for example, that, with prices at 33 per cent above the base level, the royalty equivalent for fixed and variable payments combined is about 2.35 per cent. At nickel prices above US$6.00 a pound, I estimate the royalty equivalent figure at about 3.9 per cent. The 'base' figure of 1.35 per cent is well above the equivalent figure for Ekati (see Chapter 8), while royalty rates in the region of 2.0–4.0 per cent have few precedents in IBAs in Australia or Canada. In sum, the agreements represent a strong financial outcome for the Innu and Inuit.

The goals of the employment and training provisions are to maximise Innu and Inuit employment at all levels of the project workforce and to promote equality of Innu and Inuit men and women. 'Minimum' requirements and 'objectives' for combined Innu/Inuit employment are established for the construction phase (25 per cent minimum and an objective of 40 per cent) and for the end of year one of commercial production and during the remainder of the project (25 per cent minimum and an objective of 50 per cent). It is stated that these figures are not 'quotas' and shall not be legally enforceable. The company undertakes to work with the LIA and the Innu Nation to identify and remove any barriers to the employment and advancement of Inuit and Innu, particularly Innu and Inuit women.

To assist in achieving these broad goals, a wide range of education, recruitment, training and employment initiatives are provided for. These include measures to promote the value and importance of good education, for instance achievement awards in schools and a scholarship trust for post-secondary education; pre-employment training for Innu and Inuit recruits; and a construction training program with a specified budget and number of trainees. Innu or Inuit completing the training program are accorded a preference for employment during construction and production. The company undertakes to hire one Innu person and one Inuk (singular of Inuit) to work as employment coordinators in the company's human resources department, and the employment coordinators are involved in each step of the company's recruitment and hiring processes. To assist in identifying suitable recruits, the company and the Innu/Inuit will establish a master database covering all of the Innu and Inuit communities and including details of individuals potentially interested in obtaining employment. VNBC undertakes to hire a specific number of Innu and Inuit trainees for positions that may lead to supervisory and management roles. The company will report on a quarterly basis on the number of Innu/Inuit hired, and specifically on the number of women hired.

The agreement also includes provisions designed to make the workplace conducive to effective operation of the project and respectful of Innu and Inuit culture and values. These include rotation schedules and a cultural leave policy that respect the importance of traditional activities; provision for job-sharing to facilitate the practice of traditional activities; evaluation of all potential employees for the sensitivity to and respect for intercultural relations; and cross-cultural and gender sensitivity training for the project workforce. The agreements also prohibit workers from bringing firearms on site and from hunting, fishing or trapping during their employment rotation. Alcohol and non-medical drugs are banned from the mine site.

VBNC shall require contractors to provide training programs for Innu/Inuit and shall evaluate bids for contracts on the basis of whether an appropriate amount has been provided for such training. All tender documents shall specify that the evaluation of bids for contracts will include an assessment of the proportion of Inuit/Innu men and women to be employed during the contract.

Each year the company and the Innu/Inuit will undertake a comprehensive review of the employment objectives including barriers to employment and actions to be taken to overcome these.

The employment and training provisions are extensive and detailed, addressing each stage of the employment process from education, through identification of potential employees, recruitment, training, creating an environment conducive to retention of Innu and Inuit workers, and career progression into supervisory and managerial roles. They set clear goals to be achieved within specific time frames, though the targets established are not legally enforceable. They also provide for the application of substantial resources, for instance to the construction training program and through the ongoing funding of two employment coordinators. They display none of the ambiguous wording and conditionality that, as noted earlier, characterise the Ekati agreements.

The business development provisions seek to maximise Inuit and Innu participation in business opportunities associated with Voisey's Bay and to assist with the development of business skills amongst the Innu and Inuit. The provisions are based on the concept of Innu or Inuit businesses, that is entities at least 51 per cent owned and controlled by Innu or Inuit or which have a significant percentage of Inuit/Innu employees and significant Innu/Inuit ownership and control. As with employment, 'minimum requirements' and 'objectives' are set for the share of specified goods and services that Innu/Inuit businesses are expected to provide during construction and operations. In this case also, the figures involved do not represent 'quotas' and are not legally enforceable.

Initiatives designed to support Innu/Inuit businesses in pursuing contract opportunities include negotiation of contracts with qualified Innu or Inuit businesses, rather than an open tender process; a repayable loan of $10 million by VBNC to set up revolving loan funds for Innu and Inuit businesses; a simplified contract process for contracts up to $250,000 to assist smaller businesses; and the establishment of a Business Development Committee, consisting of two members nominated by each of VBNC, the LIA and the Innu Nation. The company shall inform contract bidders that the participation of Inuit and Innu businesses is an important consideration in the evaluation of tender bids and the awarding of contracts.

The IBAs contain provisions in relation to environmental protection that are in my experience unique, by providing for the creation of monitoring partnerships between VBNC and the LIA and the Innu Nation. These require that the Aboriginal groups be involved in all phases of the development of a comprehensive monitoring program for the project, the integration of traditional knowledge into the monitoring program, Inuit/Innu participation in all biophysical monitoring activities of interest to them, and an annual review of the company's management plans related to the monitoring program and its emergency response and contingency plans. The company undertakes to fund full-time Aboriginal environmental monitors who are employees of LIA and the Innu Nation, for a period of six years. One monitor from each group is present on site at all times.

Upon permanent closure of the project, VBNC undertakes to prepare a reclamation plan in consultation with the Innu/Inuit and to restore the Voisey's Bay area as close to its initial state as possible. The final status of all project infrastructure is to be negotiated with the Innu/Inuit as well as relevant government authorities.

Innu or Inuit heritage resources (such as artefacts or burial sites) shall not be disturbed without the consent of the LIA/IN. Each IBA provides for an immediate payment of $1 million to provide compensation for negative impact on harvesting caused by the project, and for additional compensation for damage resulting from any unplanned events such as a major shipping accident. Inuit and Innu are allowed access to the Voisey's Bay area for harvesting and 'reasonable access' to infrastructure and facilities including the airstrip, roads, docks and port facilities.

The Inuit IBA has extensive provisions dealing with project shipping, and requires the negotiation of a shipping protocol to cover the construction phase and a shipping agreement for the operation phase. The IBA sets out a range of issues that will be addressed in the Shipping Agreement, and states that VBNC will pay the LIA's costs in negotiating it. VBNC undertakes to conduct winter shipping only to a single point, Edward's Cove, and also to conduct all shipping through this access point during construction. The project must be designed so that fuel shipments through land-fast ice must not be required, and the number of shipments through land-fast ice must be minimised.

Both IBAs establish joint committees to oversee implementation of the agreements. They consist of two members nominated by each of VBNC and the LIA/Innu Nation. Their role is to monitor and report on the effectiveness of the implementation of the IBAs, to develop action plans related to their major provisions, and to regularly review and modify these plans if necessary. The chief executive officer of VBNC and the President of Innu Nation/LIA will meet twice a year to review implementation of the agreement. The company and the LIA/Innu Nation undertake to each appoint an IBA coordinator to oversee the daily administration of the agreements, under the supervision of the joint committees. While the IBAs do not nominate monetary amounts that are explicitly designated for implementation, the appointment of the IBA co-ordinators and VBNC's funding of full time

Innu and Inuit employment and training coordinators and environmental monitors represents substantial support for implementing key areas of the agreements.

Assessing and explaining outcomes

In combination, these agreements represent a strongly positive outcome for Innu and Inuit from their negotiations with the project proponent and government. In each of the major areas they address (financial payments, employment and training, business development, environmental management, rights and interests in land, and implementation) they represent positive outcomes in terms of the evaluative criteria discussed in Chapter 4.

In relation to employment and training and business development, the fact that targets for Innu/Inuit involvement are not legally enforceable does detract from the outcome to some extent, but on the other hand the measures to promote Innu/Inuit employment are comprehensive, based on clear goals and specific time frames, and involve application of substantial resources by VBNC. Their efficacy is indicated by the fact that the initial production workforce for the mine exceeds the 50 per cent Innu/Inuit combined employment objective in the IBAs, while in excess of $250M of contracts were awarded to Innu and Inuit businesses during the construction phase (pers. comm. Innu Nation Advisor, 4 November 2005).

In relation to environmental management, a key issue for the Innu and Inuit, the agreements represent one of the strongest outcomes gained by Aboriginal people from any comparable negotiation in Australia or Canada. The Environmental Management Agreement combined with the relevant provisions of the Interim Measures Agreements and the IBAs (including the Inuit-VBNC Shipping Agreement, signed in March 2005) provide the Innu and Inuit with a substantial role in environmental decision-making and a major and direct role in environmental monitoring and management. For the first 5–6 years of the agreements, VBNC, Canada and Newfoundland provide the Innu and Inuit with substantial, dedicated funding to support their participation. The Innu and Inuit were also able to achieve a key goal by reducing project scale and extending mine life, assisting both to reduce environmental impacts and to increase their ability to take advantage of economic opportunities.

From another perspective, the agreements address in a substantial manner virtually all of the concerns and aspirations raised by Innu with the Innu Nation Task Force on Mining Activities.

The Innu and Inuit provide their consent for the Voisey's Bay project and undertake not to exercise their Aboriginal rights in ways that might interfere with project development. However the Crown (and Inco in the IBAs) acknowledges the existence of those rights and the ability of the Innu/Inuit to continue to exercise them, for example by harvesting wildlife. The Interim Measures Agreements prevent the alienation of land within the area without the consent of the Innu/Inuit. The agreements do not place limitations on the Inuit/Innu in exercising their rights under general legislation.

How can we explain this outcome? Key factors, which are interlinked, relate to the nature of the project itself and of Inco's investment in it; to the character, behaviour and strategies of the Innu and Inuit; to the prevailing legal and regulatory regimes; and to changes in provincial government policy in the later stages of negotiation.

Voisey's Bay is a rich and large ore body and investors and governments were very anxious to see it developed. Two things followed. First, any credible threat by the Innu and Inuit to stop or slow its development would be taken seriously. Second, the non-Aboriginal parties would be prepared to put substantial financial benefits on the negotiating table and make considerable efforts to meet the non-financial demands of the Innu/Inuit in order to secure their support for the project. Inco's decision to pay C\$4.3 billion for Voisey's Bay added another dimension to this situation. The company deferred negotiations when they were not yielding the desired outcome, indicating that it was not prepared to accept agreement at any price. However it would have been enormously difficult for Inco to 'walk away' from Voisey's Bay and fail to generate a return on its very substantial investment (see for example Stueck 2004; Lowe 1998: 59, 94). It was therefore under considerable pressure to achieve negotiated agreements, and this strengthened the position of the Innu and Inuit.

However, the Innu and Inuit needed to take advantage of the potential bargaining power provided by this favourable combination of geology and corporate imperatives. They did so, and also further enhanced their bargaining position, in a number of ways. The Innu in particular left no doubt as to their willingness to resort to direct action if companies or governments sought to ignore them or deny their aspirations. By 1997, it was clear to all concerned that a failure to reach agreement with the Innu and Inuit would result in physical disruption of any attempt to proceed with development of Voisey's Bay. While their opposition might eventually be overcome, the potential delays and adverse publicity associated with direct action created a major incentive for Inco and Newfoundland to achieve a negotiated outcome.

In addition, the Inuit and Innu had shown their capacity to act together in using the courts to prevent activities they had not agreed to. The successful Court of Appeal ruling that permits issued to VBNC for its 'advanced exploration infrastructure' were invalid was particularly important. More generally, almost every major action or decision taken by VBNC or government that the Innu or Inuit opposed was followed either by direct action or by court action.

When the Supreme Court's *Delgamuuk* decision strengthened the requirements for government to consult with Aboriginal peoples affected by their proposed actions, Newfoundland would have been aware that the Innu/Inuit stood a strong chance of using the courts to create significant project delays. In a reversal of the policy position announced after release of the Environmental Review Panel's report, the Province imposed a requirement that IBAs be concluded before it would allow Voisey's Bay to proceed. This further reinforced the negotiating position of the Innu and Inuit in their dealings with VBNC. *Delgamuuk* also influenced the recommendations of the EAP, which lent support to the position of the Innu and Inuit by recommending that development not be allowed to proceed until IBAs and land claims agreement-in-principle were in place. Thus changes in the wider legal framework served to reinforce the Innu/Inuit negotiating position. As Lowe commented, 'In theory Inco might try to go ahead [with Voisey's Bay], but it would undoubtedly be met with Aboriginal injunctions that could tie the project up for years, even decades' (1998: 134).

In this way, the Innu and Inuit effectively countered the adverse effects on their negotiating position of the fact that their land claims were not settled and that, as a result, their consent for development of Voisey's Bay was not required under Canadian law. They asserted the position, from their very first response to DFRL in 1994, that their consent *was* required, and for eight years they never wavered in supporting this assertion through political action, litigation and negotiation.

The ability of the Innu and Inuit to work together was critical. Any substantial division between them would have undermined the Aboriginal negotiating position. While their overlapping land claims created the potential for conflict, there was an underlying commonality of interests and of action based on a mutual acceptance that each had legitimate interests in the Voisey's Bay region. This acceptance was reflected in the understanding between Innu and Inuit elders referred to earlier, and also in the attitudes of respondents to the Innu Task Force on Mining Activities. As one Innu elder stated:

> I think the Innu Nation and the LIA should work together. In the past we have shared the land with the Inuit. We used to hunt together and grew up together. I think it is very important that we work together. If we work together we should have a strong voice.
> (Innu Nation Task Force on Mining Activities 1996: 78)

In working together, the Inuit and Innu were able to devise a division of labour (especially in relation to environmental issues) that allowed an efficient use of available resources. Their good working relationship also allowed extensive information sharing, especially during the final stages of the IBA negotiations, negating any possibility that the two groups might be played off against each other and allowing each to capitalise on gains made by the other. This situation stands in marked contrast to Bielawski's description of relations between the Dogrib Treaty 11 and Akaitcho Treaty 8 in the final stages of their negotiations with BHP (see Chapter 8).

The way in which the Innu and Inuit planned for and undertook negotiations was also important. The Task Force on Mining Activities and the range of similar processes undertaken by the LIA and the TIA provided the Innu Nation and the LIA with clear and comprehensive goals to pursue in the negotiations. Both groups were able to make good use of technical expertise, as for example when the Innu Nation's technical expert questioned Inco's economic rationale for basing its project design on a throughput of 20,000 tonnes a day.

This raises a wider point. Voisey's Bay was the first major mining project dealt with by the LIA or the Innu Nation, but both were engaged in extensive negotiations in a range of forums during the 1990s, including the land claims negotiations, the MoU for the Environmental Review, and discussions in relation to service provision with Canada and Newfoundland. As the decade progressed, they were building up substantial experience and skills in negotiation, reflected for instance in the strategic use of litigation as well as in the competent application of technical expertise. This pattern is also evident in the experience of individual negotiators, with the LIA's chief negotiator for the IBA discussions during 2001–2002, for instance, having previously worked as chief negotiator on the LIA land claims.

The LIA and the Innu Nation lacked access to resources on the scale enjoyed by Inco or Newfoundland and at times felt overwhelmed by the demands generated by Voisey's Bay, the subsequent staking boom and by land claims negotiations (pers comm. Innu Nation Adviser, 22 April 2005). However, both organisations had sufficient funds to undertake key tasks, derived for instance from intervenor funding provided by the EAP and from negotiation funding provided by VBNC. On a more basic level, the Innu and Inuit both had a single, functioning, well-established organisation that was able to represent their interests throughout the period from the discovery of Voisey's Bay to conclusion of the IBAs and other agreements. The timing of negotiations was important in allowing the Innu Nation and the LIA to manage multiple demands on their limited resources. For example Inco's withdrawal from negotiations in 2001–2002 provided some breathing space and an opportunity to focus on land claims negotiations. Had multiple negotiations been compressed into a shorter time frame, the pressure on human and organisational resources might have become unsustainable.

The Innu and Inuit also benefited from the political support of non-Indigenous groups. For example a number of NGOs formed the Voisey's Bay/Innu Rights Coalition in January 1997, which included supporters from the Anglican Church, the Toronto Catholic Workers Movement, the Canadian Environmental Defence Fund, Citizens for Public Justice and the Voice of Women for Peace. In April 1997, the Coalition attended Inco's annual shareholders' meeting in Toronto, forming a picket outside and distributing leaflets in the meeting to increase shareholder awareness of Innu and Inuit claims to Voisey's Bay and their concerns about Inco's project (Lowe 1998: 70, 124). Such support was important in increasing media coverage and public awareness of Innu/Inuit perspectives on Voisey's Bay and of Innu/Inuit protests and legal actions and the factors underlying them. It also assisted in ensuring that a comprehensive environmental assessment would be undertaken with appropriate terms of reference.

It can be argued that Inco's corporate culture and history adversely affected its negotiating position by reducing its ability to respond appropriately to the Inuit and Innu. According to Lowe, in the 1990s Inco and its senior management 'failed to recognize and respond to most of the changes that lay outside the narrow ambit of their business world and therefore of their own experience'. Lowe attributes to this failure Inco's inability to respond to the clearly enunciated demands and warnings of the Innu and Inuit, with whom Inco needed to develop partnerships if Voisey's Bay was to proceed (1998: 191–2). As mentioned earlier, Inco certainly lacked experience in dealing with Aboriginal groups in the contemporary legal and political context, which may explain for instance its attempts to push ahead with infrastructure development over the strong opposition of the Innu and Inuit. The company not only failed in its attempt, it further strengthened the resolve and unity of the Innu and Inuit and provided then with an opportunity to demonstrate their political power and build political support.

References

Ali, S. (2003) *Mining, the Environment and Indigenous Development Conflicts*, Tucson: University of Arizona Press.

Archibald, L. and Crnkovich, M. (1999) *If Gender Mattered: A Case Study of Inuit Women, Land Claims and the Voisey's Bay Nickel Project*, Ottawa: Status of Women Canada.

Bartek, T. 1998. *Voisey's Bay Nickel Mine – Mill Project Environmental Impact Statement: A Critique of Economic Related Issues, Report to the Innu Nation*, Ottawa.

Canada, Newfoundland and the Labrador Inuit Association (2002) *The Voisey's Bay Interim Measures Agreement*.

CHRC (Canadian Human Rights Commission) (2002) *Report to the Canadian Human Rights Commission on the Treatment of the Innu of Labrador by the Government of Canada*, Online. Available http://caid.ca/InnuRepHRC2002.pdf.

Gray, J. (1996) 'Labrador's natives determined to reap Voisey's riches', *Toronto Globe and Mail*, 17 February.

Innes, L. (2001) 'Staking Claims: Innu Rights and Mining Claims at Voisey's Bay', *Cultural Survival Quarterly*, 25(1): 12–16.

Innes, L. (2002) *The Voisey's Bay Project*, unpublished paper, Faculty of Law, University of Victoria.

Innu Nation (1999) *Innu Nation Mounts Court Challenge over Voisey's Bay Project*, Press Release, 3 September.

Innu Nation Task Force on Mining Activities (1996) *Ntesinan Nteshiniminan Nteniunan: Between a Rock and a Hard Place*, Sheshatshiu: Innu Nation.

Innu Nation and VBNC (1998) *Status of Impact Benefit Agreement Negotiations*, Joint Submission to the Voisey's Bay Mine and Mill Environmental Assessment Panel, November.

LIA (Labrador Inuit Association) (n.d.) *Seeing the Land is Seeing Ourselves*, Nain: LIA.

Lowe, M. (1998) *Premature Bonanza: Standoff at Voisey's Bay*, Ontario: Between the Lines.

Newfoundland and the Innu Nation (2002) *Memorandum of Agreement Concerning the Voisey's Bay Project.* Online. Available www.laa.gov.nl.ca/laa/land_claims/MemorandumAgreement.pdf.

Newfoundland, VBNC and Inco (2002) *Voisey's Bay Development Agreement*, Online. Available www.nr.gov.nl.ca/nr/royalties/legal.pdf

Stueck, W. (2004) 'Voisey's Bay at Last Getting off the Ground', *Globe and Mail*, 17 June.

VBMMEAP (Voisey's Bay Mine and Mill Environmental Assessment Panel) (1999) *Voisey's Bay Mine and Mill Environmental Assessment Panel Report*, Online. Available www.ceaa-acee.gc.ca/default.asp?lang=En&xml=0a571a1a-84cd-496b-969e-7cf9cbea16ae.

VBNC (Voisey's Bay Nickel Company Ltd) (1997) *Voisey's Bay Mine/Mill Project Environmental Impact Statement*, St John's: VBNC.

VBNC (1998) *Presentation to Voisey's Bay Mine/Mill Project Environmental Assessment Panel: General Session IBAs and Land Claims*, St John's: VBNC.

VBNC (2005) *Project Overview*, St John's: VBNC.

Williamson, T. (1997) *From Sina to Sikujaluk: Our footprint*, Main: LIA.

10 Conclusion

Explaining and improving negotiation outcomes

Structure, agency and negotiation outcomes

This book set out to explain outcomes from real-world negotiations between mining companies and Aboriginal peoples, and in doing so assist Aboriginal people to achieve more positive results from mineral development on their ancestral lands. In the process, it sought to contribute to our understanding of how negotiation outcomes more generally can be identified, evaluated and explained.

The existing research literature on negotiation proved of limited utility in providing appropriate analytical frameworks. The heavy use of experimental approaches and the related emphasis on the individual as the unit of analysis means that negotiation outcomes are often equated with negotiation behaviour, and attention focuses heavily on the latter. However, studies of actual negotiations make it clear that negotiator behaviour is only one component in explaining outcomes. In addition, the conditions under which negotiation research is undertaken often bear little relationship to those in which actual negotiations occur, and key issues such as relationships between negotiators are often downplayed or ignored. More broadly, there is a strong tendency in the literature to focus on factors internal to negotiation processes (negotiator behaviour, the sequence and character of offers and counter-offers, negotiator access to information, the cultural background of negotiators), and to pay little attention to wider, structural factors that shape the context in which individual negotiations occur. There are few attempts, in particular, to integrate analysis of 'internal' and 'external' factors in a coherent way so as to explain outcomes.

Some negotiation studies do focus on the real world and recognise the need to take into account wider structural influences as well as factors internal to the negotiation process. However, many of these studies encounter another problem in that they lack explicit, robust and credible criteria against which to assess negotiation outcomes. The criteria widely used in the literature either focus on an individual negotiator's profit and so are inadequate in addressing negotiations involving communities, corporations and the state, or are conceptually flawed. An example of the latter is the focus on achievement of agreement. Given imbalances of power between negotiators, the fact of agreement may say little about whether negotiations have been 'successful' for the less powerful party or indeed in the longer term for either party (see Chapter 2). In the absence of criteria to determine whether or not negotiations have been successful, it is impossible to identify the causes of success or failure.

To address the issue of evaluating negotiation outcomes, I have adopted an approach that involves establishing the interests of a negotiation party (in this case Aboriginal peoples) in relation to key negotiation issues and then developing explicit criteria for gauging negotiation outcomes in relation to these issues. At a conceptual level, there are certainly issues about accurately identifying 'interests' in negotiations (see Chapter 2). However, in practice there is a great deal of relevant information available from data on the social and economic circumstances of Aboriginal peoples in Australia and Canada, from the pattern of issues they have pursued at the negotiating table, and from the literature that analyses the impact of large-scale mineral development on Indigenous societies. On the basis of this information, seven key issues, and Aboriginal interests in relation to these issues, were identified. An appropriate scale was developed for evaluating outcome of agreements in relation to each issue (see Chapter 4). A similar approach could be applied to negotiations in other areas, for example those involving labour and management over working conditions, trade negotiations between governments, and commercial negotiations between firms.

This approach produces criteria for evaluating negotiation processes and outcomes that are explicit, empirically verifiable and capable of being applied in practice, as demonstrated by their use in Chapter 5 to evaluate agreements emerging from 45 negotiations between Aboriginal peoples and mining companies in Australia. It thus provides a solution to one of the major problems with the existing negotiation literature, which is that the evaluative criteria used in many studies are implicit, self-referencing and not amenable to external verification, or difficult or impossible to apply in the real world (see Chapter 2).

A number of important points emerged from the analysis of agreements in Chapter 5. One relates to causality. Perhaps the strongest argument in favour of an experimental approach to negotiation research is that it can assist in establishing causality, and so in allowing explanation, by analysing interactions between a limited number of variables in a 'controlled' environment. However, Chapter 5 demonstrates that where real-world negotiation outcomes are characterised by differences on a range of variables, comparing a substantial number of negotiations can allow important conclusions about the salience or lack of salience of specific causal factors.

For example, the analysis of 45 agreements shows that 'weak' or 'strong' negotiation outcomes do not, at a broad level, reflect trade-offs made by Aboriginal parties between outcomes on different issues within individual negotiations. If this were the case, we would typically find a mix of 'weak' and 'strong' outcomes on individual issues from most negotiations. In fact we find the opposite. With few exceptions, individual agreements tend to be strong across all or most issues, or weak across all issues.

Comparing a large number of negotiations allows clear conclusions regarding other potential explanations for the variance in outcomes. Neither the scale of the mining project involved, the type of company concerned, corporate policies, or the timing of negotiations and agreements can explain overall negotiation outcomes. On the other hand the analysis clearly demonstrates the strong impact of prevailing legislative frameworks on negotiation outcomes, and in particular the negative effects of the *Native Title Act* on outcomes for Aboriginal people. A closer analysis of relevant provisions of the Act reveals the nature of the mechanisms at work. These serve to create a *structural* inequality in negotiating positions by generating differential pressures and incentives on Aboriginal groups and mining companies, creating an unattractive BATNA for the former and a very attractive BATNA for the latter.

Further comparative analysis reveals that this causal link, while powerful, need not be determinative. A number of agreements strongly favourable to Aboriginal interests have been negotiated pursuant to the NTA, while some groups that lack even the minimal legal rights offered by the NTA have also been able to secure favourable outcomes. A spatial analysis of these and other 'strong' outcomes for Aboriginal people indicated the existence of another powerful, causal factor. This involves the influence of regional Aboriginal land organisations in north Australia which, working alongside individual Aboriginal communities, have been able both to negate the structural disadvantage created by the NTA, and to engage in productive negotiations with mining companies even where there has been no legal requirement on the latter to negotiate. The fact that many of the 'strong' agreements are accounted for by 'clusters' of negotiations occurring close together in space and time indicates that outcomes have also been affected by learning processes within individual regional organisations, with a succession of negotiations over short periods allowing an accumulation of relevant skills and experience.

The impact of structural and institutional factors external to individual negotiation processes is indicated by the fact that not one 'strong' agreement is found outside regions where legislation or/and powerful regional land organisations create structural distributions of power that are more favourable to Aboriginal negotiators. If factors 'internal' to specific negotiations were of similar importance, one would certainly expect to find a significant number of strong agreements in other regions. This finding does not mean that individual negotiation processes or the 'performance' of negotiators are unimportant. As the case studies reveal, these factors may either reinforce, or moderate, the impact of broader structural and organisational forces and so are certainly worthy of attention. But the findings strongly suggest that the current heavy emphasis in the literature on negotiator behaviour and more broadly on factors internal to negotiation processes is misplaced. They also highlight the importance of combining analysis of factors internal to and external to the negotiation process.

A possible defence of existing approaches to negotiation research is that structural and institutional factors are not easily amenable to change, whereas negotiator behaviour and other 'internal' factors such as the sequencing of offers and provision or withholding of information are so amenable. Two points should be made here. First, the evidence from 45 negotiations presented in Chapter 5 strongly suggests that, in the absence of structural change, even the adoption of optimal 'internal' negotiation approaches will have effects on outcomes that, while perhaps not insignificant, will be limited. Second, the operation of institutional and structural factors can be modified, even if this does take time. Neither regional land councils, nor effective working relationships between themselves and individual Aboriginal communities, appeared out of thin air. The institutions were created and relationships developed by Aboriginal people *precisely because* they understood that in their absence structural factors would operate so as to seriously disadvantage them in dealing with mining companies. But here also the wider context for individual negotiations is critical. Aboriginal people in north Australia have been better placed to exercise agency and modify the impact of structural factors because of the nature of their contact history with settler society and, in particular, because they were not systematically dispossessed of, or moved away from, their ancestral estates (see Chapter 3).

The Australian and Canadian case studies provide specific illustrations of the impact of wider institutional and structural factors, but also of the capacity of Aboriginal groups to counter or mitigate that impact. For instance, important structural limitations reduced the Western Cape York Aboriginal Community's bargaining power and forced it to relinquish some key demands. These limitations included an historical context in which its rights and interests were ignored, and a legal regime in the form of the High Court's *Mabo* and *Wik* decisions and the *Native Title Act*, which validated Comalco's interests and ensured it could continue to mine bauxite without legal hindrance. The Aboriginal groups affected by the Ekati project were disadvantaged by the fact that their land claims had yet to be resolved and that, as a result, BHP had no legal obligation to conclude agreements with them. The Innu and Inuit were in the same situation, but they employed direct action and legal challenges to enhance their bargaining power. They were also assisted by Canada's Supreme Court, whose decisions regarding government obligations to consult have increased the leverage of Aboriginal groups in Canada when faced with activities that affect their Aboriginal rights. These developments ultimately led to the *Interim Measures Agreements* with Canada and Newfoundland, and the requirement that IBAs be concluded before the Voisey's Bay project could proceed. This marked the effective reversal of the structural weakness in bargaining power resulting from the absence of settled land claims, highlighting the point that structural factors are not immune from change.

The case studies: specific explanations for outcomes

The role of the Innu Nation and the LIA in Voisey's Bay and of the CYLC in the Comalco negotiations illustrate the importance of regional institutional arrangements for outcomes from negotiations. For instance the CYLC played a key role in providing the Aboriginal Community with access to technical expertise and to government decision-makers, access not available to traditional owners or individual communities. A case in point involved the Land Council's ability to secure substantial funds from ATSIC to sustain the negotiation effort and continue to pursue a more favourable outcome, at a time when corporate funding was exhausted and conclusion of an agreement would have required the Aboriginal community to give ground on issues of fundamental importance. The ACI–QLC negotiations provided a further illustration of the importance of institutional frameworks. The QLC's strong and positive relationship with the original Native Title Representative Body for South-East Queensland allowed it to help build its own capacity and expertise. This was important, for example, in allowing it to insist on undertaking the social impact assessment in relation to ACI's original proposals and to force a substantial amendment of that proposal to move mining further away from Brown Lake, a place of great cultural significance to the Quandamooka people. On the other hand, the QLC's inability to establish a positive and supportive relationship with a new regional organisation, the QSRB, undermined its ability to successfully prosecute negotiations with ACI and the Queensland government.

The case studies reveal starkly the enormous impact on negotiation outcomes of internal political process within Aboriginal 'communities'. This raises a wider issue regarding the nature of the entity that is involved in negotiations. As Putnam (1994) notes, much of the literature assumes that negotiations are carried out by individuals representing single interests (in experimental settings, their own interests). In fact many real world negotiations involve groups that represent multiple parties. Sitting behind negotiators are complex and diverse groups and organisations, and their actions can have a major bearing on outcomes. This results not only from the fact that negotiators have a 'constituency' that will be more or less active in directing them (Sebenius 2013). The particular character of the constituency, its composition and the nature of relationships between different components of it, and the question of whether there is in fact one constituency or many, can all have a major effect on outcomes.

This is illustrated by the issue of unity and cooperation (or in some cases the lack of it) among the various components of the Aboriginal 'constituencies' for the case study negotiations. It should be stressed that the issue here is not one of diversity or complexity. The Aboriginal peoples affected by the case study projects were all characterised by diversity, by a range of different historical, linguistic and cultural backgrounds, and by different priorities regarding economic development opportunities and protection of culture and environment. However, not all of the groups displayed a similar capacity to *manage* difference and diversity in a way that helped them achieve their objectives in negotiations.

The Innu and Inuit, despite their traditional differences, exchanged information at key points in the negotiation, supported each other in undertaking direct action and legal challenges, and agreed a 'division of labour' in taking responsibility for certain negotiation issues. It is important to remember in this regard the agreement reached by elders of both groups, prior to the discovery of Voisey's Bay, to recognise each other's interests in the area in which their claims overlapped. The Western Cape York Aboriginal Community, consisting of 11 traditional owner groups and descendants of people from other regions of Queensland brought to the Mapoon and Napranum missions in earlier decades, managed to maintain their solidarity even when negotiations were deadlocked, a key factor in explaining their ability to secure many of their key goals.

The Aboriginal groups affected by the Ekati mine acted separately in relation to the IBA negotiations and did not share information at key points. One result was that the Akaitcho feared the Dogrib would do a deal with BHP and leave the Akaitcho without an agreement, placing the Akaitcho under considerable pressure to accede to BHP's demands. Thus BHP's ability to negotiate separately with Aboriginal groups that were not communicating about the negotiations strengthened the company's bargaining position, and prevented favourable clauses negotiated by one group from being used as precedents by other groups. In contrast the Innu and Inuit, working closely together as the negotiations moved to a conclusion, were able to build on each other's successes. The NWT groups were able to cooperate in relation to the Environmental Agreement and BHP's Water Licence, and this helps explain the difference in outcomes in relation to environmental issues and the IBAs (see Chapter 8). The Quandamooka native title group, ironically perhaps the least heterogeneous of the case study Aboriginal 'constituencies', was unable to apply even the most basic level of unity or common purpose to negotiations, and suffered a disastrous outcome from the negotiations as a result.

The reasons for this lack of unity and purpose are instructive. It was due at least in part to the activities of Queensland Government officials, who encouraged a dissident group to disrupt and ultimately undermine the QLC's negotiating effort, in pursuit of their goal of ensuring that ACI could exploit MLA 7064 rather than having to mine ML 1032. Government actions, or inactions, had a major influence in other ways. It was Government that suggested to ACI that it relinquish the southern portion of MLA 7064, undermining the unity of purpose that had characterised the community's initial reaction to ACI's proposal because of the proximity of the southern portion of the lease application to the highly significant Brown Lake. Critically, Government refused to provide the QLC with the time and resources that were required for a thorough consultation exercise that might have allowed the Aboriginal community to achieve a consensus regarding the approach it should adopt in negotiations. By linking its willingness to progress the Quandamooka native title claim to the QLC's approval for MLA 7064, Queensland severely limited the options facing the QLC. Particularly when a judicial decision deprived the QLC of the ability to invoke the RTN provisions of the *Native Title Act*, it had little choice but to become involved in negotiations with ACI, despite the Government's failure to meet the preconditions the QLC had set for doing so. The QLC was thus immediately in a weak bargaining position and unlikely to secure a positive outcome from negotiations.

More generally, it could be argued that the QLC was seriously disadvantaged by having to engage in a tripartite negotiation in which the other two parties had common interests that they pursued jointly. This raises the broader issue of the role of government in negotiations between mining companies and Aboriginal peoples. What light do the other case studies cast on this issue? Government did not play as direct a role in the other negotiations, though it certainly did have an impact in all three. In relation to Ekati, both Canada and the GNWT made their support for the project very clear, and were unwilling to consider delaying the project until land claims were settled. This weakened the negotiating position of the Aboriginal parties. Canada did insist on substantial progress on IBAs and the EA within 60 days as a condition for granting project approvals, but, on the other hand, amended BHP's land use permit to allow construction to begin during the 60-day period, reducing the pressure on BHP to quickly reach agreement. The time pressure on the Aboriginal parties caused problems for Akaitcho Treaty 8 in particular in the IBA negotiations, and Aboriginal leaders believe it further weakened their negotiating position, especially in a situation where they had limited resources and were required to participate simultaneously in multiple negotiation and regulatory processes. However, Canada's position did create the opportunity for the Aboriginal groups to achieve a significant role in environmental management through the Environmental Agreement.

In Voisey's Bay the provincial Government was strongly supportive of Inco. The Federal Government insisted on negotiation of a legally binding EA as a condition of project approval, and after the Supreme Court strengthened the requirements for Aboriginal consultation, the province imposed a requirement for IBAs to be negotiated before the project could proceed. The Queensland Government played a major and positive role in facilitating the Comalco agreement, by contributing a share of its statutory royalty and facilitating land and title transfers. However, in this case Queensland was brought to the table by agreement of the mining company and the Aboriginal Community, after they had settled many aspects of the agreement as between themselves.

The case studies illustrate the importance of careful preparation for negotiations, especially in terms of setting clear goals and establishing structures to ensure broader community support for negotiating teams.

The importance of both is illustrated by the Comalco case study, where the articulation of a clear and comprehensive negotiating position and the steering committee structure was critical in sustaining a strong negotiation effort under conditions that were often adverse. The Innu and Inuit also established clear goals for the negotiations and undertook extensive preparations, including community consultations and the commissioning of technical studies. On the other hand, in the Ekati and ACI/QLC negotiations the Aboriginal parties did not have clearly articulated goals based on a thorough community consultation process, placing them at a significant disadvantage in the negotiations. The value of even limited preparation is highlighted by the Ekati case. The Dogrib did start to plan for negotiations earlier than the other Aboriginal groups and developed their own draft agreement. As a result, they were better prepared for the time pressure generated by the Federal Minister's '60 day deadline', and their agreement contained a number of positive elements missing from other IBAs.

Preparation is just as important for corporate negotiators. BHP had a clearly formulated position on all major issues, which it presented to the Aboriginal groups in its template agreement, and this enhanced its negotiating position. It appears that Comalco was initially hampered by lack of a position that reflected a careful consideration of its underlying interests, whereas the negotiations were able to proceed to an agreement that generated important benefits for both parties once Comalco established such a position. Inco does not appear to have considered the likely response of the Innu and Inuit to some of its actions, resulting in significant costs to the company.

The availability or the absence of human and financial resources is another critical factor in shaping negotiation outcomes. This is an obvious issue but one whose importance is often underestimated in the literature. Its relevance is especially obvious in negotiations between Aboriginal peoples and mining companies because of the serious imbalance in resources that exists between the two. None of the Aboriginal groups included in the case studies were able to dispense anything like the level of resources available to the companies and governments with which they dealt. However, the capacity to mobilise and efficiently apply even a limited quantum of resources greatly enhanced the capacity of Aboriginal negotiators to secure positive outcomes, a point that emerges clearly from each of the case studies.

The availability of resources was critical in allowing the Western Cape York communities and the Innu and Inuit to establish clear negotiating positions, and in permitting the Aboriginal groups affected by Ekati to intervene in the regulatory process and secure a favourable Environmental Agreement. Access to technical advice and skilled negotiators allowed the Innu to effectively question the basis for Inco's determination to develop Voisey's Bay at a scale much larger than the Innu and Inuit wanted. It allowed the CYLC to critically analyse a succession of financial offers from Comalco and ultimately to accept an offer that, as Comalco's subsequent expansion highlighted, served the Aboriginal community's interests. The paucity or absence of resources prevented the CYLC from producing a draft agreement in a timely manner in 1997; made it impossible for the QLC to undertake a consultation process that might have restored a degree of community cohesion; and made it very difficult for Akaitcho Treaty 8 to secure relevant advice and develop proactive negotiating positions.

The case studies also highlight the important role of alternatives to negotiation in shaping outcomes, a point illustrated starkly by the ACI–QLC case study. ACI had an alternative, mining of its granted lease ML 1132, that would ensure its supply of silica sand without the need to negotiate with the QLC. The Government did not wish to see ML 1132 mined, a position ACI had to take into account, and this helped explain its willingness to negotiate with the QLC. However, given the availability of ML 1132, the onus was on the government to secure an alternative for ACI. For the QLC, on the other hand, alternatives to rapidly reaching a negotiated outcome were few and unattractive. It did not have the resources to pursue legal avenues that might have improved its bargaining position before entering negotiations, and its ability to pursue political strategies was limited by the Aboriginal community's lack of unity. Against this background, the only alternative to a speedily negotiated agreement for mining of the northern portion of ML 7064 was that ACI would mine ML 1132 in the absence of any agreement with the Aboriginal community, an outcome entirely unacceptable to the QLC and its constituency. The position in Voisey's Bay was reversed. The Innu and Inuit were effective in maintaining alternatives to negotiation through litigation and direct action. Inco on the other hand would have found it extremely difficult to walk away from a rich nickel deposit for which it had paid C$4.3 billion. Especially when the provincial Government indicated that conclusion of IBAs was a prerequisite for the grant of project approvals, the company had little choice but to achieve an agreement with the Innu and Inuit.

A number of other points emerge from the case studies. Political alliances with third parties can serve to enhance Aboriginal negotiating power. This is illustrated by the role of environmental NGOs, and in particular the Canadian Arctic Resources Committee, in supporting the desire of Aboriginal groups to play a major role in the Ekati Environmental Agreement and in increasing media and public awareness about the goals of the Innu and Inuit in relation to Voisey's Bay and about the reasons for their protests and legal action. On the other hand, the ambiguity of environmental groups in relation to mining of ML 7064 served to further undermine the QLC's tenuous bargaining position.

Time is an important influence on negotiation outcomes, though its impact is not straightforward. In the case of the QLC, the absence of adequate time to undertake community consultations in relation to ACI's revised proposal seriously weakened the Aboriginal negotiating position. Canada's imposition of a 60-day time frame created major difficulties for the NWT Aboriginal groups, especially the Akaitcho. On the other hand, the CYLC was able to turn the time pressures faced by Alcan to its advantage, facilitating a speedy conclusion of negotiations with the company and in turn securing substantial benefits for the traditional owners of Alcan's lease and at the same time for creating an important precedent for the Comalco negotiations.

A specific and final point that emerges from the case studies involves the relationship between individual negotiations. It is rare in the literature to see a negotiation, whether it is simulated or occurs in the real world, analysed in any way other than as a single event or process. However, links between individual negotiations are in fact very important. Such links can involve learning processes that may enhance negotiation performance and outcomes, as occurred for example when the CYLC applied its earlier experience with other companies to the negotiations with Comalco and when the Innu and Inuit applied their experience in negotiations over land claims and service delivery, and the Innu their experience in fighting against low-level flying, to Voisey's Bay. Outcomes achieved in one negotiation can help achieve stronger outcomes from another, as illustrated by the CYLC's use of negotiations with Alcan to improve the Aboriginal community's bargaining position vis-à-vis Comalco. However, linkages between negotiations can also have negative effects, illustrated when the community conflict that arose from negotiations between ACI and the QLC fatally undermined the position of the Quandamooka community in negotiations with another mining company and with the Queensland Government in relation to the Quandamooka native title claim (see Chapter 7).

There will always be ambiguity about the effect of links between one negotiation and another because of the fact that the impact of any negotiation strategy depends on how the other side responds to it. In the Comalco negotiations, for example, the CYLC used extensive consultations to formulate and obtain community endorsement of a comprehensive negotiating position, an approach it had developed in earlier negotiations. However this approach had previously been applied in situations where mining companies needed to reach a speedy agreement, but Comalco was under no such pressure. In addition, the company responded very quickly with a position that was a long way from that of the Aboriginal community and did so, it appears, without giving adequate consideration to where its own fundamental interests lay relative to the Aboriginal position. This set the stage for a long and hard-fought negotiation that imposed significant costs on both sides.

Improving negotiation research

I have already illustrated the importance for negotiation research of not focusing exclusively or excessively on negotiation behaviour, on the 'performance' of negotiators or on the 'profit' gained from negotiations between individuals. The analysis of 45 agreements and the case studies show very clearly that to do so is to exclude from the picture most of the factors that are critical in explaining negotiation outcomes. It is also to eschew an explicit and direct focus on negotiation outcomes, without which the explanatory power of research is inevitably limited. Research on real-world negotiations and their outcomes is absolutely essential to advance knowledge, because it is simply impossible to mirror in experiments the impact of structural and institutional factors and of the agency of organisations and constituencies which seek to mould these factors in their favour. This applies even to interactions between negotiators which is a major focus in the literature because, in the real world, negotiators do not interact in controlled environments but in complex institutional and social contexts that shape their goals and behaviour. In the absence of more research on negotiation and negotiation outcomes in the real world, Menkel-Meadow's conclusion that, after 25 years of research, scholars are often unable 'to fully or correctly describe negotiations, let alone explain their outcomes', is likely to remain valid for another 25 years (Menkel-Meadow 2009: 423).

A comparative approach to research is especially valuable, particularly where it includes a large-N study of the sort described in Chapters 4 and 5. Comparison has been critical in allowing this study to demonstrate which structural features operate to influence outcomes, and so in moving beyond excessively broad categories such as Weiss's 'environmental forces affecting each party' (see Chapter 2). A comparative approach has also helped identify how structural factors operate and how their impact can be modified. In other words, it can provide a window not just into *causal connections*, the holy grail of experimental studies in negotiation research, but also into *causal processes*. An understanding of the latter, as stressed in Chapter 1, is essential if negotiation research is to result in improved outcomes for those involved in negotiations. This is a critical issue for groups, including Indigenous peoples, who are often seriously disadvantaged by the legal, political and economic status quo.

The study provides support for and builds on the work of authors such as Bacharach and Lawler (1980, 1981) and Drahos (2003) on bargaining power. In addition to showing how it is possible to modify the impact of structural factors and so enhance weak bargaining positions, the case studies provide examples of situations where asymmetry of power, as Bacharach and Lawler predict, does not necessarily lead to outcomes that are exploitative of the weaker party. The Comalco negotiations offer a case in point. Comalco was in possession of all the interests it required to continue mining and had access to extensive financial, technical and organisational resources. The Aboriginal community had no clear legal rights on which it could rely in the negotiations, and had few resources at its disposal. Yet the outcome that eventuated, while certainly offering Comalco significant benefits, also offered substantial gains to the Aboriginal community. In achieving this outcome the Aboriginal community certainly made use of other sources of power of the type identified by Pfetsch and Landau (2000: 33–8). These included the ability to infuse moral principles into the negotiations, which was done for instance by the insistence of the Aboriginal traditional owners that they had moral and cultural obligations to protect country, and so needed to be involved in environmental management and secure effective measures to protect cultural heritage.

As in the labour-management negotiations analysed by Bacharach and Lawler, Comalco and the Aboriginal community are involved in a long-term relationship, reflecting Comalco's long history at Weipa and its expectation that it will mine there for many decades to come. This may have had an impact on the outcome, a possibility also suggested by the highly inequitable outcome that occurred in the ACI negotiations. In this latter case, no relationship existed between the parties prior to the negotiation, and ACI's priority was to deal with its urgent need to secure silica resources rather than to build such a relationship.

Finally, this study illustrates the importance of heeding Dononue's call, mentioned in Chapter 1, to extend the range of contexts within which negotiation analysis is conducted. It is the particular circumstances and histories of Aboriginal peoples, their position of structural inequality, their paucity of resources, and their efforts and in some cases their success in minimising the impact of these factors that yield many of the insights about negotiation outcomes contained in this and earlier chapters. These insights will, I hope, in turn help Indigenous people to overcome the barriers they face in seeking to negotiate acceptable conditions for commercial developments on their ancestral lands. The final section considers what lessons the study provides in that regard.

Improving negotiation outcomes for Indigenous peoples

The most important way in which negotiation outcomes for Indigenous people can be improved is through the reform of structures and institutions that serve to undermine their negotiating positions. This point highlights the importance of national and international campaigns for constitutional and legislative recognition of Indigenous rights, because in the longer term this recognition profoundly affects the context in which negotiations occur. As I have argued elsewhere (O'Faircheallaigh 2012), Indigenous action 'on the ground' in relation to specific developments projects is important both in promoting the wider recognition of Indigenous rights and also in ensuring that the legal adoption of norms such as the principle of Indigenous Free Prior and Informed Consent translates into changes in government and corporate behaviour.

Thus every negotiation should be approached from a strategic perspective, both in the sense that the relevance of structural and institutional constraints is recognised, and that opportunities which arise in negotiations to negate the impact of these constraints, and ultimately to remove them, are fully exploited.

Development of appropriate institutional arrangements, and in particular of regional organisations that can support individual Aboriginal peoples or communities in negotiations, is critical. Most Indigenous communities are small, and cannot mobilise the human and financial resources to negotiate on anything like a basis of equality with large corporations and with state agencies. The case studies highlight the value of regional Indigenous organisations in helping to overcome these constraints, and the adverse impact on negotiation outcomes when Indigenous communities are unable to access the resources they need. Involvement of regional organisations also facilitates learning and the transfer of information and expertise from community to community. This is highlighted by the fact that many of the 'strong' agreements identified in Chapter 5 were generated from a succession of negotiations involving the same regional organisation, allowing an accumulation and transfer of relevant skills and experience.

Careful planning is required to ensure that adequate resources are available and that there is enough time to apply them effectively. It is significant that both the CYLC and the Innu and Inuit negotiated written agreements with the mining companies concerned to provide funding and support for community engagement processes. There can be risks for communities in relying on company funding of negotiations. For example, companies may try to influence the community's choice of advisers or, when negotiations are deadlocked, may threaten to withdraw funding for the community, placing it under pressure to accept the company's offer and undermining the Aboriginal negotiating position. To help deal with these risks, communities should avoid a 'drip feed' funding approach. where a company agrees only to provide funding on a piecemeal basis, for instance only paying for one set of meetings, or provision of a single piece of advice. This leaves the community particularly vulnerable to pressure. A proportion of funds received can be set aside as an emergency fund that can be used if a company cuts off funding, for example by incorporating an administration charge into budget estimates and retaining this to use in 'emergencies'. A community can seek additional sources of funds or other resources to support negotiations, for instance by supplementing corporate funding with funds from governments or private foundations, and/or by locating legal advisers or researchers who will be willing to undertake voluntary work if company funding is exhausted. University-based advisers, for instance, may be in a position to continue to support a community through a crunch period in negotiations, even if the community does not have the funds to pay them, or faces delays in obtaining these funds (for a full discussion of funding issues and options see Gibson and O'Faircheallaigh 2010: 80–2).

Availability of adequate resources for Indigenous peoples involved in negotiations is also a major issue for corporations and governments. Virtually every Aboriginal organisation discussed in the case studies struggled for resources at some stage of negotiations. This is likely to cause delays in reaching agreement and so in project development and often results in outcomes that disadvantage Indigenous people. Such outcomes are not conducive to the long-term stability required if corporations and states are to maximise returns from mineral development.

The case studies illustrate only too well the importance of maintaining unity and cooperation within Aboriginal groups engaged in negotiations. I have stressed that the issue here is not about denying diversity of interests or views within Indigenous communities. Mining raises contentious issues and there will inevitably be differences about whether to negotiate with mining companies and what values and goals should be prioritised in any negotiations that do occur. The issue is that if a decision is made to negotiate, internal conflict should not be allowed to intrude into the negotiations. The two pairs of case studies in Australia and Canada illustrate dramatically the benefits of ensuring that this does not occur, and the dangers involved if it does. Achieving consensus can take time, and Indigenous groups may have to resist pressure from companies and governments to ensure that they have the time they need.

Time devoted to building unity is well spent, as is time devoted to mobilising community support and clarifying community goals. The value of entering negotiations with clearly articulated goals that reflect community priorities is vividly illustrated by the case studies. Similarly, careful attention needs to be paid to identifying and augmenting alternatives to negotiation. Once a decision is made to negotiate, there is a natural tendency, particularly when resources are scare, to focus solely on negotiations and ignore other potential avenues for influencing outcomes in relation to mining projects. Indigenous groups should resist that tendency, and always maintain a focus on the alternatives to a negotiated outcome (for a detailed discussion of this point see O'Faircheallaigh 2010).

While Indigenous communities need to create the time required to build unity and prepare, they also need to be aware of time pressures on companies and governments and on the way in which these can be turned to their advantage in negotiations. In some cases it may be to the advantage of Indigenous peoples to accelerate their internal processes because a capacity to help meet company deadlines can offer them a powerful lever in negotiations. Equally, it may be important to understand the implications of a situation where a company is *not* under pressure of time, a factor which had significant implications in the Cape York negotiations.

This raises a wider point. It is critical for Indigenous groups to understand, as best they can, the structures, values and imperatives of the corporate entities with which they negotiate. This may not be easy, given that corporate processes are often opaque and, especially where trust is slow to develop between negotiation parties, there is likely to be withholding of information or deliberate obfuscation. Absence of trust can be a particular problem in negotiations between mining companies and Indigenous peoples, given the power imbalances that typically exist between the two and Indigenous histories of dispossession and marginalisation. Yet trust can be developed if both sides are open to positive engagement. It was essential, for instance, to the capacity of the CYLC to quickly negotiate a favourable agreement with Alcan Ltd (see Chapter 6). In summary, it is important for Aboriginal groups to approach corporations with critical but open minds and use every opportunity to understand the forces driving particular companies or subsidiaries in specific circumstances. This is especially so given the wide variety of outcomes negotiated by a single company that was involved in six of the 45 agreements analysed in Chapter 5. This variance in outcomes shows that companies adjust to particular contexts, and the capacities and approaches of Indigenous groups constitute one critical variable in shaping those contexts.

Turning to government actors, a similar point can be made. The case studies support the view that Aboriginal groups should be wary of government involvement in their negotiations with mining companies; should assume that government will generally be supportive of mining interests except when, or to the extent that, some specific legal or political imperative inclines them otherwise; and should seek to carefully manage government involvement where it does occur. On the other hand, government also has imperatives which can modify its behaviour and even, as the Cape York case study illustrated, lead it to play a supportive role and facilitate favourable agreements. A strategic appraisal of government interests and of how these can be influenced is important for Indigenous success.

In conclusion, the key implications of this study are, in a sense, similar for Aboriginal peoples and for negotiation scholars. A focus on both internal negotiation processes and on wider structural factors, and on the interaction between the two, is essential. For scholars, it offers the prospect of greater success in explaining negotiation outcomes. For Aboriginal peoples, it enhances their capacity to shape negotiation outcomes to their advantage and so to start reversing the unfavourable balance between costs and benefits which they have historically endured from mining on their ancestral lands.

References

Bacharach, S. and Lawler, E. (1980) *Power and Politics in Organisations*, San Francisco: Jossey-Bass Publishers.

Bacharach, S. and Lawler, E. (1981) *Bargaining: Power, Tactics and Outcomes*, San Francisco: Jossey-Bass Publishers.

Drahos, P. (2003) 'When the Weak Bargain with the Strong: Negotiations in the World Trade Organisation', *International Negotiation*, 8(1): 79–109.

Gibson, G. and O'Faircheallaigh, C. (2010) *IBA Community Toolkit: Negotiation and Implementation of Impact and Benefit Agreements*, Ottawa: Walter & Duncan Gordon Foundation.

Menkel-Meadow, C. (2009) 'Chronicling the Complexification of Negotiation Theory and Practice', *Negotiation Journal*, 25(4): 415–29.

O'Faircheallaigh, C. (2010) 'Aboriginal–Mining Company Contractual Agreements in Australia and Canada: Implications for Political Autonomy and Community Development', *Canadian Journal of Development Studies*, XXX (1–2): 69–86.

O'Faircheallaigh, C. (2012) 'International Recognition of Indigenous Rights, Indigenous Control of Development and Domestic Political Mobilization', *Australian Journal of Political Science*, 47(4): 531–46.

Pfetsch, F. R. and Landau, A. (2000) 'Symmetry and Asymmetry in International Negotiations', *International Negotiation*, 5(1): 21–42.

Putnam, L. (1994) 'Challenging the Assumptions of Traditional Approaches to Negotiation', *Negotiation Journal*, 10(4): 337–46.

Sebenius, J. K. (2013) 'Level Two Negotiations: Helping the Other Side Meet its "Behind-the-Table" Challenges, *Negotiation Journal*, 29: 7–21.

Index

Page numbers in *italics* denote tables, those in **bold** denote figures.